Jane,

Thank you for y

and support. It has been
a real honor and pleasure
to know and work with
you at Rutgers. Keep up
the great work MARINE!

Semper Fidelis
&
God Bless

1stLt Matt A. [illegible]

(0302, USMC)

SECOND PLATOON: CALL SIGN HADES

A Memoir of the Marines of the Combined Action Company

FIRST LIEUTENANT MARK A. BODROG
Exclusively for Always Faithful LLC

iUniverse LLC
Bloomington

SECOND PLATOON: CALL SIGN HADES
A MEMOIR OF THE MARINES OF THE COMBINED ACTION COMPANY

iUniverse books may be ordered through booksellers or by contacting:

iUniverse LLC
1663 Liberty Drive
Bloomington, IN 47403
www.iuniverse.com
1-800-Authors (1-800-288-4677)

ISBN: 978-1-4917-1141-5 (sc)
ISBN: 978-1-4917-1142-2 (hc)
ISBN: 978-1-4917-1143-9 (e)

Library of Congress Control Number: 2013918798

Printed in the United States of America.

iUniverse rev. date: 11/13/2013

WELCOME TO HADES
WARNING
HADES 1ST PLATOON
HADES 2ND PLATOON
ANA
COMBINED ASSAULT
TASK FORCE
NO UNAUTHORIZED
ENTRY

This memoir is dedicated to the Marines and
Navy Corpsmen of Second Platoon.

CONTENTS

PREFACE

I was born in the former steel mill town of Roebling, New Jersey. I am the son of a United States Marine. My commissioning as a Lieutenant in the United States Marine Corps adds to the history, tradition, and bloodline of the Marines and military servicemen in my family. Being a part of the tradition and history of servicemen in my family is a goal I have strived to attain all my life. I grew up in a family in which I was constantly surrounded by great men, and I emulated them as a child and as a young adult. At even my youngest age, I wanted nothing more in life than to live up to my family name and share in the experiences and history of which they were a part.

My great-grandfather came to America from Europe prior to World War I. Loving this country very much, he served first in the Army and then joined the Marine Corps once World War I started. During World War I, as a Private First Class in the Corps, he fought in the Battle of Belleau Wood and many other decisive combat engagements. It was in Belleau Wood that he sustained multiple non-life-threatening machine gun wounds to his legs and received a Purple Heart.

His son, who is my grandfather on my paternal side, joined the United States Navy during World War II. He saw combat action in the Pacific Theater of the war during his service. He was directly involved in the historic Naval Battle of Guadalcanal as a Coxswain on the USS *Aaron Ward*. During the Battle of Guadalcanal, his destroyer went toe-to-toe with the Japanese Imperial Navy and was eventually sunk in the Iron Bottom Sound as a result of constant barrages of Japanese guns, bombs, and torpedoes.

My grandfather on my maternal side fought with the Army Airborne as a Soldier during the Korean War. During his time in Korea, he saw direct combat and kinetic action during heavy engagements with both North Korean and Chinese enemy forces.

My father was a Corporal in the United States Marines Corps during the years directly after the Vietnam War ended. He was stationed in North Carolina, California, and Okinawa. He took part in Operation Beacon Cherry, which prevented the North Koreans from infiltrating South Korea through tunnels dug underneath the Demilitarized Zone (DMZ). After his time of service, he returned home and married my mother. Currently, I have a younger brother who is a Staff Sergeant in the Marine Corps.

I graduated from Rutgers, the State University of New Jersey, earning a BA in criminal justice. During my time in college, I worked at various places of employment. I helped out family with backbreaking landscaping and construction work. I worked in the culinary and patient transport departments at my local hospital. I taught part-time at my local high schools as a substitute teacher and volunteered at my local library. Although they were all rewarding experiences, I still felt like I was not doing enough with my current life, and I wanted to do more. It was a confusing and uncertain time for me, as I had already changed my major twice, and I knowingly had zero real-world experiences.

I grew up in a competitive household with my brother and sister, and I knew I could not settle for second best. After all, my parents and family always pushed my siblings and me to do our best. As the older brother, it was my job and responsibility to set the example for my siblings. With college graduation looming and unanswered questions about my future lurking in the background, I was uncertain what to do with my life, but I knew it had to do something with the Marine Corps.

Like a silent calling, I began to look much harder at serving in the Corps. Knowing it was our country's most elite fighting force and prided itself on being the best, I was drawn to it. Subconsciously, I was convinced that somewhere in my genetic code I was supposed to be a Marine. By the time of my college graduation, I prepared my mind, body, and soul as best as I could for the hardest training my country had to offer.

I reported to Officer Candidate School (OCS-197), Quantico, Virginia, in January 2008. Upon completion of Officer Candidate School, I reported to The Basic School (TBS), which is also located in Quantico. After graduating from TBS, I received orders to Infantry Officer Course (IOC 4-09). Upon successfully graduating IOC, I received orders to Lima Company, Third Battalion, Third Marine Regiment located in Kaneohe Bay, Hawaii.

During my time in Third Battalion, Third Marine Regiment, I was honored to have held the billets of Platoon Commander, Weapons Platoon Commander, Assistant Operations Officer, Executive Officer, and Company Commander. I have conducted two successful combat deployments to Afghanistan in support of Operation Enduring Freedom (OEF) 10.1 and Operation Enduring Freedom (OEF) 11.2. My personal awards include letters of appreciation, a certificate of commendation, the Navy and Marine Corps Achievement Medal, the Navy and Marine Corps Commendation Medal, and the Combat Action Ribbon.

During my first deployment, I deployed as a Platoon Commander to the Nawa-I-Barakzayi (Nawa) District, Helmand Province, Afghanistan, in support of Operation Enduring Freedom (OEF) 10.1. Throughout this deployment, my Marines and Navy Corpsmen performed in an outstanding manner. Within our second month in the Helmand Province, both my platoon and First Platoon from Lima Company were hand selected by our Battalion Commander to form a combined operational maneuver element with Afghan Army (ANA) Soldiers. This maneuver element would become known as the combined action company (CAC). It would consist of two rifle platoons of Marines and two platoons of ANA. These platoons within the CAC were known as combined action platoons (CAPs).

This combined action company would be my battalion's secret weapon against the Taliban. It would employ integrated combat techniques, tactics, and procedures (TTPs) to disrupt and interdict kinetic areas in both the Nawa District and adjacent areas in the Helmand Province, Afghanistan. The CAC was utilized as the main effort in numerous battalion- and company-level named combat operations and missions. My CAP was involved in frequent combat engagements with the Taliban during deployment and received many honors and awards for bravery and commitment to the mission.

All Marines are the product and result of the history and traditions of the men and women who have come before them. The war in Afghanistan and the Global War on Terrorism are both arguably America's longest and least talked about wars to date. To all who read this, let the lessons of this memoir and the stories of the men in it never become a lost chapter in our nation's history.

The point of this book is ultimately to honor the men and women who came before us and to immortalize my Marines by writing their part of history. It is out of their honor and the honor of those who came before us that I chose to write this memoir. In writing this memoir and chapter in our great nation's history, I encourage people who read this book to visualize their own loved ones and family members through the stories and experiences of my platoon during their time in Afghanistan. It is in this manner that we can all share in the honoring of our servicemen and never forget their sacrifices.

I have always loved the Marine Corps and consider it the greatest and most elite branch of military service in America. I have had the unique privilege of leading and serving with the greatest men and women our nation has to offer.

All the events in this book are known to me and a matter of fact and record. Names of certain Marines have been changed or altered to protect their privacy, safety, and identities.

I was able to complete this memoir through the use of personal testimony, logbooks, and journals and limitless motivation from my Marines, family, and friends. In no way is this book meant to shape foreign policy or bring disrespect or discredit on the Marine Corps, our great American leaders, or America.

A portion of the royalties from the sale of this memoir will be honorably donated to support wounded and fallen warriors who took part in the Global War on Terrorism. You will never be forgotten.

On behalf of the Marines of Second Platoon, I would like to give thanks to all our friends and family members for supporting our efforts and keeping us in their thoughts, memories, and prayers. Without your tireless dedication and compassion to take care of us, especially against those who speak ill either at home or overseas, many of the achievements and sacrifices we made on behalf of our country and loved ones would not have been possible.

It is you, the "civilian cultural warriors," who recognize, share, and feel the trials and tribulations we encounter in the service of fighting for our great nation. It is you who live this fight every day, either at home or when you are at work, when many people would rather turn a blind eye or sit in their own comfort zones. Thank you all for the care packages and the glimmers of hope and for fighting for us at home. You all ensure that our voices and silent prayers are heard and never forgotten.

To my fallen brothers from IOC 4-09 and the Marines who lost their lives during the deployment of Third Battalion, Third Marines to Operation Enduring Freedom (OEF) 10.1, Helmand Province, Afghanistan: Private First Class Suter, Sergeant Joe Wrightsman, First Lieutenant Scott Fleming, First Lieutenant Robert Kelly, First Lieutenant William J. Donnelly IV, Major James Weis, and Lieutenant Colonel Mario Carazo. God bless you all, and may your sacrifices never be forgotten by the country for which you gave all.

Frater Infinitas, Ductus Exemplo, Semper Fidelis.

Introduction

The events of this memoir are meant to describe in detail the military actions and combat operations undertaken by the United States Marines and Sailors of Second Platoon, Lima Company, Third Battalion, Third Marine Regiment between May and December 2010 in the Nawa District of the Helmand Province of Afghanistan during Operation Enduring Freedom (OEF) 10.1.

This memoir will give readers a true story of the brave and the bold few who still fight for our American freedom and way of life. Through the stories of my Marines and Sailors, I will attempt to immortalize every Marine, Sailor, Soldier, Airman, and civilian who gave the ultimate sacrifice to our great nation and asked nothing in return.

The focus of this book will be to detail the events that took place in the Nawa District of Helmand Province during the time period in which my infantry platoon conducted its deployment.

The focus of this book will then shift to the specific combat operations that were conducted once my platoon became detached from Lima Company and became directly attached to our battalion's Headquarters and Service Company (H&S) to form a combined action company (CAC) consisting of both United States Marines and Afghan National Army Soldiers (ANA).

This combined company, in its principal, was based purely on Marine Corps doctrine; however, the idea of a combined company and platoon is not new. Marines have been conducting counterinsurgency (COIN) operations for more than a hundred years since the days of the Banana Wars. The utilization and efficacy of combined action platoons

(CAPs) was made famous by Bing West in his book *The Village* in which he and his Marines directly partnered with the South Vietnamese and conducted COIN operations against the enemy during the Vietnam War.

With all of these lessons to learn from and stories to read, my Marines and I, as a CAP and as part of the CAC, were personally responsible for taking all of these historical documents and facts on COIN and directly applying them in our partnership with Afghan Soldiers.

CAPs consisting of both Marines and Afghan Soldiers were an idea I had not heard of being utilized during the Global War on Terrorism. I had never heard about CAPs in Iraq or Afghanistan other than the term *transition teams*, which are utilized to educate and train foreign police and military.

My Marines and I were not only given the mission to create a combined unit by our battalion, but we were also ordered to be fully capable of conducting sustained combat engagements against the Taliban once our Afghan counterparts were proficient and capable. Even though our country had been fighting in Afghanistan for more than a decade, there were zero historical documents or after-action reports on combined Marine and Afghan units. I soon realized that what my Marines and I were about to embark upon was something that had not been seen or possibly conducted since Vietnam. It was now my platoon's responsibility to document and record in detail the techniques, tactics, and procedures (TTPs) used in the creation and execution of this unit to help enhance future COIN operations and save lives in the process.

The intent of this book is to dispel rumors the American audience sees and hears from media-driven television, Internet, and daily life. The intent is meant to counter the negative news articles and one-sided opinionated views that my platoon and me read and witnessed while deployed in Afghanistan and continue to read now at home.

It seems that average Americans are socially disconnected with many issues and military-related topics in the media. One cannot dispel the factual and logical assumption that negative social agendas (even global social agendas) drive many of our media outlets to the general population, and certain factions are conducting reporting based on political correctness and opinion rather than factual data. These same media outlets report losses instead of wins and display a feel-sorry sympathetic attitude toward our men and women in the military service. This is wrong and should be challenged. It is time for all of us to question what is real, question the truth, get involved, get interested, wake up, break the chains of our shackles, and become unplugged from our video games before it is too late.

I will attempt to dispel these reports by giving documented firsthand accounts of the reality of the situation on the ground from Marines and Navy Corpsmen who were physically in Afghanistan, living in the dirt for months under the hot and unforgiving desert sun. In doing so, I am determined to clarify for everyone reading this book who and what United States Marines are and how they act and operate on a daily basis inside the Afghanistan war zone.

Many Americans have a mental image of what a Marine is, but they cannot put this image into tangible words. Many people have a formed opinion that Afghanistan is a country in which war is ever present; however, more Americans are being murdered on our own streets than on the unimproved dirt roads and challenging terrain of Afghanistan.

Little do people know that after one year of United States Marine presence and strategy, the Nawa District became one of the safest places in all of the Helmand Province. Consequently, the Helmand Province started becoming one of the safest provinces in the country of Afghanistan. The opinion that the Helmand Province was a lost cause (as was the case with Ramadi and the Sunni Triangle in Iraq) was an unsubstantiated claim that was driven by some of the unsupportive media and forced on the civilian populace with zero factual basis. Instead of many media outlets rallying support for our troops and reporting our wins and progress, it seems they have an agenda of showing only the dark side of our great military and leadership. Consequently, like many suppositions made by the media, the Marine Corps was able to prove them wrong again by bringing the Helmand Province area greater peace, stability, and security.

This memoir will give readers realistic accounts of the various combat operations conducted by my platoon, by painting the picture of how my men and I viewed, observed, and conducted everyday life in Afghanistan. Ultimately, this memoir will describe in detail the creation and implementation of two Marine and Afghan combined action platoons (CAPs) and the combined action company (CAC) by my infantry platoon and the leadership of Third Battalion, Third Marine Regiment. This was a task many can argue had not been accomplished for more than forty years, since the author Bing West detailed it in the book *The Village* while deployed in Vietnam.

Throughout this story, I will highlight the sacrifices the United States Marine Corps and military servicemen of all branches are making on behalf of the American and Afghanistan population. These highlighted sacrifices will support the notion that this war is winnable and that we must win at all costs, or else all who have given their lives will have died in vain. All the sacrifices, many at the hands of our fallen and wounded warriors, will be forgotten in the hourglass of time if we allow the enemy to achieve victory in Afghanistan and in the Global War on Terrorism.

The events of this book solely demonstrate the actions of my platoon, with references to my company and battalion, from the personal views and opinions of me, my Platoon Sergeant, and my Marines. Our personal views by no means reflect or are representative of the thoughts and feelings of the entire United States Marine Corps or its Marines. This memoir is in no way meant to be a political tool to shape foreign or domestic policy.

The stories and accounts mentioned in this book are but a mere microcosm of all the Marines, servicemen, and civilians who sacrificed everything they had to make the United States and the world a better place for our children. In no way is the publishing of this book a means to profit from the sacrifices of our fallen Marines or the service members who gave their lives.

Instead, this book is meant to honor all our troops who are involved in the Global War on Terrorism and every war America has fought. I would like to reemphasize that a portion of the royalties from this memoir will be donated to charitable military organizations, wounded warriors, and veterans of the Global War on Terrorism.

This book is formally dedicated to the Marines of Second Platoon, Lima Company, Third Battalion, Third Marine Regiment, who achieved so much during their time spent in Afghanistan during Operation Enduring Freedom (OEF) 10.1.

Gentlemen, this memoir is for you. Without you, my highly motivated overachievers, I would not have been able to document this part of history. You are all my silent professionals, my brothers in arms, and the men who inspired me every day. You are truly in every essence of the word *heroes*! I could not give you all the awards or medals you deserved and earned, but forever in the eyes of God and through the fabric of space and time you will be remembered for all you did and accomplished during your deployment in Afghanistan.

Against all odds, you continued to persevere in the face of adversity and extremely confusing times both at home and abroad. Your COIN mission was not always clear, and the rules of engagement made your jobs difficult; however, you always came out on top. You always gave me your 110 percent at every task, mission, and operation that came our way. This memoir is for all of your hard work and efforts to make the country and world a little bit better. You have all made your mark on history.

PART I

What It Means to Be a United States Marine, a Short History of Afghanistan's Past and Present, and Patrol Base Brannon

Remember, upon the conduct of each depends the fate of all.
—Alexander the Great

A leader leads by example, not by force. A Commander who advances without any thought of winning personal fame and withdraws in spite of certain punishment, whose only concern is to protect his people and promote the interests of his ruler, is the nation's treasure. Because he fusses over his men as if they were infants, they will accompany him into the deepest valleys; because he fusses over his men as if they were his own beloved sons, they will die by his side. If he is generous with them and yet they do not do as he tells them, if he loves them and yet they do not obey his commands, if he is so undisciplined with them that he cannot bring them into proper order, they will be like spoiled children who can be put to no good use at all.
—Sun Tzu, *Art of War*

If you do not like the image in the mirror, do not break the mirror, break your face.
—Afghan Proverb

CHAPTER 1

Before we can start with the events surrounding my platoon between May and December 2010 in the Nawa District of Helmand Province, Afghanistan, it is my platoon's duty to dispel all rumors and falsehoods by explaining in our own thoughts and words exactly who and what United States Marines are.

When people hear the word *Marine*, they immediately recall scenes or quotes from the famous movie *Full Metal Jacket*. Viewers can connect with this movie because they get a sense of the rigors young civilians face as they undergo the fundamental transformation process it takes to become a United States Marine. This movie is timeless in the sense that although generations change, the brotherhood and camaraderie in the Corps remain the same, if not grow stronger over time.

In this movie, viewers can look into the eyes of Gunnery Sergeant R. Lee Ermey as he plays the role of the fearsome Senior Drill Instructor Gunnery Sergeant Hartman and feel as if they are his recruits in boot camp. Observers feel Hartman's ice-cold gaze mentally projected upon them and hear his frightening yell. They can almost smell his rotten breath that tastes of death as he motivates his Marines and chokes out Private "Gomer" Pyle, the platoon "fat body." Viewers feel the intensity and stress associated with boot camp and catch a glimpse of the harsh reality seventeen- and eighteen-year-olds go through as they are voluntarily plucked from the civilian world and begin the transition and evolution to become our nation's fiercest and most elite warriors—United States Marines.

People may hear the word *Marine* and remember another movie titled *A Few Good Men*. Jack Nicholson's portrayal of a Marine Officer in the movie and his famous line, "You can't handle the truth," earned this movie notoriety and fame. People see Nicholson's neat and clean uniform and steadfast bearing as Tom Cruise (a United States Naval Officer) questions him during a military trial. During the movie, the audience can physically see the divergence between the different branches of the military and can see the discipline, loyalty, and obedience portrayed by the Marines in the movie. Although this movie depicts Hollywood's interpretation of the Corps, Marine Officers strive to be the antithesis of Nicholson's character and will give their lives to fight for the enlisted men of whom they are in charge.

Much of what people visualize a Marine to embody stems from both personal knowledge and Hollywood's depiction of us. Movies like *The Siege of Firebase Gloria; Ears, Open. Eyeballs, Click.; Heartbreak Ridge; Generation Kill; Jarhead; The Pacific;* and *The Marine* all display a unique charisma and attitude in their depiction of Marines. An objective viewer can distinguish between reality and fiction; however, there is always enjoyment in the depiction of Marines as Titans or Spartan-like warriors defeating the enemy in an intense battle.

There is a fraternity-like bond commonly shared between all Marines that is uncommon in the other branches of service. We take pride in our education, history, and those who came before us. We remember the Marines who gave some, and we honor the Marines who gave all. No matter what generation of Marine we are, we will always be brothers to one another. The same determination, motivation, and discipline is ingrained in us through constant hardships and sacrifices. These commonalities set us apart from the rest and make us truly elite warriors.

When people hear the word *Marine*, they may think of the holidays or Christmas season and identify a United States Marine with the Toys for Tots program, handing out gifts to our nation's unfortunate children who otherwise would not receive any. They may also think of the numerous volunteer projects and networks we as a Corps conduct and recognize our determination to ease the pain and suffering of the noble warriors who were injured or killed during the Global War on Terrorism and previous wars.

Other patriotic Americans may view us as the men and women who guard the President of the United States of America, with our squared jaws, bulldog-like faces, and sharp dress blue uniforms that perfectly complement our Spartan-warrior-shaped bodies. Everyone knows of and recognizes all the prestige, glamour, and glitter that are bestowed upon us. Our roars of "Oorah" and the Latin catch phrase "*Semper Fidelis*" are both feared and respected by everyone around the world.

CHAPTER 2

Ninety-nine percent of the population in the United States has never stood in the historic yellow footprints located at Parris Island, South Carolina, or at the Marine Corps Recruit Depot San Diego, California. Those footprints ultimately mark the start of the transformation from civilian to Marine. There are even fewer who make the choice to become Commissioned Officers in the United States Marine Corps by completing Officer Candidate School located in Quantico, Virginia.

Even fewer individuals who make this life choice actually survive the rigorously intense second-to-none physical, mental, and spiritual education and training it takes to transform into a United States Marine. However, the lucky few family and friends who see their sons or daughters on graduation day witness and feel the transformation their loved ones have gone through to shed their societal images and civilian beliefs in order to live, act, and breathe as and become a United States Marine.

Less than 1 percent of the country fights for the very same ideals and beliefs that 99 percent of the population feel they are entitled to have. For this reason, there are disconnects in the understanding and interest in the military by our civilian population, almost to the point of indifference and sympathy. Many Americans have forgotten and fail to appreciate that their God-given right of freedom is only God-given because men and women have made the sacrifice and died for it.

Our inherent rights of life, liberty, and the pursuit of happiness were words our Founding Fathers chose carefully. These specific rights that are endowed by our Creator are only apt when people can fight for them to be in place. If we place the value of these rights ahead of our inherent duty to fight for and maintain them, our great nation will effectively cease to be. Thus, in the words of Thomas Jefferson, "The tree of liberty must be replenished from time to time with the blood of patriots and tyrants." If it is not, failure to fight for our liberties and rights will result in their loss.

Of the less than 1 percent of the American population serving in the Armed Forces, the total population of the United Marine Corps is presently about two hundred thousand strong. By comparison, in a country of more than 350 million legal Americans and illegal human beings, we as United States Marines are a very minute and elite branch of the Armed Services. This happens to be a unique point I continually stress to my Marines. They are doing a job no one else wants and only a few can do. We are one of the oldest and most elite fraternities and brotherhoods in America.

Does this make us better than the 99 percent of the population who choose different life paths? Some will argue yes, and others will argue no. All I will say is that we are elite warriors, nobly fighting for the ordinary men and women who cannot fight for themselves. Whether because of loyalty, determination, family tradition, or patriotism, we as Marines chose the path to become the greatest warriors of our time. We heeded the call of our great nation and volunteer to fight for our great American countrymen and women.

We as United States Marines are given the ability to kill the enemies of this great republic with the realization that we may also be asked to give up our lives while defending it. There is no greater honor or sacrifice a person can give to his or her country or fellow warriors than his or her own life.

We as United States Marines are protectors of the American way of life, holding infinitely true to the United States Marine Corps motto: *Semper Fidelis*, Latin for "always faithful." *Semper Fidelis* is our esteemed and timeless quote of the few and the proud throughout the ages. We are the keepers of more than two hundred years of tradition. We are the time-traveling life vessels that create and carry on our own history and legacy.

CHAPTER 3

A Marine by definition is a "Sailor" of the sea. I caution against using the word *Sailor* because Marines aren't Sailors, or Soldiers. A Marine is a warrior, comparable to a modern-day Spartan. A Marine is someone who is capable of achieving power projection through the mobility of the Navy and can conduct amphibious combined arms operations from the ocean or sea to a body of land.

In the past, and arguably still to this day, Marines were and are the Navy's right-hand punch. During battles at sea when two or more ships were close enough for gun battles, close engagements, or hand-to-hand combat, Marines were the ones called in to achieve decisive victory. This is where the term *leatherneck* came from. During hand-to-hand combat on Naval ships in the 1800s, Marines would wear leather around their necks to protect themselves from the deadly sword slashes of their enemies.

Presently, Marines engage in myriad combat and noncombat operations. Many of these operations range from conducting combat missions in the Middle East, disrupting pirates off the coast of Africa, or supporting humanitarian operations in countries suffering from natural disasters or other crises. We as Marines are by precedent required to be at the direct dispersal of the President of the United States of America whenever he needs us. We are America's 911 forces in readiness. Therefore, when issues like these occur, Marines are on standby to react to any number of circumstances, foreseen or unforeseen.

These are still very vague descriptions that do not fully highlight or capture all the battles, wars, climbs, and places we have been to, fought at, and won. These descriptions still do not capture every drop of blood shed over the centuries in numerous terrains, climates, environments, and continents. They still do not fully paint the picture of all the men and women who have fought for the colors of this country and ran to the sound of the gun when all hope seemed lost.

In making that statement, I asked my Marines during a professional military education (PME) study class located at Forward Operating Base (FOB) Geronimo in the Nawa District of the Helmand Province, Afghanistan, to explain in their own words what they believe a United States Marine is. It is the words of the men on the ground who are fighting for our American freedom and way of life that truly capture what a Marine is.

The Marines of Second Platoon describe Marines as the most disciplined, morally and ethically upright, honored, and elite force in the entire world. A Marine is a subunit of a larger culture known as the United States Marine Corps, where history, traditions, and memories live on forever. Destiny or not, the ability to become a Marine is either passed through our bloodlines through reproduction or genetically written in our DNA. We are, as Commandant James Conway said, a "breed apart," genetically codified differently than the majority through years of hardship, evolution, and natural selection.

We are the leathernecks of ancient ships, the *Teufelhunden* (devil dogs) from Belleau Wood, the destroyers of the Imperial Japanese, the "Walking Dead" from the A Shau Valley, the jarheads from the Persian Gulf War, and now America's 911 force in readiness in the Global War on Terrorism.

All Marines, whether they are male or female, uphold the three Marine Corps values of honor, courage, and commitment under the umbrella of his or her God, country, and Corps. A Marine wants to be the best at everything he or she does, and he or she constantly trains and studies to be the best warrior possible. Marines recognize that when you are the best, someone is always trying to be better than you. Therefore, we are the best and constantly try to be better at every task we do, lest we give our enemy an advantage over our destiny.

Willing obedience to lawful orders and the ability to improvise, adapt, and overcome any obstacle are traits we live by and continually achieve. United States Marines cannot and do not know how to surrender, and they push themselves to the limits of everything and every task they encounter.

We as Marines are motivated and dedicated in upholding our honor, beliefs, and values. There is a sense of overwhelming pride that exists among us that is insurmountably higher than any other branch of service in the world because of our love for our heritage, history, and culture. We are masters of our destinies and fate and skilled in the arts of survival and modern warfare. We are the living testaments of time-honored traditions and the physical embodiment of the Marines who came before us.

According to my Marine Corporal Adam Mount, a Fire Team Leader for Third Squad, "A Marine is an individual who thinks of others before himself. A Marine is a leader who motivates, encourages, and always sets the highest standards. He lives to accomplish even the hardest mission. He does not know how to quit and cannot quit, for quitting is failure. A Marine is tough and hardheaded and at the same time understanding of the sacrifice he is willing to give for others. He himself comes last; others come first. A Marine is a true professional."

The views of my Squad Leaders are a little different but along the same lines. My First Squad Leader and most aggressive Marine, Sergeant Brent Olds, says, "We can church up a United States Marine with all types of meaningful words and names for ourselves and try to add depth and purpose. When you get right down to it though, United States Marines are little red buttons for the government that are pushed when a crisis or emergency arises and an immediate response is needed. We are America's right-hand punch. We guard the sheep from the wolves like a sheepdog that has been crossbred with a pit bull and German shepherd. If you try to harm innocent lives, we will be there to stop you. We are the most morally and ethically upright military that has ever defended a nation. The only true Marine is an Infantry Marine."

You would have to know Sergeant Olds to understand where he is coming from, because he is the type of Marine who tells you how it is, not what you want to hear. He is like an animal in this respect; he will challenge anything that is different because that is his job and what he was trained to do. He is my First Squad Leader, and the alpha male mind-set comes with the territory. This is a rare quality to find because many people are afraid to speak their minds for fear of political correctness. He is right though; we are trained to kill when we have to, but we are also trained to be ethical and moral warriors capable of respecting all human life when the time arises.

My First Squad, First Fire Team Leader, Corporal Matthew Garst—who subsequently became known as the battalion's "Unbreakable Marine" for actions during Operation New Dawn—describes a Marine as "the individual who grew up being all of the trouble a town could handle. Fathers watched him around their daughters, and mothers thought he was a bad influence. When the time came and the drums were beaten and the trumpet was sounded, he had the courage to become the nation's elite warrior who would channel all of his aggression and anger toward an enemy, using large amounts of firepower and violence among other brothers with the same mentality." Much like his Squad Leader, Corporal Garst displays the aggressiveness that is fundamentally inherent in a United States Marine.

My Second Squad Leader and a most methodical Marine, Sergeant Tyler Brown, describes a Marine and his Marines as "well-trained warriors capable of completing any task or mission set before them in any climb or place. Marines are trained to fight on land or at sea and are able to adapt and overcome any situation or obstacle that stands before them. He never leaves another Marine behind and lives to fight for his brothers to his left and his right." This is a very true description of all the ways we are capable of fighting and our belief that no one should ever be left behind during conflicts with the enemy.

Lastly, my Third Squad Leader and most comedic Marine, Sergeant Lawrence Guthrie, believes Marines must be "professional, disciplined, physically fit, and confident. These traits give Marines the ability to rise above the rest, enabling them to have the willingness to learn and accomplish any mission at hand. They are trained to ignore any and all discomfort, friction, and pain they may encounter."

Some of these views from my Squad Leaders may seem either odd or right on point, but you have to know my Marines to understand where they are coming from. They are leaders and must at all times show strength and set an example for the men under their charge.

The men writing these descriptions have seen the "real world" and the face and adversity of war. They have been trained and educated by the finest military branch in the world, the United States Marine Corps. They have fought for and earned the right to voice their opinions and views under the protection of the freedom of speech that they defend. These men are some of the smartest individuals I have ever encountered. They all have twenty-twenty vision to recognize anomalies or inconsistencies with the status quo and will not hesitate to let you know if something is wrong or not right. They put the mission and their Marines at the forefront of every decision and task that comes their way.

My Platoon Sergeant, Staff Sergeant Daniel Lebron, sums up the description of a United States Marine as follows: "When describing a Marine, there are many facets and factors one has to take into account in addition to choosing a dimension that highlights who we are. A United States Marine is an American: a student, a country boy, a farmhand, a hay bailer, a city slicker, a delinquent, and everything in between. They come from all types of backgrounds, be it rich, middle-class, or poor. They are the youth who find themselves called forth for a greater purpose. They are extraordinary individuals with a special set of character traits that draw them to this illustrious gun club. They are trained the hardest, given the least, and expected to do the most. They do the jobs no one else wants to do, and they do them without hesitation or grief. They do not become United States Marines for the paycheck or for the college funds. They do it for the dedication to the men who serve to their left and right. They do it because they want to be challenged and be the best. No other branch fights for the will of the men to their left and right better than the Marines. When the gunshots ring out, we ultimately fight for each other."

Someone who has never served would not understand, but those who have honorably served can agree that there is no bond greater than the one shared between platoon members and teammates during times of battle, hardship, and adversity. This unspoken bond we share as brothers in arms is the fuel that propels us to do whatever it takes to complete the mission and bring every man home.

From the time an individual steps on those yellow footprints to the day he or she puts on the uniform for the last time, that individual is thoroughly indoctrinated in the traditions and ways of the brothers who served before us. We are the finest embodiment of the phrase "*E Pluribus Unum*." From the ones who committed great acts of bravery to those who gave all, we as individual Marines take pleasure ingraining our history and traditions, never forgetting where we came from, and holding ourselves infinitely true to the same standards and beliefs of the many who came before us.

General James Amos, the thirty-fifth Commandant of the Marine Corps stated, "There is no such thing as a former Marine. You're a Marine, just in a different uniform, and you're in a different phase of your life. But you'll always be a Marine because you went to Parris Island, San Diego, or the hills of Quantico. Whether you served four years or forty years, regardless of age, time, or era, one truth is self-evident and unavoidable: once a United States Marine, always a United States Marine—never an ex-Marine."

From these statements, you now have a better insight into what exactly a Marine is in contrast to how we are depicted. My Marines are the real deal, and their views and opinions are the closest anyone will get to truly understanding the mentality, mind-set, and image we see in ourselves and how the rest of the population perceives us. As anyone reading this can see, we hold ourselves to a very high standard.

CHAPTER 4

Throughout written history, Afghanistan has been a necropolis where countless superpowers and empires have come to fight and eventually die. Afghanistan is a country that has been invaded and conquered since before the days of Alexander the Great and all the way up to present time. Many former superior forces of the world, including Genghis Khan, the Royal British Empire, and Soviet Russia, can trace their military demise, in part, to their defeat at the hands of the Afghan people.

The Afghan people are the embodiment of the face of war. For many Afghans, war is all they know. Many of these people have been fighting all their lives, some since they were old enough to hold a gun. The Afghans have a proverb that says, "If you do not like the image in the mirror, don't break the mirror; break your face." It is a true description and passage that captures the brutal and harsh life and reality these people live every day. *Peace* is a novelty word that is virtually meaningless in the mentality and minds of the people of Afghanistan because many have been at war literally since they were in their mothers' wombs. They are warrior people who live to fight and will continue to fight long after America has come and gone.

Setting up a legitimate federal government is something that has never been accomplished in Afghanistan, and it is an idea many of the locals cannot even contemplate or fathom. In this country, the indigenous people do not have a concept of time, what is morally right and wrong by civilized standards, or even a basic education. There is not even a fundamental understanding of what a federal government is and how it can be useful for its people, because Afghans utilize tribal law and code.

What people throughout the rest of the world need to take into account is that since 1893 when the British Empire created the borders of Afghanistan through the establishment and enforcement of the Durand Line, many tribes—both friendly and hostile—were split apart or moved next to one another. This created a country that benefited British necessity rather than Afghanistan unity and is largely the reason for the ongoing violence and disunity seen in Afghanistan today. The splitting of these tribes has had a catastrophic effect on attempts to achieve regional stability and unity to this day.

Having a strong federal government is something the people do not want, yet our current government and Hamid Karzai's want nothing more than to establish one for the overall benefit of the people. The Afghan people fear having a powerful government that tries to enforce federal law on their traditional regional beliefs and customs, which go back thousands of years. They reject the idea of a modern federal government having power to direct their tribes and village elders on what to do and how to live.

The people in Afghanistan, both as a civilization and culture, have not evolved and progressed like much of the world. Many of their tribal laws and codes of conduct, such as *Pashtunwali*, have been in place for hundreds if not thousands of years. These people are set in their ways and have no reason or desire to change. The last thing they want is some politician or president enforcing federal laws and democracy on their local culture and customs. It is a great idea; however, it is a shortsighted false reality once America decides to leave.

To paint a picture of what I mean when I say the Afghanistan populace has not evolved, I will make a comparison between Roman Soldiers during Caesar's rule and United States Marine forces today. United States Marines are one of the most technologically advanced military branches in the world, much like the Roman Empire and the legions of Praetorian Soldiers during Roman reign. As Marines patrol and walk through the countryside, it almost feels like we are modern-day Praetorian Soldiers traveling back in time, walking through a Roman desert wilderness, giving security to people who still live in mud houses, lack running water and electricity, and travel by camel or mule.

All attempts we make to civilize these people are met with resistance and in many cases violence. For the average Marine, each patrol is like stepping into a time machine and going two thousand years into the past. The Afghan people look at us like spacemen with all of our advanced technology and knowledge, while we look at them as savage and uncivilized more than anything. They resort to violence to solve disputes, use primitive irrigation methods, ride donkeys instead of vehicles, conduct daily trade in bazaars, live with their livestock, utilize witch doctors, etc.

What we must understand is that the people of this region have lived exactly the same lives for centuries and have their own laws, beliefs, and values. We must respect this logical fact and realize that a loose centralized government that empowers tribal leaders is a course of action that should not be taken off the table. The Taliban realized this, and that is why they are more effective than Karzai's government and maintain some form of power in the country to this very day. As bad as the Taliban are, they understand that controlling a population is achieved by empowering tribal leaders, allowing village customs to exist, and having a structurally weak central government.

The United States of America, as the world's only superpower, has the unique ability to redraw boundaries and borders to unite this country and end much of the bloodshed caused by warring tribes. We have the power to destroy the Taliban once and for all. The only question is if we are willing as a nation to invest the required troops, time, and money on a goal that will take decades, if not a century, to accomplish.

People alive today in Afghanistan are the ones who were not killed by the British, Russians, mujahedeen, warlords, criminal factions, Taliban, and the United States of America over the past century. Progress is defiantly a sluggish and time-consuming course of action, and as we patrol and conduct COIN operations, we must remember that not everyone is the enemy or Taliban.

A good portion of the Afghan people distrusts America because of both a lack of education and the fact that we have never stayed long-term during previous Afghan conflicts. We have a pattern of supporting a side that benefits a shortsighted foreign policy and then pulling out and leaving people in turmoil to fend for themselves (as was the case during the Vietnam War and Soviet-Afghan War in which millions of human beings were slaughtered once America withdrew its forces and support).

However, our patterns have never pointed to us oppressing or abusing the people of Afghanistan, and we have always acted on the side of good rather than evil. If anything, over the last half of this century, all American efforts and dollars have improved life and helped liberate the people of Afghanistan from their tyrannical rulers and the forces of darkness. This is a fact to which most educated Afghans will attest.

We as Americans must remember that we are not the bad guys, and history will prove this fact. We protect the sheep from the wolves. We are the light of the world and must stand strong because the world is being consumed by many forces of darkness even as we speak. Historical evidence of our great American deeds and footprints can still be seen and felt today, especially in the Helmand Province of Afghanistan.

Many of the canals and roads in the Helmand Province and adjacent areas that give life and transportation to the region were built by American contractors and groups like the United States Agency for International Development (USAID) back in the 1950s. The people of this area still recall Americans vacationing in the Nawa District as far back as the 1960s, just before the Russians occupied. Many elders still remember the humanitarian aid our government has given them over the last half century. The American government gave support and funding to the Afghan people in the 1970s to help them end Russian war and oppression—a fact that many who are still alive will never forget.

The people of this country desperately want to be liberated from the Taliban culture and oppressive rule. No one, no matter who you are or where you are from, wants to be controlled by an oppressive regime. No matter what anyone thinks, the voices on the ground sing a different song and paint a different picture than what most media outlets and news stations would have us believe. The Afghan people for the most part vehemently hate and despise the Taliban, but they lack the power and educational assets to oust them. Without our help to legitimize the government and military, the Afghan people will be forced to live under the extreme and fanatical Taliban regime.

The Taliban are not some unstoppable terrorist force capable of amassing great armies and weapons of mass destruction against our military. They are not genius tacticians or capable of starting nuclear war and global annihilation. Sure, there will always be a brain in any operation, but for the most part, the Taliban are poor and uneducated evil religious fanatics. They are no more fearsome than petty thugs, criminals, or occultists who just want to control everyone and everything in Afghanistan.

They are not hungry for world power like al-Qaeda. Let us not forget that although the Taliban commit human rights violations and are inherently evil, they did not blow up the Twin Towers on 9/11. Al-Qaeda and other Muslim terrorists, the majority of whom were from Saudi Arabia, were the ones responsible. The training they received to commit this act of war, however, was learned in Afghanistan in the training camps of the Taliban. Without the help of the Taliban, 9/11 might never have occurred. Eradication of the Taliban has been our mission from the beginning of this war and needs to remain a focus. It is possible. The Taliban are on the run, disorganized, and weak. There should be no reason to stop eradicating them at this point while we have the momentum and are winning.

Many Taliban fighters are just as scared of dying as many Americans are. This is why they hide among the population like cowards, sometimes wearing veils, burkas, or other female garments. The Taliban willingly sacrifice women and children by strapping bombs to their chests or using them as human shields in firefights to further their cause and agenda.

That said, it is important to note that many of these same evildoers do not even care about Osama bin Laden or even want to spread their hate, discontent, and religion on the world's stage. Sure, to many locals he is a dead inspirational hero who ousted the evil Russians, but he is not the reason they fight. But make no mistake: they want nothing more than to kill every American in Afghanistan and will do so with every ounce of breath they have.

There is no doubt that every last Taliban member should be killed and sent to meet his prophet Mohammed way up high in the sky for judgment for all the atrocities and war crimes the Taliban have committed against the innocent people of Afghanistan. It will be time-consuming, but in a war, albeit a global war, you go in to win no matter the cost, or you will lose.

The Taliban have to be ruthlessly hunted down and eliminated, which will take years and decades to accomplish. The military training camps Islamic jihadists used for the planning and preparation to commit 9/11 have to be denied and destroyed. It is possible. It can be done. But in a country the size of Texas and in which our military forces are limited, it will just take a long time.

CHAPTER 5

The Helmand Province is the most notorious and one of the most dangerous areas in all of Afghanistan. It is known for murder and intimidation campaigns by the Taliban against the local population, especially women and children. For military units, it is a devil's snare of rugged terrain and harsh, unpredictable weather. It is a province notorious for unexploded ordnance and improvised explosive devices (IEDs). For Marines, it was a playground, and we were the bullies sent in to keep the peace and bring justice to those who could not fight for themselves.

The Taliban had numerous strongholds and jihadist sleeper cell networks in this area from which to plan their attacks. Many of the locals sympathized and supported them out of necessity or fear of being killed. This afforded the Taliban the capability of cowardly blending in with the local population and hiding themselves among the men, women, and children in the rural villages.

During the conduct of their daily operations, the Taliban used Afghan people and children as human shields for protection in firefights, intelligence gathering, and during engagements with military forces. The Taliban murdered free-thinking village elders and district councilmen, raped children (especially little boys), and pillaged villages if anyone chose to not do what they commanded. The Taliban used women and children as shot spotters in firefights to help them achieve accurate fires on our forces.

The Taliban enemy is so distinctively immersed in the local nationals' day-to-day lives that there is almost no escaping the fact that they are always watching them, either visually or through informants. For the Taliban, Afghanistan is their turf, and the people are their possessions. They are not going to give them up without a fight.

The Helmand Province is also infamous for its drug cultivation and the Taliban's use of profits from these drugs to fund their terrorist operations. A billion-dollar industry in itself, poppy and marijuana fields stretch over many kilometers of lush, green farmland, starting at water-filled canals and ending in desert areas of knee-deep sand. On every one of my patrols, Marines saw endless drug fields and the remnants of dead poppy plants from which opium had been extracted. Drugs were everywhere!

Luckily for the Marines of Second Platoon, many of the local nationals during our deployment started the transition from growing drugs to growing other crops such as wheat and corn through Afghan and United States government-led eradication (GLE) programs. This process helped break the ties and bonds of exploitation the Taliban held over locals. Slowly, we saw the effects as the Taliban's ability to exploit and profit from the cash crop grown by poor farmers began diminishing thanks to our eradication and transition efforts.

In reality and on a macro scale, transitioning from poppy to wheat or corn was like putting a Band-Aid on a bullet wound. Afghanistan is a country that supplies the majority of the world with opium and drugs, and the supply and demand for the product is too great to shut off completely. The ever-increasing demand for opiates in countries like Pakistan, Russia, and China, as well as European countries, always slowed down our efforts to eradicate the supply. Certain villages ultimately transitioned during our deployment; however, the majority of the country still conducts business as usual in supplying the world with drugs.

The area in which we were located was only a small piece of the larger puzzle in which the United States, ISAF, and NATO forces eradicated these drugs. Sure, our area of operations (AO) was getting better, but making a significant impact to the drug trade in a country the size of Texas would take decades to accomplish. It is very hard to change a culture and way of life that has roots that stretch back for thousands of years.

The biggest problem United States Marines faced was their center of gravity, or in other words, the Afghanistan populace. These were the good Afghan people who were not Taliban and did not involve themselves with the degenerates and thugs in the illegal drug business. The local nationals' lack of education and understanding coupled with the fact that every major force that has entered the country has always demoralized, oppressed, and exploited them has always impeded efforts to better their lives. Although we never abused the people and always acted legally, ethically, and morally in all of our decisions, earning the trust and confidence of the Afghan people was a battle in itself. My Marines and Navy Corpsmen truly do not get the credit they deserve for the countless hours of patience it took to earn Afghans' trust and confidence.

Knowing these facts, educating the people, and explaining our intentions became one of the main strategic goals in our COIN fight. To the people of Afghanistan, the generosity of our American culture was an unbelievable spectacle that they took greedy advantage of. Witnessing a foreign military go out of its way to help with the problems of the people definitely earned us their trust and confidence; however, these actions were hard for Afghans to genuinely interpret because previous military units had never cared about their well-being. As Americans, we go out of our way to ensure the safety and welfare of those who are less fortunate and oppressed.

The people of Afghanistan are so illiterate and distrustful of each other that they cannot fathom the decency and generosity of our American democratic culture. This is the truth of the matter I want everyone to know. Many of the people are simple in their ways. They are concerned with the very things Americans are concerned about; however, they do not know kindness and decency. As Americans witnessing this, we tend to get bitter because Afghans almost never return our kindness and decency in full.

Having food, water, and money and being able to provide for themselves and their families is the primary concern of the local Afghan nationals. Many are not the religious fanatics they are portrayed to be. I cannot tell you how many times my Marines and I were invited into mosques and compounds for *shuras* (tribal or religious consultation meetings) or just a meal. I cannot even begin to recount all the acts of generosity bestowed upon us in support of our forces securing their population centers and bazaars.

If anything, the people of Afghanistan do not want us to leave because of all money and random acts of kindness the United States Marines are known for providing. With respect to the words of the Roman General Lucius Sulla popularized by the great Marine Corps Officer General James Mattis, we as Marines truly are "no better friend and no worse enemy" to the Afghan people.

CHAPTER 6

As far as the Taliban goes, I am going to say here and now that they are afraid, disorganized, defeated, and on the run. The only way for them to ever come back is if America pulls out of Afghanistan and Hamid Karzai's government crumbles. They cannot provide the same resources and strength for sustainment that Marines are able to provide, and they know it. They run from us when we are in sight and hide from us when we go hunting for them. They are no match for our superior strength and firepower. They bastardize the people because they know that is our critical vulnerability.

We as Marines, and furthermore as Americans, fight for individual human rights. The Taliban see this as a weakness and choose to kill the people and blame it on our morally and ethically right way of life by using illogical religious perspectives and interpretations to justify their evil actions.

The government of Afghanistan is slowly starting to legitimize, and the people want to believe it is there to support and fight for them. We must remember that in all reality, Afghanistan has truly never had the luxury of a government or military that could provide for and defend its own people. In fact, it has been quite the opposite.

There is corruption on both sides of this fight between the Taliban and the Afghan government. What people fail to realize is that new governments are not created overnight. Our American government has been around for a little more than two centuries, and we still have crooked and corrupt individuals in powerful positions who target, deceive, lie, and steal from the people. For as great as our country is, it is still plagued by secret societies, factions, and agendas that want nothing more than to restrict the rights and freedoms guaranteed by our Bill of Rights and Constitution so they can control our daily lives and bring down the very fabric of our government. America still has corruption that continues to afflict the lives of everyday law-abiding citizens and civilians. Afghanistan faces many of the same problems.

On the other side of the argument is factual actuality that the COIN strategy the United States Military utilized for this war limits our forces' capabilities to track down and hunt the Taliban enemy. Therefore, this war will take a long time to win. Our rules of engagement (ROEs) under the stellar Generals McCrystal and Petreus were very strict and felt like punishment for a crime that we as service members did not commit. It felt like a social agenda of tolerance and welfare was being forced upon my Marines, tying their hands in firefights. Although correct in intent, in a war these ROEs had the potential to get Marines into trouble. Government officials thousands of miles away made social decisions that turned into policy for my men when we engaged the enemy.

The Taliban knew we could not shoot unless shot at, they knew we could not go in mosques, and they knew we would be blamed for all civilian casualties as a result of battle. This was their wild card, and they played it. They knew our ROEs and therefore adapted and used them against us.

The enemy benefited from our ROEs because they knew how much it limited us when we were hunting them down. The ROEs are probably the hardest policy for the Marines to grasp because the rules are based largely on political correctness and defined by not upsetting or offending the culture of the local population at the expense of killing the bad guys. Marines were even told not to offend the Afghan people or else they would create more Taliban in the process. This was just absolutely absurd.

Marines were not allowed to go into compounds or pursue their adversaries without approval, sometimes at the battalion or regimental level, and the enemy knew this. It was almost as if the rules of engagement were exclusively in place to extend this war so those in charge of the military industrial complex would continue to profit because there was no end in sight with respect to the War on Terror.

We are fighting terrorists, not an organized or recognized military. Many critics argue that they do not fall under the protections of the Geneva Convention. They are not a formal military group identified by the Government of the Islamic Republic of Afghanistan as part of the military. Therefore, the Taliban can be interpreted as not falling under the auspices of the Geneva Convention, and we should not be limited as a military and should be able to use any means necessary to destroy them all.

CHAPTER 7

The President of Afghanistan, Hamid Karzai, made his own rules for ensuring cultural sensitivity in planning and executing operations for the United States and their coalition forces very clear in respect to what we could and could not do when conducting combat operations.

To clearly demonstrate the restraint my men faced during daily operations in Afghanistan, I have listed the rules Hamid Karzai enforced on the ROEs of United States and coalition forces below. It is no wonder why my men and Marines especially felt limited and hindered in everything they did while in Afghanistan. These rules had the potential to allow insurgents and terrorists to escape or unnecessarily put our forces in harm's way for the achievement of purely political purposes.

Hamid Karzai's Twelve Points (within hours of issue, the Taliban and our enemies all had copies of these Twelve Points):

1) Gain COMISAF approval before arrest, apprehension, or detainment of a current or former government appointed official.
2) Conduct coordination with local government officials and tribal leaders when conducting searches.
3) Ensure the return of materials/documents taken during searches, unless the owner is detained and the property becomes evidence.
4) Ensure personnel receive training on local customs and courtesies prior to conducting authorized searches.

5) Ensure Soldiers/Marines conducting searches ask for doors to be opened by occupants rather than Soldiers/Marines forcing entry.
6) Avoid the cuffing or binding of hands, unless required for security.
7) During low-risk operations, use a local person to enter the home or business of the person to be searched to explain what is happening.
8) Conduct of night searches needs to be led by ANSF (Afghan National Security Forces).
9) Ensure there is an infusion of reconstruction funds to areas where local people were detained and subsequently released.
10) Sustain the use of interpreters for direct interpretation while conducting raid or detaining GOA (Government of Afghanistan) personnel.
11) Deliberate detention operations.
12) Must operate within ten kilometers of the border of Iran or Pakistan.

After reading this, if one does not agree that this is an unmistakable enforcement and blatant attempt at socialism in a war zone, he or she is foolish. Marines and coalition troops had to inform locals of their intentions, ask permission to enter a compound, and only bind the hands of people if deemed absolutely necessary so as not to offend or hurt the local nationals' cultural feelings.

Not to mention the fact that Marines now had to coordinate with local police forces before conducting searches. Why? So the Afghan Police could tip off the bad guys? The reality was that most of the time when Marines coordinated with the local police, many of whom were affiliated with Taliban, the enemy would leave the village or compound and live to fight another day.

From the experience of the Marines of Hades Second Platoon and my CAP and CAC, the majority of Afghan people we encountered in the Helmand Province were very greedy and conniving. There is a saying in Afghanistan that if you give 50 percent in generosity, the Afghan people will give you back 100 percent in generosity. They also say in Afghanistan that if you are offered three cups of tea, the Afghan people will protect you with their lives, and if you are invited into a home, it is rude not to eat or drink the meal provided. That is a load of baloney for the most part, and our generosity and hard work were hardly ever rewarded in kind.

The worst thing Marines could do and were doing was buying into this type of pseudosocialism, because it limits the potential to find the enemy by forcing Marines to place trust in a third-world people whose culture essentially makes them into liars and thieves. This had the potential for Marines to become complacent, let their guard down, and get killed.

Now this is not to say that we should not follow the rules and act in a civilized manner toward the Afghans. The majority of Afghan units and civilians are probably great people; they are also the third-world's greatest warriors.

The majority of locals my platoon encountered were probably the few who did not meet that criteria. Regardless, the best advice for units conducting COIN is to obey the law at all times and not lose focus on the mission by thinking you are going to offend the local population and create Taliban from the locals you offend in the process of conducting daily combat operations. Keep your personal opinions to yourself and carry out the mission until it becomes unethical, immoral, or illegal.

If the Afghans want to fight, they will. If the Afghans don't want to fight, they won't. If they want to become Taliban, they will. If they don't want to be Taliban, they will not. The biggest mistake my Marines and I saw in Afghanistan was the manipulation, indoctrination, and brainwashing of junior Marines and ground units by senior leadership to be afraid to socially or culturally offend the population because it would supposedly create more Taliban.

Spending unlimited money, bending over backward to promote the Muslim culture and Islam, and offering projects to buy and pay the local nationals not to shoot at us was not counterinsurgency in the *Galula* sense. It was a hybrid farce being called COIN to justify the waste, fraud, and abuse of taxpayer money.

CHAPTER 8

It is a very hard concept for Marines, who are trained to kill and win at all costs, to grasp COIN and hit the "off switch." It is not impossible, however, and once United States Marines are trained to conduct counterinsurgency and three-block warfare, they do it very well. After all, counterinsurgency is nothing new to Marines historically. We conducted this type of warfare in the Banana Wars and in the Vietnam War. It is only recently that we started to conduct this type of warfare again, after years of not practicing it.

This does not mean that we as Marines cannot do it and be the best at it, because we are doing it, and we are excelling at it. As Marines, we pride ourselves on improvisation, adaptation, and overcoming obstacles. In this fight, the best strategy to win, according to our Commanding Generals, is to demonize the enemy and turn him against the population, resulting in the population having a greater trust and confidence in our forces rather than in the Taliban. I agree with this strategy, and my Marines and Navy Corpsmen followed the letter of the law down to the smallest detail.

Essentially, that means Marines go around on patrol and interact with the local population to legitimize themselves in the local nationals' eyes and show them our determination to rid their country of the Taliban and the tyranny they impose. The goal is to win the trust and confidence of the locals to turn them to our side and against the Taliban.

In a modern three-block war scenario, the proponents of counterinsurgency argue that it may be better to let the enemy go today at the risk of killing or injuring civilians, and find and kill the enemy tomorrow. The people are the center of gravity, and through a ruthless campaign of goodwill and kind gestures, the people will turn against the insurgents and effectively eliminate their control over the population.

What this *really* means, however, is that Marines patrol their specific areas of operation in Afghanistan as poster boys for this COIN strategy, waiting to get shot at because our ROEs limit us to the point that it is nearly impossible to even hunt down the Taliban because we may alienate the local populace in the process. We cannot go into compounds or buildings, we cannot interrogate, and we cannot offer monetary compensation for critical information. When Marines ask the local nationals for help or information in tracking down the enemy, the results are usually unsuccessful. Unless we are directly engaged, we are very limited in what we can do as a military.

However, this is not to say people are not helping us, because little by little, some are. The Afghan people fear for their lives and are deathly afraid to go against the Taliban because getting caught aiding our forces will unquestionably result in harassment, murder, or execution. Although many of my Marines felt indifferent to this policy of counterinsurgency, we still obeyed it and carried it out as we were told even though it felt like our leaders were turning their backs on us while giving more rights to the enemy.

By the time my Marines arrived in country, this counterinsurgency strategy—which was supposed to win the trust of the people—had evolved into a giant unaccountable welfare project of government waste and abuse. Interacting with the local population was geared toward offering them jobs and projects that would better their lives, not collecting intelligence that would win the war. Basically, my Marines were told to become glorified project managers and welfare agents, paying people and the enemy welfare money not to shoot at us. This was the outcome and endstate of the type of COIN we were enacting. We were not using money as an end or as a weapon but rather as a means.

David Galula would roll over in his grave if he saw what we were being told to do.

The downside to this, as the Marines of Second Platoon soon found out, is that the people, no matter how many projects they were given, would not give up any hard evidence or information about the location, structure, or whereabouts of the Taliban. Throwing money at a problem was only a temporary solution, not a permanent one.

But who can blame the Afghan people? We are throwing United States taxpayer dollars right in their faces while writing international welfare checks that make them rich and their wallets fat. If you think the Taliban aren't cashing in on it, you are wrong. For every project the United States government gives the local people, the Taliban, through murder and intimidation campaigns, take a certain percentage of the money. They then use those funds to purchase weapons and materials to harm United States and NATO forces.

The local nationals are smart too. They know our deployment rotation cycles, and they know the vulnerability, generosity, and compassion toward the local Afghan civilians new units bring into an area. Local nationals will take advantage of new units and new Commanders because they know they can. Therefore, when a new unit comes into an area, it is no wonder bridges, roads, and compounds are blown up and schools are intentionally burned down because of the "Taliban." The locals are greedy and smart. They will look for any excuse to profit from our generosity, even if it means burning down shops or compounds repeatedly for more funding. As long as they are getting money out of the deal—and trust me, they are—they will continue to undermine our efforts unless we truly use money as a weapon.

Soon after learning of these facts, the Marines of Second Platoon began to have enough of the charades and political butt kissing. We never gave out money or projects to local nationals. We made it our mission to cut down on the flood of money flowing through our area of operations that had been established by previous units, and we opted to create a little drought. We even took lessons learned from Iraq and made ultimatums with village elders that an attack on our Marines would lead to us damming their canals or cutting off government support. We impressed upon them their responsibility toward us to work together to defeat the enemy.

The population became upset, but not to the point of being hostile. They could feel their wallets getting smaller and were willing to work with us now more than ever so they could stay rich. We did not care. As long as we were not indirectly or directly supporting the enemy with United States taxpayer dollars, we were doing the right, noble, and honorable thing.

It was through these actions that Second Platoon started to see a drastic increase in intelligence and reporting on Taliban who lived in our area from the locals—all because we started to use project money as a weapon. The Afghan people started to see that as the new unit on deck we meant business, and they slowly came around to our side more and more. My Marines knew that when people are hungry, they want your support; however, when they are full, they do not need you anymore. We also knew the Afghans were warriors, and if we showed weakness, they would exploit it. They had to know who was in charge the entire time.

Money is a great motivational weapon that should be utilized with great responsibility in the theoretical "Galula" approach. It should not be used in a manner of fiscal carelessness with an endstate of waste, fraud, and abuse.

What the counterinsurgency strategy creates is a war that will be drawn out for years because the enemy becomes well-funded, motivated, and knowledgeable of our weaknesses. It is a hard thing to grasp, but the only way to win this war is to kill every last terrorist without remorse. America has to go in it to win at all costs. Contrary to what some in the media or select politicians would have you believe, wishful thinking, ideals of grandeur and social harmony are dreamworld nonsense. People fail to realize that the bad thing about the Global War on Terrorism is that it will be a long, costly war with potentially no end in sight.

CHAPTER 9

The Nawa District is a region in the Southern Helmand Province of Afghanistan directly north of the Garmsir District and east of Marjeh. It is the area to which my platoon deployed. It was an area the media cursed and declared lost to the Taliban by US and NATO forces. Just like the Sunni Triangle or Ramadi in Iraq, the United States Marines quickly turned the area around, making it one of the safest places in the entire country.

Take that, you cowards and negative journalists and reporters with your pessimistic views on the war that spread fear and lies rather than the truth! It amazes me how quickly the media turns its back on the American military while protecting and glorifying the human rights of the villains who speak out and conduct violence against innocent human beings. Rather than report our wins, they report our casualties and the loss of life and at no time report the damage we inflict on our enemies to defeat them. When did our own media become propaganda machines for the enemy and terrorists?

What made the Nawa District a very hard fight to win was the fact that the Taliban were so immersed in the people's daily lives and the fact that they were much better at local justice and settling disputes than President Kharzi's Afghan National Army or Afghan Uniformed Police (AUP) forces. Afghanistan is an enormous country, and being able to influence every part of it with elements of this new Government of the Islamic Republic of Afghanistan (GIROA) would only be possible in time. Immediate and tangible results were just not logical.

Don't get me wrong. From everything my platoon saw and every person we encountered, the majority of people in many different tribes and areas generally supported us and fought for the Marines and Afghan government in some way, shape, or form if they could. Many preferred our method of justice to the Taliban's because it is more civilized and fair.

We are not the bad guys, and the people of Afghanistan know it. We give the people life through creating jobs, enhancing their crops, securing their areas, and bringing them justice without oppressing them in return. We build roads, bridges, and schools to enhance their education and transportation. We are not the wolves; we are and have always been instruments that protect innocent sheep from the wolves.

The area of the Nawa District in which my Marines were located consisted of five companies that made up our battalion. From north to south there was India Company, Kilo Company, Headquarters and Service Company, Lima Company, and Weapons Company. These five companies together made up Third Battalion, Third Marine Regiment. Inside Lima Company, which was the Rifle Company my Marines and I were part of, were four platoons that were located at four separate patrol bases (PBs), and one company operations base (COB).

COB Toor Gar was where First Platoon, under the command of First Lieutenant Seth Miller and Staff Sergeant Matthew Salazar, and the central leadership of Lima Company were located. My Commanding Officer (CO), Captain Shields; my Company Executive Officer (XO), First Lieutenant Freedman; and my Company First Sergeant, First Sergeant Mize, were in charge of the conduct of the entire Lima Company area of operations from Toor Gar.

COB Toor Gar was a very well-fortified base with its own helicopter landing zone (HLZ). At Toor Gar, Marines were fully partnered with the Afghan National Army. The company-sized base was surrounded by green fields, luscious farmland, civilian compounds, and canals on all sides. It was here that all helicopters and convoys taking part in our company operations arrived and departed.

COB Toor Gar was the central hub for all contracting projects and monetary transactions in the Lima Company AO. It was here that all shuras, or tribal meetings, took place between village elders in the Lima Company AO and our Commanding Officer, Captain Shields. Toor Gar was where the local nationals came to discuss any issues they had, regardless of the problem.

Patrol Base (PB) Noba was to the southeast of Toor Gar, and it was fortified by Third Platoon under the command of First Lieutenant Vali. PB Noba was partnered with the Afghan Uniformed Police Officers and United States Marines. What made this patrol base vital was that it was strategically important in the counterinsurgency aspect of the war. It was located right next to a bazaar where thousands of people goods. Having a strong Marine- and Afghan-led partnered presence in the area to provide security to the local populace was imperative to the success we needed to achieve. It was a great deterrent for the Taliban as well because it prevented them from committing suicide bombings and vehicle IED attacks against both us and the civilians at the local bazaar.

PB Jengali and PB White Twenty were north of Toor Gar, fortified by the Marines of Weapons Platoon and the Afghan National Army and Police and under the command of First Lieutenant Alex Hartsell and Staff Sergeant Fields. PB Jengali was probably the most civilized of the bases. It had showers, air-conditioning, and electricity. For these reasons alone, it rivaled every other position in the battalion AO, especially during the triple-digit temperatures of the long, hot summer months. It was a very well-fortified base. Its only weakness was a tree line directly north of its defensive perimeter that could be used by the Taliban as cover and concealment to plan an attack.

PB White Twenty was controlled by a squad from Weapons Platoon and an element of the Afghan Uniformed Police and under the charge of Staff Sergeant Tyr Jackson. It was a small area between FOB Geronimo and COB Toor Gar that was very vulnerable to attacks because of the minute presence of coalition forces. It was a vital position because it was a buffer or staging area for both combat and noncombat operations conducted between FOB Geronimo and COB Toor Gar.

PB Brannon, which was named after Corporal Brannon, a Marine who gave his life during the Vietnam War, was located eight kilometers (clicks) southwest of Toor Gar. PB Brannon was where the Marines of Second Platoon and a platoon of the Afghan National Army were centrally located during the first month of deployment. I arrived at the PB on approximately 18 May 2010 as part of the advance party deployment to conduct my leader reconnaissance of the area before my Marines arrived on 25 May 2010.

PB Brannon was surrounded on all four sides by uninhabitable desert. Visibility from the guard posts ranged up to two clicks in every direction on a clear day when there were no sandstorms. This was good because the enemy would either have to be foolish or have a death wish to think he could successfully attack our base without being seen.

The living situation at PB Brannon was less than decent at best. There were no showers, cold water, air conditioners, Internet, or bathroom facilities. All creature comforts had to be made by my men. Many Americans would go crazy at the thought of these meager conditions. This did not matter though, because as Marines we feed off each other and motivate each other to build morale.

As far as our defensive capabilities were concerned, to complement our entire standoff we had three M2 .50-caliber machine guns, two MK19 grenade launchers, and two M240B machine guns on our guard posts, covering every possible avenue of approach the enemy could utilize to his advantage. It would have been a meat grinder for the Taliban if they decided to commit jihad against us at PB Brannon, but my Marines of Second Platoon would have gladly arranged a meeting between them and their god. In every aspect, if the Taliban were to attack us, it would be like "hugging a chainsaw." This quote was one my Marines loved to use and was made famous by our Regimental Commander when he said it to his Marines conducting combat operations against the Taliban in the Korangal Valley, Afghanistan, a few years earlier.

What made PB Brannon great was the work ethic and nonstop determination of my Marines to continually improve its defensive capabilities and fortify it. My Marines are the select few, the ones movies and books are written about, because they are the best leaders and followers I have ever come into contact with. I am blessed to have been in charge of them, and I thank God every day to have been their Commander.

A Platoon Commander's biggest worry when he receives his first platoon is having an undisciplined, weak, lackadaisical Platoon Sergeant and immature Squad Leaders that walk all over him. This was not the case for me, and I could not have asked for a better group of Marines and Navy Corpsmen than those who were under my charge.

Upon their arrival, they all tirelessly worked to fortify and sustain our patrol base day in and day out. My Marines constantly police called, improved our fortifications, stacked sandbags, and improved the quality of life and defense positions.

Staff Sergeant Lebron and I had trained our Marines and Sailors to have the highest standards of physical, mental, and ethical conduct. Our Marines knew we demanded results and if expectations were not met, he and I would enforce these standards of conduct and discipline. However, that rarely, if ever, occurred.

Chapter 10

On 25 May 2010, my platoon of Marines arrived at PB Brannon to link up with me and conduct their relief in place and transfer of authority (RIP/TOA) with our First Battalion, Third Marines (1/3) counterparts of Cobra Company, who were still at PB Brannon.

During the first day of our occupation and inheritance of the patrol base, my First Squad discovered their first IED. Subsequently, this was the first IED discovered by any unit, respective to Third Battalion, Third Marines, since we arrived in Afghanistan.

On a routine dismounted joint security patrol with Marines from First Battalion, Third Marines, which was conducted to familiarize my Marines and Navy Corpsmen with the surrounding area and terrain, Sergeant Olds and Lance Corporal Hall from First Squad, acting on a tip from Second Squad's Sergeant Brown and Corporal Berry, who had patrolled earlier that day, confirmed the explosive device's existence.

The IED was snugly nestled between two compound walls and underneath a hedgerow of shrubbery so Marine units would be unable to see or detect it until it was too late. This IED, made up of a mixture of ammonium nitrate, fertilizer, and motorcycle parts, was exploited by Sergeant Olds's squad directly following their five-hour cordon of the IED. Because our AO was so vast, it took five hours for a team of Explosive Ordnance Detail (EOD) to arrive on scene to support my squad.

Finding this IED was a great discovery in itself because if any of my Marines had walked by the fifty-pound explosive device, it would have detonated and killed a minimum of half the squad. It was also a great discovery because we gained fingerprints and now had real-time knowledge of the TTPs our enemy was using to make these bombs, which would enable us to defeat them in the future.

Communication between my two Squad Leaders and their Marines undoubtedly saved lives that day. Already, on day one, my platoon had set the bar for the rest of the company and battalion by finding the first IED in our AO and destroying it.

Within the first week of occupying PB Brannon, just about every one of my Marines and Navy Corpsmen, including myself, had some type of gastrointestinal parasite or virus that became known as "the demon." It was awful! Constant diarrhea, dehydration, delusions, and vomiting were the common symptoms. Those not affected by the demon laughed like hyenas as Marines ran to the toilets a few times every hour in agony. Our Platoon Corpsman gave us stomach relaxers and medicine to treat the symptoms, but to no avail. When one became stricken with the demon, he was out of commission for twenty-four to ninety-six hours and lost at least fifteen pounds of body weight.

We soon figured out that parasites contained in the local food and water supply were the cause of the sickness. In Afghanistan, when a person is invited into a home and offered food, it is generally rude to refuse a meal or drink (or so we were trained to believe in our Afghan culture courses). Marines who were lucky enough to be offered a cup or two of chai tea made from the bacteria- and parasite-infested water of the canals or eat undercooked chicken or beef usually fell victim to the illness within twenty-four hours. It was a risk we all had to take at some point because refusing the gesture could insult the Afghan people and have a negative impact on our COIN strategy (or so we were led to believe). We did not want to turn good people into Taliban.

Marines have a unique ability to immerse themselves in a culture and live among the people. We can adapt and live in any environment with any group of people. Marines work with less, and we do not quit, because a situation can always be worse. Even though we all became sick, did not have running water, had inadequate bathroom facilities and zero air-conditioning in the triple-digit climate, our PB was a tangible entity we all helped build and create. It was ours, it was alive, and like a well-oiled machine, it ran smoothly and took care of us. After all, it was named after Corporal Brannon. That alone was motivation in itself.

During our downtime, we built guard posts, a weight room, a combat operations center (COC), and even a barbeque grill made out of old HESCO barriers. This especially came in handy when Lance Corporal Evola (whose family owned an Italian restaurant) decided to cook meals for the platoon at night.

My innovative Marines built an animal coop that was filled with many living creatures such as chickens, goats, and ducks. My Marines cooked and ate these animals when our Unitized Group Ration-A's (UGR-As) and meals ready to eat (MREs) started to run low.

PB Brannon was our home, the surrounding villages were our community, and the people were our citizens. Responsibility for their lives and the stability of the community depended on the stellar lawful, moral, and ethical conduct and resolve of each of my Marines and Navy Corpsmen.

A typical day at PB Brannon was complex in its design but simple in its execution. At all times Staff Sergeant Lebron and I had our Marines and Afghan National Army Soldiers either on post, conducting combat security patrols, or manning vehicle checkpoints (VCPs). When not doing these three daily tasks, they rested, improved the defensive capabilities of the PB, or made the most of their free time by conducting PME and classes. Our Navy Corpsmen were constantly studying or attending to the medical needs of the local nationals, who visited our PB daily.

Staff Sergeant Lebron and I ran our own patrolling schedules. Our Marines covered approximately ten to fifteen kilometers daily and conducted four squad-level dismounted combat patrols a day. This totaled more than one hundred dismounted security patrols and more than three hundred kilometers covered per month. Combine this with triple-digit temperatures, eighty pounds of gear, chow, water, and ammunition and these patrols over a period of time became a great physical fitness workout.

We were eight kilometers away from any friendly ground support unit. It would take the nearest infantry unit up to an hour just to reinforce our position on foot if we were in a contact situation. We were truly on our own at the edge of the empire, not as cowboys but as elite warriors ready and willing to take on the Taliban enemy.

Each day at 0430, reveille sounded for the Marines not manning a guard post. Chow would then be prepared and administered by my Navy Corpsmen, either Doc Greenough or Doc Williams. By 0600, the first patrol of Marines and Afghan National Army Soldiers patrolled from the PB and covered various sectors of our platoon-assigned AO. Two hours later, at around 0800, our next patrol commenced and covered areas the first patrol had not been to. Never setting a pattern, our patrol times varied each day based on a number of reasons, including atmospherics, biometrics, and intelligence, but we generally conducted them two times in the morning and two times in the evening.

On average, each squad I sent out patrolled up to a minimum of five kilometers over rocky, muddy, and sandy desertlike terrain and through arid climates that reached temperatures as hot as 140 degrees. On every patrol, a Marine was expected to get wet and be up to his waist in water because of the many canals and creeks running through the area. My Marines and I eventually had to cut holes in our combat boots with knives because water would not drain from them fast enough. The benefit of going through the canals was there was a less likely chance for IEDs, and it gave us the ability to cool down our constantly high body temperatures, which were normally 101 degrees or higher. I made it known to my Marines that they were never to follow straight lines or use roads or trails as guides for their patrols. These were havens for buried IEDs.

It was a little known secret that both the enemy and Afghan Soldiers hated getting wet and immersing themselves in water. My Marines used this opportunity to teach the Afghan Soldiers at PB Brannon how to be comfortable in water and why it was safer to patrol this way rather than on improved roads and linear trails. To set the Afghan Soldiers up for success, they needed to know how to defeat IEDs and enemy tactics.

On a daily basis, our combat security patrols focused on interaction with the local national populace and having lunch and dinner with the elders in the area to foster and build our relationships with them. We handed out *Kalam*, the Pashtu word for pens, to the children because for some reason they just loved "ink sticks." We patrolled local stores and local markets to buy food or drinks and interact with the local population.

My Navy Corpsmen routinely treated sick village members and gave medical support to injured children and adults. My Platoon Corpsmen were like manna sent from heaven to the local nationals because all the villagers had prior to the Marines arriving were the village witch doctors who used inferior medical practices to treat ailments.

In the Pashtu culture, particularly in the Helmand Province, when infants cry or misbehave, their parents will throw boiling water on them as punishment, causing second- and third-degree burns. Unlucky children who do not have this done to them are immersed in boiling water and subsequently killed. Life meant nothing to the people who lived in our AO. The Marines at PB Brannon encountered at least five boiled baby situations during their first month there. It seemed almost biweekly, little babies with third-degree burns would come to PB Brannon for treatment. Some were lucky; others were not.

Up until the point my platoon arrived, the local Afghan village witch doctors usually treated burns by putting canal water, which was basically the equivalent of raw sewage, on the burn wounds, further infecting the children. Obviously, most of the time when parents burned their children the endstate was death by serious infection.

Life has zero value in Afghanistan, and many people stab or assault each other over the most minor disagreements. My Corpsmen did their best to save these babies' lives even though most of the time their efforts were unsuccessful.

Within our first week at PB Brannon, my Marines and I arrested a local national who threw his neighbor into a wood chipper over what he described was a minor dispute. The local national accused his neighbor of stealing one of his rakes and gardening tools, and because the neighbor had offended his honor in the process, the Afghan man felt justified in regaining his honor by throwing this man into his wood chipper. Obviously, by the time my Marines and I arrived on the scene, all that was left of the man's body was little bloody pieces. To make the situation even more bizarre, the local national man who killed his neighbor even had the audacity to ask my Marines and me for money to fix his now-broken machine. Little did he know that he had committed an act called murder and would soon be in an Afghan Police jail.

The locals knew if they faced some type of medical problem or emergency, they could always come to see our Navy Corpsmen or me for help. However, if they did something morally and ethically wrong, such as killing one another, they would answer to us and face some type of justice.

When my men first arrived in the country, their initial expectation was to be shot at during routine security patrols and encounter IEDs everywhere they went. After all, Afghanistan as a country has millions of undiscovered landmines and IEDs and has a great history of instability.

The reality was that our area was generally safe, and my Marines routinely reentered friendly lines at my patrol base angry that they were not being shot at. When I say generally safe, I mean that more people were killed by violent crimes on the border between Mexico and the United States and on our own American streets than where we were located.

Many of my Marines started to feel weak having to promote a social agenda of interaction through project management and friendliness rather than doing what they had been trained to do since their inception at boot camp, which is to kill. It was also hard for some to see the multitude of dead babies or children and the crimes against humanity being committed by the people we were there to help and protect against the Taliban.

I recall asking Sergeant Olds one day as his squad was coming back from a security patrol, "Give me a debrief. How did the patrol go?"

His response was, "Sir, I am shattered, and every time I get back with my squad, I am shattered. I walk around patrolling all day throughout our assigned sectors of responsibility, and people ask me for projects and money instead of shooting at me. I wake up daily, not to the sounds of gunfire but to the screams of a boiled baby or an idiot Afghan Soldier who just shot himself with his own weapon. I am not a social worker or Red Cross employee or a welfare agent. I joined the Corps to kill, not to become a project manager and ask grown men about their feelings.

"We are in a Global War on Terrorism, and my Marines are at the mercy of bureaucratic policy makers with no military experience. They sit behind desks and make decisions on what we do here on the ground without ever stepping foot on it. How can they ever know the value and feeling of leading Marines in combat? This is depressing, sir."

Obviously the counterinsurgency aspect of the war has its critics, but it is a known fact that Marines are not happy unless they are being shot at. I fully agreed with my Squad Leader. However, we knew our mission, and we had to execute it regardless of our personal beliefs.

By 1000 each day, my first dismounted security patrol reentered friendly lines at the PB and executed their rest plan. Around 1200, my second dismounted security patrol entered friendly lines and executed their rest plan. Between the hours of 1200 and 1600 it was very rare for my platoon to conduct patrols because of the extreme temperatures and blinding sandstorms. Sandstorms were a particular problem during our deployment to the Helmand Province. My platoon encountered numerous sandstorms during a seasonal phase in Afghanistan known as "the winds of 120 days." This act of nature occurs primarily between June and September in Afghanistan, and the storms can reach a wind velocity of 180 kilometers per hour.

It was generally understood that when temperatures were in the triple digits and sandstorms were occurring, the Taliban would not want to fight. Therefore, our patrolling efforts were geared toward early mornings and late afternoons when the temperatures were cooler and the storms were less frequent.

Usually around 1600 and 1900, the same two squads from the morning executed the conduct of their security patrols by concentrating their efforts on areas missed during the morning. At night, these same squads set up listening post and observation post (LP/OP) positions in the vicinity of our PB to look for any anomalies or patterns of life that would indicate the enemy placing IEDs or planning an imminent attack on us. Nothing came in or out of PB Brannon unless it went through my Marines, who watched everything.

The patrolling squads were usually on a two-day rotation with two squads tasked as the patrolling elements and one squad guarding the posts. Each squad member averaged between five to six hours of rest a day, while Squad Leaders averaged even less.

This is what we are trained to do. United States Marines are trained to conduct operations in the face of adversity, in the harshest conditions, and under intense sleep and food deprivation. We all know it, we all do it, and we all recognize that it is expected of us. We are the best at what we do, and we work harder than everyone else to prove it.

CHAPTER 11

One of the most unique events that came from our time at PB Brannon was the measurable improvement of the working relationship between my Marines of Second Platoon and the Afghan National Army Soldiers. At PB Brannon, successes and failures were a direct result of how hard my Marines and our Afghan partners worked together and how much both were willing to sacrifice for each other.

If my Marines and our Afghan counterparts were enthusiastic and wanted to learn, we would get better as a fighting unit. However, frustrations with the language barrier and cultural differences with this less equipped, educationally deprived third-world military impeded progress and evolution and frequently took us right back to square one. Examples of this included the inability to have a simple, basic conversation or mistakenly patrolling over a cemetery during a night dismounted security patrol.

This way of thought directly applied to our relationship with our Afghan National Army Soldier counterparts, who were led by their Commander, Captain Baz Mohammed. Captain Baz Mohammed was a very crusty, salty, and rotund man. He was stern in his posture and demanding of his Soldiers. At age forty-nine, this man had lived through the Russian, mujahedeen, and Taliban tyrannical rule and had a great deal of experience in conducting counterinsurgency operations. What made him even better was that he despised the Taliban because they had tortured and tried to kill him a few years earlier, and he wanted nothing more than to help the American military destroy them altogether.

He knew the Taliban were like wolves. Any offering of peace would be seen as weakness to them. Baz often said if you give a mouse a crumb, he will be back and want more next time. Speaking in parables and proverbs or quoting religious scripture was Captain Baz's way of conversing. If I wanted to get work done with respect to the Afghan Soldiers or the local Afghan villagers, Captain Baz Mohammed was the guy I had to talk with to make it happen. It was incumbent on my platoon to utilize the knowledge of our Afghan partners to achieve mission success.

From my experience in dealing with the Afghan National Army, many of the Soldiers were young, scared, addicted to drugs, or looking for any reason to just quit. They were very untrustworthy, and my Marines always treated them as if they would turn on us and try to shoot or kill us at any moment. We had to, especially with all the acts of violence Afghan Soldiers were committing against coalition forces.

There is a saying about Afghans: "You can't buy an Afghan's loyalty; however, for the right price you can rent it." My Marines always knew the Soldiers could be bought by the Taliban and infiltrate the PB. We were always on guard against it and slept with one eye open and a guardian angel present at all times. For all we knew, a few of these Afghan Soldiers living with us were Taliban. It was a shame that even though these were our partners and we were forced to live with them, we could not trust them at all.

This is not to say there were not good Afghan Soldiers because some of them would have given their lives to protect my Marines and Corpsmen. Many of the good Soldiers were put in positions of leadership to benefit our success in the fight against the enemy. The key element that was lacking was strong and dependable leadership throughout the Afghan ranks. However, this was not the case with Captain Baz Mohammed at PB Brannon. If his men could not cut it professionally or acted like schoolgirls when it came time to work or go out on patrol, he would not hesitate to enforce capital punishment on them and beat their bodies half to death.

One night as I was sitting in my hooch, finishing an after-action report for my daily squad combat patrols, Staff Sergeant Lebron came storming in looking very upset, to say the least.

"Hey, sir, come with me. I saw something outside the PB, and I need you to get out here with me now before there is an international incident!" He said these words to me in an uproar that was coupled with a deep professional concern and a hint of sarcasm—a skill Staff Sergeant Lebron had gained from his years of heckling recruits on the drill field in Parris Island as a drill instructor.

In a stunned and uncertain manner, I replied, "What's going on? Is everything all right?"

"No time to explain, sir. I saw a few of our Afghan Soldiers doing some shady activities outside the wire, and you need to come with me right now so we can rectify this," he replied in a furious manner.

"Got it. I am right behind you," I replied with an obvious tone of uncertainty. I grabbed my M4 rifle while Staff Sergeant Lebron explained to me that he had alerted our Marines on guard to watch our backs through the scopes of their rifles.

We exited my hooch and walked outside the southern entrance of our PB in the pitch-black of night. I noticed Staff Sergeant Lebron walking very cautiously and cunningly toward where the Afghan Soldiers' vehicle was parked. Anytime my six-foot-seven Platoon Sergeant walked cautiously, I knew we were going to get into some type of action. He was doing a complete combat glide to ensure no one heard his footsteps as he approached the Afghan vehicle outside the wire.

"Right here, sir. Tell me what you smell," my Platoon Sergeant said to me as he pointed to a vehicle with the windows rolled up, lights on, and music playing.

"Is that what I think it is? Are they smoking hashish right now?" I replied quietly in order to not give away our position or alert the drug-smoking Afghan Soldiers to our presence.

"Yes, sir. I was out here messing with our Class IV lot and followed the smell to their vehicles. These simians are smoking dope and getting stoned on my patrol base, around my Marines and Corpsmen," he replied.

At the realization of this fact, Staff Sergeant Lebron and I surreptitiously hurried back into the confines of our PB and grabbed our linguist by the name of Nassir. My platoon liked to jokingly call Nassir "Jesus," a nickname he received from Staff Sergeant Lebron because he thought he looked like what our Lord Jesus Christ would have looked like.

At thirty-three years old, Nassir was every bit of 110 pounds and constantly smoked cigarettes everywhere he went. This small man would smoke a carton of cigarettes a week and patrol three times a day. He was a very intellectual man and a former teacher from Kabul, Afghanistan. He had my highest respect because he patrolled hours on end and never complained. He was a short Afghan man of about sixty-four inches with olive skin and a beard that covered his entire face. The Marines got along with him very well and always heckled him in a joking way.

He was a very skinny, nonmuscular individual who loved martial arts videos and saw himself as the Afghan version of Jet Li. He also always watched movies with Arnold Schwarzenegger and quoted lines from his movies. I remember every time we went on patrol he would say things like, "Lieutenant Bodrog, come with me if you want to live" or "Get down." He was a strange bird, to say the least, but he was one of the few linguists we trusted to say the right things to the local nationals at all times.

As we went to grab Nassir in the dimly lit confines of our base, Staff Sergeant Lebron said, "Nassir, let's go. Get your butt over here now," waking him from slumber.

"I am coming, Staff Sergeant," replied Nassir with a very heavy accent.

The three of us returned to the vehicle in which the Afghan Soldiers were smoking. We then told Nassir to knock on their window and find out what the two Afghan Soldiers were doing.

"*Salam. Sen-gay*?" asked Nassir with his right hand over his heart in a formal gesture. *Sen-gay* is the Pashtu phrase for "How are you doing?"

In a very hesitant reply, one of the Afghan Soldiers said, "*Jor-ray,*" which is the Pashtu response for "Everything is well." Clearly, my Platoon Sergeant and I knew everything was *not well.*

A few long and hot seconds went by before we ordered Nassir to have the Afghan Soldiers step out and open their vehicle doors. Disoriented and with bloodshot eyes, the two Afghan Soldiers were clearly in a daze and wondering what was going on. Before anything could be asked, Nassir looked at my Platoon Sergeant and told him they were smoking hash and under the influence of drugs. He even instructed us to be careful because they were not in their right state of mind. Mental red flags automatically went up, and my Platoon Sergeant and I immediately started firing questions for translation to Nassir at the cyclic rate to find out what the two stoned Afghan Soldiers were up to.

"What are you both doing out here in the vehicle? Why are the windows up? It is over one hundred degrees out here. Why are you blasting music in the middle of the night? What's wrong with your eyes? Why is the vehicle filled with smoke? What are your names? What are you smoking? Why do you look scared and nervous? Why are you both saying two different stories and then changing them? Why does your truck smell like hash? Did you sell any of your drugs to our Marines?" The questions flowed from us through the conduit of our linguist's mouth as if we were professional interrogators trying to solve a murder mystery.

Now mind you, these Afghan National Army Soldiers did not have air-conditioning in their truck, and on this particular night the temperature was over one hundred degrees. There was no reason for anyone to be out, especially outside the safety of the PB.

One of the Soldiers in the vehicle replied, "I am out here starting the truck so the battery doesn't die."

The other Afghan Soldier stated, "I am sleeping here because it's more comfortable in the truck than outside of it."

According to Staff Sergeant Lebron, at this point I looked irate, like I was about to break both their faces for bringing this "drug pestilence" onto my base. Before we could say another word we heard footsteps coming from the darkness somewhere behind us. Instinctively, Staff Sergeant Lebron slid his hand down to his side and flipped his knife open while taking a half step back to see the growing commotion behind us.

Like a swarm of insects, more Afghan Soldiers were approaching us to see what we were doing, and they began to surround Staff Sergeant Lebron and me in a circular fashion. Staff Sergeant Lebron, out of protection and loyalty, was prepared for anything to happen and had my back, as I did his. If they were here to kill or harm us, we would counter it with the Iraqi death blossom tactic and shoot our way out.

Enraged at the Afghan Soldiers standing in front of me, I became internally focused on the situation at hand, unaware of the events unfolding around us. Luckily, my Platoon Sergeant was not. He was in a high state of alert. Realizing now that drugs were involved, logic and reason went right out the window for me like the smoke from the Afghan vehicle. We always operated under the assumption that foreign Soldiers could snap against us any minute. Now it was time to fall back on the level of our training.

This was not America, and there was not a level of civility to be measured. This was a third-world country, and when people get angry, more often than not they will resort to violence or just kill you, because human life has no value to them.

With the situation growing tense and more Soldiers appearing from out of the darkness, Staff Sergeant Lebron and I made the decision to break contact and head back into the protection of the PB, toward the security of the platoon and our Marines. With a blade in his hand and rifle at the ready, my Platoon Sergeant cleared a path through the Afghan Soldiers and the darkness that surrounded us, and we walked back-to-back into the PB.

At this time, my Platoon Sergeant looked me in the eyes and said, "What course of action do you want to take now, sir? Those bastards just surrounded us both out there!"

"Staff Sergeant, I am going to call Lima Main, inform them of the situation, and then let the Afghan National Army Commander know what is going on. Watch the Marines. Wake up a team, brief them up, and have them act as a guardian angel roving patrol inside the PB," I replied, looking to seek an avenue of justice for what we had just witnessed. I could not professionally tell him what I wanted to do even though I was sure we were both thinking the same thing. With the immediate situation de-escalated, I had to take the moral, lawful, and ethical high ground for the safety of my Marines and Corpsmen.

After I radioed our company's combat operations center and informed Captain Shields (who told us we needed to be tolerant, respect their culture more, and get over it), we headed straight toward the living quarters of Captain Baz Mohammed. He greeted us pleasantly with a smile as he held a cup of chai tea and started talking to us in Dari, his native tongue.

He took a look at both my Platoon Sergeant and myself and realized something was wrong. We were not smiling back at him, to say the least. He knew we could only understand bits and pieces of his language and realized the language barrier was not why we were angry. According to my Platoon Sergeant, I was pacing back and forth at this point, growing intensely mad, and trying to calm myself so I could articulate in a clear, concise manner what we had just witnessed. It was hard to keep my bearings after being surrounded by armed Afghans, most of whom had been under the influence of drugs. After all, these guys were supposed to be our partners, not our enemies.

Nassir began explaining to Captain Baz Mohammed what had happened outside between the Afghan Soldiers and the both of us. He gave Captain Baz the names of the Soldiers we had caught smoking drugs. Before Nassir could even finish his sentence, Captain Baz began bellowing out commands at his Soldiers. From every angle of the PB, Afghan Soldiers came running toward him, looking deathly afraid as he barked out order after order at them. As one Soldier moved slowly toward him, Baz commanded him to find whoever was outside smoking hash in the vehicle. Hesitantly, the Soldier tried to question the Commander, promptly resulting in Captain Baz punching him and throwing him outside on the ground where the vehicles were parked.

Moments later, one of the Soldiers in the truck started walking through the entrance of our PB with his head hung low and a very weak posture. Captain Baz started shouting at his Soldier in an increasingly loud manner that climaxed with tears filling the dope-smoking Soldier's bloodshot eyes. The Afghan Captain, without hesitation, immediately commenced to openhandedly slap his Soldier in the face, punch him in the chest, grab him by the throat, and shake him to the ground. It was an awesome display of power by Captain Baz.

Amazing! I thought. *Baz destroys this Soldier while Captain Shields tells me to be more sympathetic and tolerant of their culture. Did my Captain not care that they were bringing drugs onto my PB and around my Marines? Obviously the Afghan Captain does.*

I looked to Staff Sergeant Lebron during this awesome moment and said, "Is this really happening right now? I didn't expect this. The previous unit was not kidding when they said Baz rules with an iron fist. This is outstanding! Well, at least our Marines get to watch a lesson in Afghan discipline and international law. You have to admire their tactics in discipline."

He jokingly replied, "I couldn't agree with you more, sir. If I knew it was going to come down to this, I would have dragged them out of the truck myself and stomped the piss out of them to save Baz the headache. I tell you what, sir, there better not be a next time with these dope-smoking clowns. If there is, it's going to be a fight to see who gets to them first. I will not have this poison around the platoon. I do not care what the cultural divide is, and I am not playing this sensitivity card or politically correct game.

"My boys have worked too hard and have enough to worry about. They deserve better. They don't deserve to have to question if their Afghan counterpart Soldiers are stoned or on drugs when they go on patrol. They especially do not need the burden of being asked to buy drugs either. This is unprofessional and illegal, and it will eventually get our Marines killed. This situation needs to be rectified right now," said my Platoon Sergeant in an obviously infuriated tone.

"I could not agree with you more, Staff Sergeant. Sometimes a fist is needed when words are meaningless and talk is cheap," I replied. I had reported it up the chain. We now had to work twice as hard to ensure this did not poison our men.

"I feel you, sir. A physical beating is universally understood. You don't need a translator for that. Don't worry. I won't allow any of these Soldiers to be around the platoon if they are getting high," replied my Platoon Sergeant, trying to hold his bearings in the midst of the clearly deteriorating situation going on around us.

At this time, the Afghan Captain approached us and told Nassir that he would handle this and promised it would not happen again. He then further mentioned that he was embarrassed that this had happened and assured us that by morning these two scumbags would disappear.

My Platoon Sergeant and I shook his hand in a gentlemen's agreement and returned to the common area, where all of our Marines were. Staff Sergeant Lebron explained to the platoon what had taken place outside of the PB near the Afghan vehicle and everything that had led up to them having front-row seats for the 2010 Afghan Ultimate Fighting Championship.

After our Marines calmed down from watching the main fighting event of the night, all we heard were the sounds of Captain Baz yelling one last time. After the yelling stopped, the entire PB was quiet, and things started to feel eerie. White star clusters started going off mentally in our heads, sending electrical signals that ran chills up and down our spines, causing our "spidey senses" to activate.

The Afghan Soldiers who were punished earlier that night boldly walked past. As they walked by Staff Sergeant Lebron and me, they stared us down with cold, evil, nefarious glares, looking as if they wanted to take vengeance on us for turning them in to their Commander.

Infuriated, I looked to Staff Sergeant Lebron and said, "This is not good, and tonight is going to be an interesting night. You know, you always hear reports of Afghan Soldiers going rogue on coalition forces and shooting up friendlies at PBs. I suggest we both sleep very lightly tonight. Again, I will do my job and report this up the chain. If they try anything though, my gloves will be coming off."

Confidently and in a gung ho manner, he replied, "To hell with that, sir. If one of them tries anything on you or me, I will rip his face off and make him watch me feed it down his throat. I am on edge right now, and I can't sleep. These guys have the audacity to stare me down. What if they shoot up the men tonight? No way. This is getting taken care of right now. I got this one, sir. You, ANA, come here!" ANA was the acronym given for the Afghan National Army Soldiers.

Staff Sergeant Lebron eyed one of the Afghan Soldiers and ordered the Soldier to approach him. "Nassir, translate this," said my Platoon Sergeant to our linguist, who was standing next to us.

Gripping the shoulder collar of the mint chocolate chip colored military uniform the Afghan Soldier was wearing, Staff Sergeant Lebron proceeded to lift him into the air while looking into his eyes with an icy stare of death. Verbally and with godlike authority, he said to the Afghan Soldier, "If any of you want to regain your honor, get stupid, or get froggy and leap, I am drawing the line right now. If you come at my Marines or my Lieutenant, I assure you I will arrange a meeting with your maker. This ends now! Do you understand me?"

Staff Sergeant Lebron was never one to back down from a fight, and he always put the welfare of his men over himself. His years of living on the streets of New York City undoubtedly gave him the edge, attitude, and smarts he needed to sense when a situation could potentially get out of hand. Standing six foot seven and weighing 240 pounds, he was the biggest man on the base, and his sheer presence was enough to deter even the boldest enemy. As he slowly lowered the Afghan Soldier down to the ground, he kept his eyes trained on him and received a little head nod signaling that the Soldier understood. When his boots hit the ground, the Afghan Soldier looked at his comrade and signaled that it was time to retire back to the confines and misty blackness of their side of the PB. They hurriedly disappeared into the blackness without looking back at Lebron even once. They knew my Marines were in charge.

Everyone reading about this incident must understand that Afghan culture is different than American culture. These people respond better when pain and beatings are used as a stimulus rather than harsh words and rhetoric. They are a hard people, war torn, and born into a world of violence. The idea of solving all their problems by using smart words, wishful thinking, and influential rhetoric is pure dreamworld nonsense. Many of these people are illiterate and lack the ability to even have an educated debate about mundane issues, even the Koran. Therefore, they resort to solving their problems with the sword rather than the pen in many respects because it gets the job done quick, fast, and in a hurry.

CHAPTER 12

Before my platoon inherited PB Brannon, the Marines from Charlie Company (Cobra Company), First Battalion, Third Marine Regiment who were there before us had a mutual relationship with the Afghan Soldiers and laid the groundwork for the COIN strategy my company was to assume. I know that deep down Marines dislike working with other units the majority of the time because it has the potential to cause a poor quality of work and mediocrity, which is directly against our Marine Corps *raison d'être*. Besides, we have our own culture and plainly just do things differently.

Historically speaking, our country always sends the Marines Corps to any conflict first. As the tip of the spear, we get the job done right and have never lost a battle. This is where the phrase "first to fight, last to leave" comes from.

A person can be forced to work with another human being, but people cannot be forced to like each other. Marines are true professionals in this aspect because regardless of friendship, both mission accomplishment and troop welfare are paramount. We do not have the time or luxury of letting feelings get in the way of what has to be done. As much as we do not like working with other units or branches, sometimes it has to be done, and we make the best of it.

That said, living at PB Brannon was the first time my Platoon Sergeant and I knew combined action platoons were possible in Afghanistan. It was an idea formed and created through more than a century of Marine Corps hardships and sacrifices of previous counterinsurgency warfare. This same idea was one Staff Sergeant Lebron and I constantly tossed around, trained for, and thought of accomplishing with our Marines. It was a concept that, once put into practice, would enable the successful transfer of lead security from Marines to Afghan forces and would lighten the patrolling and task load of my Marines by subdividing the work. It would also allow my platoon to achieve successes and mission accomplishments that Marine-pure units could not because of restrictive ROE measures.

Staff Sergeant Lebron and I made all our Marines read the book *The Village* prior to the deployment. We had them study strategy and historical doctrine of previous military units in battle against the Afghans, especially the Russians during the Soviet-Afghan War. Now it was almost a sign that we were in charge of PB Brannon and were actually conducting integrated patrols with the Afghan Soldiers at the PB with whom we needed to start forming a fully combined platoon.

In terms of my platoon, we knew this type of "integrated" platoon was possible because we were conducting partnered operations on our own terms and had tactical control of every internal and external circumstance and situation, not the Afghans. We did not have senior leadership breathing down our backs, micromanaging us, and telling us how to run our operations. Professionally, this aspect alone was one of the greatest traits of the command climate of Lima Company and the battalion. All my Platoon Sergeant and I had was the intent from our higher command and the freedom to achieve mission success through improvisation and adaptation to the constantly evolving situation.

The progression and evolution of the Marines of Second Platoon and the Soldiers of the Afghan National Army were under the immediate control of my platoon. My Company Commander set the tone and mission, and we executed it.

My Marines slowly started integrating elements of the Afghan Soldiers into their fire teams and squads on patrol. At first, integrating Afghan Soldiers into Marine patrols resulted in friction and pushback from my Squad Leaders and Riflemen because they had obvious communication and cultural issues. My Marines and Corpsmen were all alpha males, and they learned to despise any action that might lower their standards.

I made every effort to instill in my Marines that hard work and evolution were the keys to their success. They knew to never settle for second best and maintained highly competitive attitudes everywhere they went. If I had thought this would lower our standards, I would have ended it right there.

These Afghan Soldiers knew the area better than my Marines did, and my platoon had to at least make an attempt to start forcing them to take control of their country and lead their own patrols. We could not disregard that the Soldiers at the base knew the area, people, and terrain better than we did. We were strangers in this land, and we needed the Afghan Soldiers to help us navigate through it.

Having hope and mindlessly believing integrated patrols would work was nonsense, and my Marines would not be fooled into accepting that fact. Hope is not a course of action for United States Marines. We are doers, not sayers. We live and exist in a world of reality—life and death. We do not live in a world of fantasy, sunshine, and red rose gardens. Effectively combining Marine and Afghan forces would take blood, sweat, and tears from hard work and initiative. We had to believe in it. Even the best operating units in the world train day in and day out for obstacles like this. My men were given zero preparation time and told to make it happen. CAPs and integrated combat patrols have been achieved and were utilized in Vietnam. History has proven this is not going against our Corps principals of war or doctrine. It could be done and achieved again.

The primary reason these initial integrated squads worked was because my Marines and I made it clear to the Afghan National Army Soldiers that this was the mission and we were in charge, not them. They were not given and did not have the option to question our tactics, logic, or decisions. We made sure they understood this. The Afghan Soldiers at PB Brannon were going to learn from us to become a better fighting force capable of defending their country against the insurgents.

As Marines, we are a more technologically advanced, more civilized, better trained, better equipped, and better educated force than the Afghans. If anything was certain, the Afghan National Army Soldiers feared and respected my Marines and felt honored and privileged to gain a spark of knowledge from them. It did well for them to learn from us.

Slowly, through combining Afghan and Marine squads during combat security patrols, the Afghan Soldiers started to learn and formulate their own logistical and operational self-sustaining dismounted security patrols. They became visual learners just like Marines are and learned by shadowing my "devil dogs" everywhere they went. The Afghan Soldiers even began imitating their posture and the way they carried themselves while on the PB.

We started their training and education by taking baby steps to slowly get them to a jogging level. My Marines spent hundreds of hours teaching, educating, and preparing Afghan Soldiers at PB Brannon. This gave them the confidence and ability to slowly start taking over patrols and the PB. This directly facilitated the interpretation and endstate of my Commanding Officer's intent. Transfer of lead security through the use of integrated patrolling was occurring. My Marines and Corpsmen were making it possible.

The endstate of my CO was to have the Afghan National Army Soldiers completely transition lead security operations from the Marines and take over every PB in the Lima Company AO. This would be facilitated by allowing them to conduct their own security patrols without the presence of Marine units before we redeployed out of Afghanistan in December 2010. The goal was to effectively enable the Afghan National Army Soldiers to fight for their country against the Taliban. We were off to a great start!

The achievements of the relationships built between my Marines and our Afghan Army Soldiers were not only because of my small unit leaders and individual Riflemen; almost every night, my Platoon Sergeant and I would have dinner and drink chai tea with the Commanders of the Afghan National Army. During these times, we created patrol routes and training schedules. This helped build camaraderie and foster relationships at the top level of the chain of command.

What resulted was a trickle-down effect of communication, command, and control. Once the Afghan Soldiers and my Marines realized and visually saw that the leadership was working together and getting along, they instinctively followed suit and emulated the leadership. There are no such things as bad Marines or bad Soldiers; there are only bad leaders.

PART II

Operation New Dawn and the Unbreakable Marine

Ninety-nine percent of failures come from people who make excuses.
—George Washington

Sweat saves blood, blood saves lives, and brains save both.
—General Erwin Rommel

An individual cannot carry two watermelons with one hand. Just as one stick by itself is weak and can be snapped, a bundle of sticks tied together are strong and hard to break.
—Afghan Proverb

Chapter 13

My platoon's occupation of PB Brannon and the control of its AO was short, lasting from approximately 18 May 2010 to 15 June 2010. On 16 June 2010, my Marines, First Lieutenant Vali's Marines of Third Platoon, a squad from Weapons Platoon under the command of First Lieutenant Hartsell, and elements from our company headquarters (HQ) were tasked to support the battalion's offensive operation known as Operation New Dawn. Our time at PB Brannon had been for the most part purely humanitarian and nonkinetic.

The kinetic actions my platoon witnessed were three firefights in a period of three days that were initiated by two rival Afghan Uniformed Police Officer units fighting over control of the land and villages between PB Noba and COB Toor Gar. Given the stand-down order from our higher headquarters to let the Afghan units police their own and solve this issue internally, my Marines and I watched these rivaling government agencies fight and vie for power over the local area through our various surveillance activities each day and night to ensure the fighting did not head in our direction.

My Marines discovered and neutralized three IEDs, constantly came across bomb-making materials, and witnessed the Taliban driving on motorcycles or in vehicles daily. Not one of these events resulted in conflicts, incidents, or loss of life. My platoon could never engage the Taliban on their motorcycles because our ROEs stated that without positive identification or unless we were shot at, Marines could not pursue or kill the enemy. It made no sense to be able to see the enemy but not be able to do anything about it, but the mission was the mission, and the Taliban did not carry identification cards. Shooting these terrorists in the back while they fled would certainly have led to investigations or possible brig time. In COIN, the value of human life, both enemy and friendly, is placed on a higher scale than hunting down and destroying the enemy. It was our job to be "smiling killers," taking the moral and ethical high ground to preserve innocent life.

Our humanitarian noncombat operations consisted of the approval and subsequent construction of two canal water locks, five footbridges, eight water wells, and the improvement of one vehicle bridge. My Marines refused to be project managers, and I could not blame them. To get around this, we ended up sending all our local nationals to Toor Gar to discuss all future projects and monetary transactions in my AO.

COB Toor Gar would then call me or my Platoon Sergeant on the radio and request verification and approval for the project based on our intelligence and relationship with the local national who wanted a project. I refused to allow myself or my Marines to directly fund these projects, knowing portions of the money were going to terrorists.

The only instances of loss of life in my AO in the first month of our deployment was by the local national who murdered his neighbor over a minor dispute. As far as my company AO was concerned, Weapons Platoon was hit the hardest when one of their Marines by the name of Private First Class Suter died at PB Jengali.

CHAPTER 14

Operation Moshtarak, which is a Dari word for "together" or "joint," was a successful combined combat operation between US, ISAF, and NATO forces designed to protect and liberate the innocent people of the Afghan city of Marjeh from Taliban fighters who had a command center and stronghold there. The operation involved more than fifteen thousand forces and was the largest joint operation in the war in Afghanistan up to this point. In its broader implications, it was designed to destroy vital logistical and communication ratlines the Taliban used as they traveled from Quetta, Pakistan, northwest throughout the Helmand Province to Marjeh and eventually Kandahar.

Operation Moshtarak commenced on 12 February 2010 and ended in June 2010. It was devised to be an overwhelming offensive against the Taliban to disrupt their momentum and deny them the ability to plan attacks and transport weapons and IEDs from Pakistan to the Helmand Province.

By June 2010, with Moshtarak ending, my battalion wanted to support the tail end of this operation by conducting one more offensive assault against an already weakened enemy in an area of the southern Nawa District known as Shorsurak. This operation was known as Battalion Operation New Dawn. Shorsurak was an enemy stronghold that had not seen the presence of Marines for approximately one year and was utilized by the Taliban to transport weapons and munitions from the southern Helmand Province north to Marjeh.

My platoon's mission was to assume the role of the battalion's main effort for Operation New Dawn (not to be confused with Operation

New Dawn in Iraq). This operation was a joint mission between Third Battalion, Third Marines, and our Afghan Army counterparts. As the main effort, my Marines were tasked with executing a clear interdict and block in the vicinity of Shorsurak to disrupt Taliban operations south to north from Shorsurak to Marjeh. My platoon's follow-on task was to leave one reinforced squad, along with my Platoon Sergeant, behind at PB Brannon to continue conducting combat operations and patrolling efforts throughout the AO.

It seemed a little ridiculous at the time for any military Commander to either read or be tasked with, but my platoon had three simultaneous tactical tasks. When I asked my Company Commander about this fact, his reply was, "Yes, three tactical tasks. That's right. This is direct from Operations." Little did I know this was only the beginning of things to come.

Shorsurak was a tribal region of the Nawa District located five kilometers south of PB Brannon. As far as the landscape in Shorsurak goes, the areas to the north, south, and west consist of very arid, waterless, and barren terrain, but the east is thriving and luscious farmland. Mud compounds litter these areas and form numerous tiny villages and towns all along the region. The farmland in Shorsurak flourishes with crops such as pomegranates, watermelon, corn, wheat, okra, and of course, cannabis and poppy.

The poppy fields in this area were untouched by United States and NATO forces, and the local farmers had not made the transition to cultivating wheat instead of poppy. Government led eradications (GLEs) had not yet been conducted in this area by the time my Marines arrived, and we were tasked with initiating contact with the locals to enable this process during the operation.

According to intelligence reports and operational briefs from my Company Commander, the last units in this region had been the British a year or two prior to us. The Marines of Lima Company and Second Platoon were to be the first foreign military to step foot on land that had not been seen by friendly forces for a year or more.

CHAPTER 15

By June 2010, the unforgiving weather phenomenon in Afghanistan known as the winds of 120 days was fully underway as my Marines prepared for Operation New Dawn. Essentially, until the month of September, the Marines of Second Platoon, who were already constantly braving the triple-digit temperatures, now had to face the literal fog and friction caused by relentless sandstorms that could reach 180 kilometers per hour. These sandstorms prevented mounted and dismounted patrolling, grounded most flights, and severely limited line of sight as it choked men and women who tried to breathe in the dust and metallic particle filled air.

The indigenous people of the Shorsurak region were mostly poor farmers and village elders who tirelessly worked from sunup to sundown on their farms, land, and compounds. Many of the elders thought we were the Russian military at first until we explained who we were and the reason we were there. Generally, the elders and the local nationals supported our role to eliminate the Taliban threat and wanted us to be there. More often than not, the local people were very wary of giving us their full support because the Taliban thrived in the area and profited off the locals in the drug trades, and the Afghan government did not have a strong enough presence to combat them.

No matter where a person goes in Afghanistan, he or she is always being watched by someone, whether it is by local nationals or the Taliban; these people have nothing better to do. We are their television sets and their daily news channel.

The desert area of Shorsurak was inhospitable to growing vegetation, but it spawned bugs and insects. Camel spiders, mice, ants, mosquitoes, snakes, and scorpions ran rampant and soon became a greater threat than the Taliban for Second Platoon. My Marines constantly had to empty their boots, daypacks, ILBE packs, and sleeping systems because these creatures always found shelter in them. Hundreds of things have the potential to kill a Marine in Afghanistan; the Taliban are just one.

As my Second Squad Leader, Sergeant Tyler Brown, found out during a brush with death during the first week of the operation, a scorpion sting to the back of the neck is one of the last things a Marine considers could happen when hunting for the enemy. However, his response to getting stung was comical in itself.

On the sixth day of operations, while conducting rest and refitting during the peak daylight hours of the day, with the sun at the highest point in the sky, amplifying its rays down on us, heating up the environment to 135 degrees Fahrenheit, our conduct of operations suddenly became interrupted by a loud yell from Sergeant Brown that emanated from the murky sandstorm that covered our base.

"Doc! Son of a—I just got stung by something! It came from one of the sandbags I was lying on. I think it was a damn scorpion!" yelled Sergeant Brown in an obviously distressed manner.

"What happened? Show me where you were stung," said Doc Greenough, our Platoon Corpsman, as he fiddled with his medical bag while trying to identify the area of Brown's neck that had been penetrated by the venomous stinger.

"On the back of my neck, Doc! That little thing stung the back of my neck," said my Squad Leader, clearly uneasy because he knew the venom would soon start taking effect.

"Roger. I am going to call in a helo to get you evac'd! Did you catch the scorpion that stung you, because we will need it to identify the toxin to get the appropriate antivenin. What size was it, big or small?" replied Doc. A rule of thumb was that the bigger the scorpion, the better because they were usually less venomous or emitted less venom.

The smaller scorpions were more dangerous because they were usually more toxic or emitted more venom in a sting.

"Yeah, I killed it and have it right here. It is a tiny thing, but forget it, Doc. I am not getting evacuated over this scorpion sting. I am staying here with my Marines. I am not going to leave my squad. I am going to wait it out to see what happens, and if I get worse, then I will leave," said Sergeant Brown calmly and confidently, always methodically weighing his options before a crucial decision had to be made.

Knowing that all the Navy Corpsman could really do was make recommendations and prognoses, he refused to be evacuated and leave his Marines. After Doc Greenough and our other Navy Corpsman examined the dead scorpion, their conclusive prognosis was that since enough time had elapsed between the sting and no effects were present in Brown, chances were that there had been little to no venom injected into him. With sandstorms raging and all flights grounded as well, this was the best news we could have received. God was truly watching over my Marines out here in the desert.

Dead serious and stubborn, thinking only of his Marines and their welfare above his own, Sergeant Brown refused to leave them without a leader, even when facing the threat of certain death. Luckily for him, the scorpion that stung him had not injected the full amount of venom it could have. After a few agonizing and painful hours, Sergeant Brown started to feel better and laughed off his close call by calling himself the "Scorpion King."

This event clearly showed me that my men would do anything for each other and would rather die than leave each other's side. However, they hadn't really had a choice in the matter, for the sandstorms prevented all flights in or out of my PB. But for the Marines, there was no question that on that day Brown exhibited the traits of strength, loyalty, and dedication everyone wants in his or her Squad Leader.

CHAPTER 16

The initiation of Operation New Dawn was poor in its planning by the leadership of Lima Company and the operations section within the battalion, but the resolve was outstanding in the execution by the junior Marines. The moments leading up to occupying our AO were borderline disastrous; however, the Marines fought through this adversity with every step.

Prior to the conduct of the operation, I received a cut, copied, and pasted order from a previous First Battalion, Third Marine Regiment (1/3) operations order detailing the TTPs my company was going to take when we made our initial entry and foothold into Shorsurak. There were no updated maps or grid reference groupings of the area. Intelligence was sketchy at best, and we were essentially going to be walking in blind. It was blatantly obvious from the tone of my Company Commander that our operations section at the time had done very little to plan this offensive.

No one minded these issues because even though we lacked intelligence resources, we would still execute the order. Our CO had decided not to coordinate with friendly units in the area except for Truck Company and Jump Platoon for support. This was his baby, and he did not want anyone dipping his or her hands in his bowl of Cheerios. This entire operation was mainly going to be a Lima Company self-sustaining operation with zero support from our friendly agencies even though we had them at our disposal upon request.

What became the icing on the cake and sealed our fate was the fact that my CO decided there would be no Platoon Sergeants or senior enlisted Marines going on the mission; only Platoon Commanders, Sergeants, and below were going. This move created the most internal friction for us and almost led us into a black cloud of uncertainty during the operation.

I remember saying to my CO, "Sir, why aren't we taking our Staff Sergeants with us? We need a buffer between the Marine Officers and the enlisted Marines. We need at least one Platoon Sergeant to go."

"Don't worry. We know what we are doing. We have done this before," was his very confident reply. I remember asking myself, *Who is "we" and what does that even mean?* The loud repetition of these words over and over in my head steadily increased.

I had even brought my Platoon Sergeant with me on the day of the initial operations order brief at COB Toor Gar while all the other Platoon Sergeants stayed back at their PBs. I knew that without a mediator between the enlisted Marines and the Officers, things could go very badly. I also wanted enlisted input and insight because I was confident in one simple fact: this was not only my first deployment but the first deployment for many of my Marines as well. I wanted enlisted Marines present and making decisions that would affect the lives of their men.

Between the elements of light and dark, there is a clear divide that separates the two. A Staff Sergeant is this connecting file in the overall divide between the light and the dark for the United States Marine Corps who resolves issues between both the enlisted Marines and the Officers. Even though my Platoon Sergeant was not on our "go" manifest for the operation, I implored my CO to reconsider taking him, almost to the point of insubordination.

"Negative. We need all Staff Sergeants to run and coordinate all the administrative, operational, and logistical duties of the patrol bases while we are gone," said my Captain in response to my recommendation.

Nothing for nothing, but I had three Sergeants and four Corporals within my platoon who were all outstanding Noncommissioned Officers and more than capable of running a patrol base. Even my most junior Private First Class would have done a decent job. However, I do not question the orders of my higher command; I respect them, carry them out, and see that they are completed. As a Lieutenant, all I could do at this point was influence decisions; however, I did feel like a bullet sponge.

Although I disagreed with my CO on these issues, he saw a larger picture than I did. I sat in my Platoon Commander box and played with my piece of the puzzle. He dealt with all four platoons and the lives of every Marine in the company. I had and still have the highest respect for my former CO, even though I knew he was wrong here. However, I would have been fired if I disobeyed him.

I stayed up around the clock with my First Sergeant and Lieutenant Hartsell that night at COB Toor Gar until the sun came up on the morning of 17 July 2010. We didn't sleep because we were busy creating vehicle load plans and personnel rosters of all the Marines in Lima Company scheduled to depart COB Toor Gar for Shorsurak at 0700 that same morning.

It was a mess, to say the least, and I wanted to kick myself in the teeth. All the while, I kept saying in my head over and over, *What is my Gunnery Sergeant doing right now, and why are we doing his job?* Accountability and logistical preparation should have been done at least a week in advance, not the night before the offensive and especially not by a Lieutenant! Lieutenants supervise the conduct of planning and lead in the operations, but Gunnery Sergeants, with the support of their subordinate Staff Noncommissioned Officers (SNCOs), plan logistics. If our Platoon Sergeant could grasp this, why couldn't the Gunnery Sergeant?

Our Company Gunnery Sergeant had Marines from different squads and platoons in the same convoys, unit integrity was compromised, there were not enough Marines to drive the vehicles from COB Toor Gar to Shorsurak, and there was an inadequate amount of vehicles to take the Marines to the objective. *Who is the one in charge of this "retarded baby"?* I kept thinking. *Am I running the company now?*

All I knew is that if this mess did not get fixed, the entire operation could be jeopardized, our company would look incompetent, and with every passing minute more lives could be at risk. With the help of my fellow Platoon Commanders and enlisted Marines, we tackled the logistical beast and rectified this slowly evolving nightmare. One hour before our scheduled time to cross our line of departure (LOD) we had a positive solution that enabled the mission to commence.

Elements of Third Platoon departed friendly lines at 0700 that morning. The devil was in the details, and without accurate accountability of the Marines and Sailors going on the mission, we could not have made the 0700 time hack of departure set by my CO.

During the movement, Third Platoon, who was being transported and supported by our Truck Company, became lost on their mounted movement to the objective site. Between taking wrong turns and having vehicles stuck in the mud and canals along the route, Third Platoon arrived at the company objective area, located twenty kilometers southwest of COB Toor Gar, roughly seven hours late. Half the convoy was still left behind, stuck in a canal and immobile, while the other half arrived at the objective.

Marines never leave each other behind, but the mission always comes first. News such as this was not uncommon, as the terrain in Afghanistan ultimately dictated movement and caused friction for any ground unit. It was in situations like these that the mentality of "mission first, Marines always" caused me to have moral and ethical dilemmas because I always feared for the lives of my Marines and Sailors. It was never about us; it was always about them.

My platoon was put on standby until 1700 that night because of this unforeseeable mishap. I remember sitting in our Lima Company COC with my Squad Leaders, amazed as we listened to the radio traffic that was going on with our sister platoon. Just like Murphy's Law, everything that could possibly go wrong went wrong. That's all right though; as United States Marines, we improvise, adapt, and overcome. If this had been kinetic, we would have certainly been in the horns of a dilemma because Third Platoon would have been on their own.

Before my platoon departed for Shorsurak, the last update we received from Lieutenant Vali's platoon was that half their Marines made it to the objective while the other half were left behind with their immobile up-armored vehicles. The convoy that arrived to the objective dropped off the Marines and went back for the stuck vehicles and the rest of Third Platoon.

The other vital piece of intelligence we learned was that the initial target house where my CO had wanted to establish a patrol base was compromised because of security reasons and its inability to have tactical advantage in a firefight. The compound was in a low area surrounded by a cemetery, a mosque, and compounds that were home to village elders. Offending or disrespecting even one of these sites could lead to a potential disagreement or, worse, an all-out fight. Lieutenant Vali made the tactical decision to find a compound with better defensive capabilities and to leave the initial one.

With Third Platoon by themselves, alone and unafraid, the situation on the deck was becoming increasingly hostile. Lieutenant Vali's primary mission had become to establish a well-fortified forward PB as soon as possible before my platoon arrived. If it had not been for Lieutenant Vali's swift ability to overcome and adapt to the environment, our mission would have been jeopardized.

At 1900 that night, my platoon and the rest of the company arrived at a compound roughly one click south of our original objective. Inside we found disorganization and chaos. There were two squads from Third Platoon, a Scout Sniper Team, an Explosive Ordinance Disposal (EOD) Team, a squad from the Lima Company HQ, a Human Exploitation Team, an Army Psychological Operations (PSYOPS) Team, two reporters, a Combat Cameraman, and a platoon (Tolai) of Afghan National Army Soldiers scattered all over the place with zero organization, control, or leadership. I am sure even Lieutenant Vali was wondering where all these units had come from, as many had not been briefed in our original operations order.

As I walked into the compound with my two squads, I remember saying to Sergeant Olds, "Find a place for the boys to drop their gear. Make it look neat and not all nasty like everyone else. Get Lance Corporal Ortiz on the radio and communications lines and make sure they are up and running. Have Ortiz give me communication checks every hour with the Lima Main COC. Be prepared to kick out an ambush patrol here shortly because the enemy is watching us right now, and he will have us by the balls if he decides to attack us."

Lance Corporal Ortiz, an 0311 Infantryman by trade, had established himself as the most competent Marine in the platoon when it came to the TTPs of the operation and utilization of our military radios and had quickly become our Platoon Radio Operator (RO).

Walking into this disaster, I was soon greeted by a colleague of mine by the name of First Lieutenant Barnley, a very witty and intelligent man. He was the Assistant Intelligence Officer for Third Battalion, Third Marines, who I met when checking into my unit at Marine Corps Base, Kaneohe Bay, Hawaii.

"Barnley, what's going on? Why are all the Marines just lying around doing nothing? Who are these Afghan Soldiers, and where did they come from? Who the hell are these Army guys? Where is the leadership at right now?" I asked him.

"Hey, buddy, I just got here myself. I was left behind in a convoy stuck in the middle of the Afghanistan desert for about five hours. Right now all I know is that the platoon that arrived here first did not have time to fully clear the compound and gain a foothold as all these units just started to pour in. These Afghan Soldiers are apparently your attachments. Hey, brother, be advised, I just found some wires, shell casings, and a plastic cover for what looks like an Italian or Chinese land mine. Come over here and I will show you," said Lieutenant Barnley, pointing directly behind him at three dark rooms inside the compound.

"Roger. What has not been cleared yet?" I said back to him, trying to maintain professionalism and keep my bearings in front of my junior Marines, Sailors, and everyone else inside the compound.

"There are a few rooms I am finishing up on now, and a door that has a lock on it seems very suspicious to me," he replied.

"I will check it out. I will send a few of my boys over and make sure it is properly cleared," I told him.

At this point, I called over my Squad Leaders: Sergeant Guthrie, Sergeant Brown, and Sergeant Olds. The five of us approached the door that was locked. At first we were going to bust the lock open until we noticed the door was actually attached to the lock with what looked like fishing string. After examining the door and concluding there were no explosive charges attached, I cut the string and immediately had my Squad Leaders search the rooms. In doing so, we discovered wires, spent bullet shells from AK-47s, powder residue from ammonium nitrate, fertilizer, and the casing to an Italian or Chinese land mine.

CHAPTER 17

According to my CO, the local national who owned the compound had given us permission to utilize it as a base and use any room in it for shelter. However, upon learning of the actions of my Squad Leaders and me, my Captain became irate and confrontational toward me because I had cleared a room that looked like it was locked and posed an immediate threat. I explained that my intentions had been for the safety of my men because gaining the initial foothold of the compound had not occurred during preliminary occupation, potentially putting the lives of all the Marines at risk. After all, hadn't we just found evidence of items used to kill friendly forces and Marines?

"Lieutenant Bodrog, I know what you did was right. However, this man gave us permission to use his compound. We cannot go around breaking locks and smashing down doors whenever we feel like it. We are not the Taliban, and actions such as those are exactly what the Taliban did and continue to do to the people. In situations like this, it is proper to bring the owner of the house with us if we want to search or exploit rooms or areas in the compound," he explained to me in a very angry tone.

"Roger that, sir. The feelings of the locals come second to the safety of my Marines and Corpsmen. I had thought the initial foothold was not gained and therefore safety was at risk."

After all, the acronym RIGS was constantly taught to all Infantry Officers at Infantry Officer Course (IOC) in Quantico, Virginia. RIGS stands for recon, isolate, gain a foothold, and secure the objective.

This was common tactic to be employed by ground units taking over buildings or compounds.

I continued, "Lieutenant Barnley just showed me some wires and a cover for a foreign-made land mine, and I figured that was reason enough to go into the room. My mistake, sir. I assure you it will not happen again," I said back to him, obviously displaying my disappointment at the direction this conversation was taking.

"Lieutenant Bodrog, you need to realize that these people *are* supporting us, and if we want to check out a room or area, we need to ask their permission first, before we make a decision to act. We need battalion approval to go into any compound in our AO. In this case, battalion gave us the approval to utilize this compound, but in a perfect situation we should have let this local national know at least a week ahead of time that we were going to use the compound.

"These are not my rules. However, we have to enforce them. We certainly are not going to leave this compound worse than how we found it. We will create more enemy in the process if we do not respect their culture and way of life. If you cannot understand this fact, there are other platoons that will be more than happy to come out here and do your job of counterinsurgency," said my CO, reinforcing his intent and hinting that me and my platoon were one phone call away from being replaced.

At this point I was furious with the cultural sensitivity agenda I was being fed as the invisible leash was tightened around my throat, restricting the actions of my Marines and me. *And give this local national knowledge of our intentions and our mission a week ahead of time? Why? So he could inform the enemy of our plan and backlay IEDs on us? Are we United States Marines, the fiercest warriors of our time, or social workers?* I was not an idiot, however, and knew my CO was only looking out for the best interests of his company.

I was racking my brain over the fact that I quite possibly could be relieved for trying to protect the welfare of every Marine in the compound. I know my captain was only acting on the order and intent of his higher command, so I was not fully mad at him. The ROEs were pissing me off more than anything, but I had to obey them. His actions in my view had always been above reproach, and I knew he would never willingly put the company in harm's way.

A few minutes later, he tasked me to send out local security patrols (LSPs) throughout the night in our immediate vicinity to conduct reconnaissance, locate a new PB, and deny the enemy freedom of movement.

Unbeknownst to me at the time, the local national who owned the compound had informed my captain that he was only going to allow us to stay for the night. I soon came to find out that this local had informed my Company Commander that there was a cemetery to our west and a few mosques to our north, and because we were infidels and not Muslim we could not stay near the area. In my mind, I thought this guy had to be on some type of drug to think he could tell United States Marines where they could and could not stay. It was not like we were walking on the graves or in the mosques.

I wondered why this Afghan was telling *us* what to do and why my CO was allowing him to do it. This was not COIN; this was politics. Going around apologizing and asking permission to patrol in an area in which we were conducting a tactical operation made us look feeble and weak—two traits that could provoke an attack if we were not vigilant.

In reality, I knew that staying true to the principals of counterinsurgency meant we had to tuck our tails between our legs to please the population. It was a demand by the local national that my CO had happily agreed to.

Already, within two hours of my being here, the locals were playing the Muslim "religion card" on us. It has been my experience that Afghans males are extremely religious and pious when it works for them and when they get something out of it. After all, this is a culture of corruption and greed.

Many Afghans are not the religious zealots we view on television or read about in books. Many are not extremists hell-bent on jihad and responsible for creating the fear that makes Americans scared to go outside, so meanwhile they stay in their homes, watching television and getting fat. All other times when religion was not involved, money fueled the decisions and way of life of the local nationals.

Political correctness and cultural sensitivity in a combat zone, beautiful isn't it? I thought. We were United States Marines, and now because of our COIN strategy, ROEs, and social-political agenda, we were essentially acting as international peacekeepers and social workers. These third-world pricks had us by the balls, and they knew it.

I hoped and prayed my Marines and Corpsmen didn't see the charades I was playing, but I knew they were smart enough to eventually figure it out. I hoped this politically correct garbage and sensitivity would go right out the window and people would not be afraid to tell the truth, even if it meant hurting someone's feelings. This was especially true because there was zero factual evidence to back up the social logic we were applying.

The experiments of social science and sympathetic compassion that were going on in this third-world country were beyond me and seriously weakened our ability to win the war and find the Taliban. As Marines, we were trained to locate, close with, and destroy the enemy by fire and maneuver or repel the enemy assault by fire and close combat, not write them international welfare checks, promote their social goals, or ensure we did not hurt their feelings, all the while being sensitive and tolerant to their culture.

CHAPTER 18

I angrily went out on patrol that night with my First Squad, partnered with our new Afghan National Army counterparts. The Afghan Army unit called the Fourth Tolai was by far the most reckless and undisciplined Afghan Army unit I had ever come into contact with. I hated to say it, but I actually wanted Commander Baz Mohammed and the Afghan National Army Soldiers with whom my Marines partnered at PB Brannon to be our partners during this operation.

Regardless of this fact, the Marines of Second Platoon knew the stakes and risks. We made it abundantly clear right off the bat to our new Afghan partners that we were in charge, not them. We were not going to hold their hands or worry about hurting their fragile feelings. They had the choice to either man up and fight for their country just like my alpha male Marines were doing or quit (as many of them were allowed to do). There were always numerous reports of Afghans dropping their rifles and body armor on the ground during a patrol and quitting the Army and Police and just leaving.

Freedom is not a God-given right; it is fought for and earned through bloodshed and hardship. If people are not willing to fight for it, it can be taken away at any time. For these people who had never tasted freedom, it was a hard concept to understand.

The Fourth Tolai Afghan Soldiers were the worst of the worst. They were the unruly elements from every PB and COB in the AO. No Marine unit wanted to work with them. These Soldiers lacked essential leadership. They were lazy, habitually used drugs, and were known to quit or go rogue at any time. These Afghan Army Soldiers reminded me of the baseball team in the movie *The Bad News Bears.* The only difference was that this was reality, and these guys did not eventually come together and get better; they consistently grew worse, more lethargic, and more reckless.

Our initial patrol from the newly established PB in Shorsurak that first night was sadistically comedic. The Marines of Second Platoon, partnered with the Fourth Tolai, departed friendly lines at 2200 to gain the initial foothold in the surrounding area and set up LP/OP positions. There was zero illumination outside, and the Afghan National Army Soldiers lacked night vision assets to see in the dark. So my Patrol Leader, Sergeant Olds, placed them at the front of our squad for command and control reasons. We did this tactically and also because we did not want to take the risk of them shooting us in the backs in the pitch-black of night.

As far as statistics were concerned, we as Marines had a higher likelihood of being shot and killed by the forces of the Government of the Islamic Republic of Afghanistan (GIROA), Afghan National Army, and Afghan Police than by the Taliban. The Afghan Army and Police were notorious for negligent discharges and had earned a reputation for going rogue and shooting themselves, each other, and friendly forces.

After a few minutes of arguing prior to departing the PB, the Afghan National Army Soldiers felt it was crucial to inform my Marines and me that they were experts at patrolling and we had to patrol their way or else they were not going. Half smiling and holding my bearings so as not to rip these third-world Soldiers' heads off for questioning the logic of me or my Marines, I told them all that they would either listen to us or they would not go. My Marines are not as patient as I am, and they did what they did best by saying some words that did not transfer over too nicely into Dari, the Afghan National Army Soldiers' native tongue. After twenty minutes of arguing through our interpreters, the Afghan Soldiers finally left the wire with my Marines at the rear of the patrol.

We only ended up patrolling a kilometer and a half out because the area was unfamiliar and we needed to be close to the base if an attack occurred. We set up a LP/OP position on the top of a hill overlooking the lower compounds to our south and west. Here, we tactically set in, searching for anomalies and patterns of nightlife or activity. The Marines then sat in a 360-degree circular security position and filled in the gaps with the Afghan Army Soldiers.

After about an hour of sitting in our security position, we noticed that the majority of our Afghan Soldiers had fallen asleep. When my Marines went to wake them, the Afghan Soldiers got very pissed off and yelled at them. Some even raised their rifles at my men. The ones who did not go to sleep smoked cigarettes or hash and even turned on their flashlights to see in the dark, which gave away our position. Still other Afghan Soldiers used their cell phones to call their friends or possibly even Taliban, which really got underneath my skin. We were compromised, and I now had to make the decision to return to the PB.

I could not make this up even if I wanted to. This was a total lack of tactical concern and professionalism. These guys were absolutely ridiculous and did not grasp the concept that their actions were giving away our position and could get us killed. I could not believe how bad of an example this foreign military was setting for my Marines.

In the Marine culture, a new join is always judged by the first impression he or she makes on his or her peers or leadership. It is a culture based on merit. There was little I could do to mend the irreparable damage of the impression these Soldiers made on my Marines the first night.

I wanted to shoot every one of them. I wanted to tell my Marines they had permission to squeeze their triggers and send their rifle rounds into the Afghans' skulls and arrange the Soldiers' meetings with their Allah. I wanted to, but I couldn't. It would have been my demise at the end of the day, and I would be the bad guy, not these pricks who were knowingly putting the lives of my Marines at risk. My Marines would have gone the rest of deployment without leadership, and this was something I had to swallow and allow so as not to jeopardize them. They were better men, and I had to do everything possible to ensure their welfare and safety.

We stayed in this position a little while longer, but soon enough was enough. Our patrol culminated prior to my order when one of my Marines named Corporal Garst taught an intercultural lesson to one of the Afghan Soldiers who was gaffing him off. An Afghan Soldier who was supposed to be holding security for our defensive LP/OP position kept shining his flashlight and talking on a cell phone, and he was constantly smoking a cigarette. After repeated attempts by my linguist, on behalf of my Marine, to correct the deficiency, the Soldier told Garst to "f-off" in perfect English.

It amazed me how much these guys played dumb and said they did not understand English when we gave them commands, but they knew almost every American curse word we used in our daily conversations. To say the least, my Marine did not react too nicely at being spoken to like that, and he quickly decided to rectify his predicament for the safety of the Marines on the patrol.

As my patrol was reentering friendly lines, Corporal Garst approached me for his debrief. "Sir, I have to let you know something," he said to me in a cool, calm, and collected manner.

Whenever a Marine starts off a sentence like that, a Commander would do well to listen.

"During our LP/OP, I punched out one of my Afghan Soldiers and dropped him to the ground. I currently have his weapon because he told me he was going to kill me. He put the security of the entire patrol at risk by smoking a cigarette and using his cell phone. It gave away our position. He even told me to 'f-off' when I explained to him that what he was doing was putting our lives at risk," said Corporal Garst, obviously upset at the conduct of the Afghan Soldier during our night operation.

Not knowing whether to reward or yell at my Marine, I simply responded in a soft tone, "Roger. I understand. We have to recognize these guys are not United States Marines. Therefore, the majority of them are untrustworthy and operate at a level mediocre and subpar to what we are used to. That being said, we still have an obligation, and it is our mission to partner with them. We are all men here, and we will not sink to their level. We are better than them. I am willing to allow a few setbacks in the name of progress and evolution. Give me his weapon. I will ensure it is returned when the time is right.

"That being said, you were in the right, Corporal Garst, and did nothing wrong, and I am here to tell you that. Just do not make this a pattern, and use it as a learning point. We just have to be careful and not spark any international incidents. This is a very fragile line we are all walking right now in partnering with the Afghans. It could break at any time," I explained to my motivator as we walked back inside friendly lines at our PB.

I probably should have reported the incident, but I did not. I let his Squad Leader know what had transpired so he could keep an eye on his Marine throughout the night. My Marine was right: our security had been in jeopardy, and the safety of my men was paramount at all times. As the on-scene Commander, I knew I was justified in my belief. Fists, not words of compassion and harmony, solved the situation that night, and my Marine did what was best for his squad.

CHAPTER 19

The next morning, Third Platoon sent out a dismounted security patrol to find a new place for us to set up our base of operations. Because of the situation with my patrol the previous night, I was able to give Lieutenant Vali very little helpful intelligence information in his pursuit of a new PB.

Within an hour, his Marines had secured an area that was roughly one kilometer southwest of our current position, on a hilltop that overlooked villages below us to the northeast and south. The selected area for the PB was a previous home that had long since been abandoned. All that was left of it was a rectangular mud wall that stood approximately one foot high. With a few thousand sandbags, we would build these walls up and make it a defensive position and new PB.

At 0800 that same day, my platoon patrolled out from the initial PB en route to our new one. By the time we arrived, it was 0830, and already the local nationals were in an uproar as they surrounded our new PB. To make matters worse, Third Platoon had not had ample time to gain a foothold in our new PB because of the local nationals with whom they were now engaged.

Explosive Ordnance Detail (EOD) was inside the PB when we arrived, and their metal detectors had detected three different areas inside our temporary PB that contained IEDs or materials to make IEDs. This meant that until EOD cleared the temporary PB and conducted a proper sweep, no one was allowed in.

All Marines are trained to know that any compound they go into in Afghanistan must be thoroughly swept with mine detectors because the enemy loves to blow Marines up with IEDs they hide underneath the ground and in entry points and doorways. In this particular case, the IEDs and the IED-making materials we discovered were buried between six and twelve inches underneath the ground and hidden in the corners of the compound walls. Thank God for EOD.

As I patrolled up to our new PB, named PB Razza, I started feeling the hatred and discontent the locals were displaying toward my Captain's and Lieutenant Vali's Marines. It made me mad to see the locals questioning my CO and talking to us like we were the bad guys. Quickly, before my squads even entered the PB, I coordinated with the leadership at the PB and made the decision to conduct LSPs in case an enemy situation escalated and the Taliban tried to surround us. My rationale at the time was that Third Platoon was more than capable of taking care of the immediate area, but the surrounding area was unknown and needed to be investigated and secured.

While I was gone on patrol with my Marines, I had zero situational awareness of the circumstances going on between the local village elders and my Company Commander. When my Marines and I returned from our LSP, I was briefed by Lieutenant Barnley. I soon learned that the locals did not want us to stay at the area designated as our new PB. They were furious that we had not given them notice of our intentions to occupy the area, and from our location they were concerned that we could potentially spy on their women and children in the lowland compounds. Obviously this was not the case, and it was a ridiculous accusation. We were there to hunt down and kill Taliban, not their women and children.

Their solution, and one my Captain almost executed, was to move all our Marines about a kilometer or two west, even farther into the desert. To my knowledge, my Company Commander was just about to tell the Marines to move again when our Company Gunnery Sergeant dropped all our packs, gear, and essential living items smack dab in the middle of the compound. All other days, my Company Gunnery Sergeant was useless, but on this day my Gunny actually did something right and came through for my Marines. He saved our butts on this one. We now had no choice but to utilize this compound and tell the locals to deal with it.

The next two days, from sunrise to sunset, began and ended with little work being done on the PB in terms of setup, fortification, and security. All our efforts focused on patrolling the immediate AO. We soon realized that waiting for our CO to make a decision about the conduct of our operations was not the best course of action, as he was continually fielding complaints and conducting meetings with the locals, which consumed his entire day.

By the third day of the operation, our PB was dimensionally fifty meters wide by one hundred and fifty meters long. It was a rectangular shell of a one-foot-high mud wall with a few sandbags on top. Up to this point it still offered zero shade to get out of the elements, sandstorms, and 130–140 degree desert sunlight. Because the logistics, camouflage netting, tents, and shelter assets had still not arrived at the PB, my Marines and I were trapped beneath the sun and caught in sandstorms.

Zero work was getting done on the improvement of the defensive capabilities of the PB. The reason no work was being done internally was primarily because the lack of coordination in receiving logistical support and the incompatibility of our current rank structure. There were six Officers, zero Staff Noncommissioned Officers, and close to 160 enlisted Marines, Sailors, and Soldiers all with the rank of Sergeant and below. Logistically speaking, we had zero assets at our disposal to get the Marines and our partners out of the elements of the weather. We had a bunch of chiefs and zero Indians.

To compound the problem, we had a reckless, drug-addicted, and rambunctious third-world military on our hands, with whom we constantly battled, which kept throwing gasoline on the fire of this perfect storm.

There were three Platoon Commanders, an Intelligence Officer, an Air Officer, an Executive Officer, and a Company Commander. We did not have one Platoon Sergeant to task delegate or create a buffer between the enlisted Marines and the Officers. The friction was apparent to everyone. Platoon Commanders and Noncommissioned Officers are not paid or trained to be Staff Noncommissioned Officers.

The gravity of the situation climaxed on the fourth morning with a verbal scolding by our CO toward all three Lima Company Platoon Commanders about why the establishment and fortification of our PB was not getting done fast enough. It is embarrassing, to say the least, when a Commander yells at his Lieutenants in front of their Marines and blames them for the shortfalls of his own planning. Fingers started pointing, and words like *relief* were not far away for all three of us.

During the afternoon of the fourth day of this operation, just as things seemed they could not get any worse, sudden relief occurred like a cold sweeping whirlwind to sooth the burning of our skulls, which were constantly being fried in the 130-degree heat.

Earlier in the morning, our Battalion Gunner arrived on the scene, along with his Jump Platoon to conduct a site survey of our slowly devolving operation. Looking confused and irate as to why our defensive plan and sectors of fire were not established, he started to take notes to document what was transpiring at the PB. His stay was short and brief because he was fed up and needed to report this situation to our Battalion Commander. After speaking with a few Lieutenants and Squad Leaders about the circumstances surrounding the planning and execution that had gone into the operation, he departed back to FOB Geronimo to formulate a report, inform his higher chain of command, and develop plans to rectify the piss-poor operation that was leading Lima Company slowly off the edge of a precipice.

Unbeknownst to me, that change was to take place a few hours later. As I briefed my Marines on their patrol routes for the day, the image of my stellar six-foot-seven, 240-pound Platoon Sergeant came into view. He approached my platoon and me with a big smile on his face and a look in his eyes that meant business.

"Hey, sir, what in God's name is going on here? The Gunner just picked me up from Brannon, apparently to save the careers of a few Officers. He told me the Battalion Commander had asked him to give him the name of one Marine who could fix this situation. So here I am.

Fill me in," said my Platoon Sergeant with his slight New York accent, looking intense and ready to begin cleaning up this mess.

"This is the current situation on the deck. There are six Officers and no Platoon Sergeants. That part you are already aware of, as we both fought for this not to happen. Nothing is getting done because there are too many chiefs running the show, and all the platoons are operating independently of one another. We are doing our thing like we always do as a platoon, but the CO is not facilitating us to work as a company and a single entity. We are working on fire plan sketches and conducting patrols, but fortification and defensive improvement still needs to be done, and everyone wants to be in charge. I need you to give me time by rectifying this internal situation and delegating my tasks to the men while I deal with the leadership issues," I replied in an almost relieved and enthusiastic manner.

"Roger that, sir. I got this. Olds, Brown, Guthrie, get over here now! I need three squads for working parties and two of your sister platoon squads for patrols. The LT wants this PB stood up in a hurry. Get as many Marines as possible and start filling and stacking sandbags. I want these walls as tall as a man. Get this cammie netting and these tents I brought stood up now, and get the boys out of the elements. All of the water and chow need to be in a shaded place. Wake up those Afghan Soldiers over there sleeping and make them help you. Get me a Squad Leader from Third Platoon and a Section Leader from Weapons and make sure their Marines are tracking on the plan. You all have fifteen minutes. Work together with the other platoons and Afghans, backbrief me on your plan, and get it done. Do not make me have to repeat myself. Go. You're your magic now," replied my Platoon Sergeant to his Squad Leaders calmly as if he had control of the world with his fingertips.

It is a very dangerous ground for a Platoon Commander to stand on when we try to task out Marines from different platoons or units. It is dangerous ground because Commanders, especially Platoon Commanders, are territorial and possessive toward their own Marines. Commanders are like father figures, and we do not want other Marines messing with "our boys."

As you can see from this scenario, it was very hard to get work done because as a Platoon Commander, I could really only task my Marines in most circumstances. I would have generated a lot of bad blood by telling the Marines of my fellow Commanders what to do. It is an alpha male contest at the end of the day, and no Lieutenant wanted to take orders from his peers at the risk of looking weak in front of his Marines. If I were to cross the line and task out First Lieutenant Vali's or First Lieutenant Hartsell's Marines, I would have been stepping on their toes and undermining them as leaders in front of their Marines, something I would never do or want done to myself.

Platoon Sergeants are unique in this aspect, as was the case with Staff Sergeant Lebron. He was the only one out there who could play the role of Platoon Sergeant for all three platoons, thereby gaining task delegation control of all the Marines at PB Razza and enabling him to get things done.

"Well, sir, tasks are issued, and the patrolling schedule is set. The boys will be filling sandbags, building guard posts, putting up camouflage netting, and establishing the new COC here shortly. Let's go have a cigarette and supervise the conduct. I know you like the Marlboro Reds, but all I have are Newports," replied my Platoon Sergeant, smiling as he briefed me.

Laughing, I replied, "Damn glad to see you, Staff Sergeant. I can already see a difference in the morale of the men. Let's go have a cigarette."

"Hey, sir, we are both bastards of the East Coast. When South Jersey and New York come together, everybody better watch out. The Statue of Liberty has just fallen on the Jersey Shore out here in this desert," he replied in a very professionally comedic manner.

Within a period of three days, my Platoon Sergeant turned our hole-in-the-ground PB into a fully functioning and operational forward command center. Through his hard work, the poor planning involved in execution of this mission soon had zero effect on the conduct of our operations out of PB Razza.

CHAPTER 20

The clearing mission of Operation New Dawn was successfully completed after the first few days of our insertion into the Shorsurak area. For the most part, my platoon—with very little help from our Fourth Tolai Afghan Soldiers—cleared all major compounds that surrounded the immediate area of our PB while simultaneously blocking all major main supply routes from south to north. We set up deliberate and hasty roadblocks and checkpoints to thoroughly gauge patterns of life and search vehicles for enemies and enemy materials.

Lima Company was now in the stages of interdicting and blocking all enemy movement south to north from our area in Shorsurak to the Marjeh District. Around the time of this transition, my CO made a truly witty decision by enabling my entire platoon to take total operational and tactical control of the Operation New Dawn and PB Razza. By the end of the first week, Captain Shields tasked Third Platoon to occupy PB Brannon and relieve in place the rest of my Marines who were still at Brannon. Once relieved, Sergeant Brown's squad would patrol south and link up with the rest of my platoon at PB Razza.

This plan was not without a little scare, however. Early that day, prior to patrolling to Razza, Sergeant Brown's Marines encountered a potential IED threat at Brannon, which delayed the relief in place with Third Platoon. A local Afghan woman had thrown a brown paper bag at the western HESCO wall of PB Brannon and then mysteriously run off. After requesting battalion support, my Squad Leader learned that EOD was engaged in India Company's AO and would take a day to get to his position. As the on-scene Commander, Sergeant Brown made the decision to confirm the IED utilizing our IED detection dog (IDD) and our compact metal detectors. After slowly approaching the potential IED and confirming it was not a bomb, Sergeant Brown opened the bag to see what was inside. In the bag, they found a deceased boiled and burned baby. At the request of the Afghan Commander Baz Mohammed, my Marines handed over the Afghan baby to be given a proper burial.

Once Brown's squad reached our PB, Staff Sergeant Lebron took control of all logistical and administrative issues, and I was now the operational and tactical Commander of all operations in and out of PB Razza. Upon hearing news like that, I couldn't wait to get my Marines to Razza and out of Brannon. With my Second Squad arrival, I was now in charge of eighty Marines, ten Sailors, eight Army Soldiers, four linguists, two civilians, and forty Afghan National Army Soldiers. My reinforced platoon was now going to be in charge of patrolling the entire AO for the battalion mission.

Captain Shields was constantly moving back and forth between COB Toor Gar, FOB Geronimo, and PB Razza during this time and usually left his Executive Officer behind with orders to execute the mission and his intent flawlessly. As tactical Commander, I could now allow my Platoon Sergeant to have the freedom and responsibility to operate effectively and enable my Squad Leaders to have more freedom to conduct their small unit leadership.

Or as my Platoon Sergeant would say, "Sir, you handle the politics on your side. You keep it from touching me and the boys so we can do the job we are here to do. You allow me to operate effectively by keeping the higher echelons from micromanaging us." It was hard for me to see where he was coming from at the time, but I slowly started to understand how much he appreciated me trusting him and letting him operate to his maximum potential.

My Platoon Sergeant had made a huge impact in Shorsurak by cleaning up the mess that was made. I am a firm believer in giving credit where it is due. However, there was one problem neither he nor I could solve. The problem that plagued the Marines at PB Razza, from start to finish, was the ragtag bunch of Afghan National Army Soldiers from the Fourth Tolai.

For lack of a better word, they were like parasites, sucking the blood out of their victims until there was nothing left. In our case, they were an infectious internal enemy and a pestilence. These Afghan Soldiers caused daily destruction and havoc on both the internal and external operations my Marines conducted, with their lack of enthusiasm, unreliability, drug addiction, and idle mentalities.

Their actions on patrol the first night of Operation New Dawn and their inability to help the Marines fortify the PB because of their constant tardiness, drug use, and laziness caused a clear divide within the first week. My Marines, who were very patient with the Afghan Soldiers for the initial few days of the operation, could no longer work with them out of fear for their lives.

At the end of the first week, combined and partnered patrols were not occurring because the Afghan Soldiers and their leadership decided they would rather sleep and do drugs than support my Marines and the mission. My Marines were going out on combat patrols unpartnered, without the Afghan Soldiers. Regardless of this fact, they worked more productively, discovering IEDs, bomb-making materials, and weapons caches in roads and compounds on their own without the help of our third-world counterparts.

A clear divide existed at the PB, with the Afghans self-segregating the camp between themselves and the Marines. The Afghan Soldiers had sectioned off a third of the PB on its eastern side and lined its borders with two-foot-high Marine-filled sandbags and cammie netting they stole from the perimeter of our PB. They decided not to help the Marines at all in building PB Razza and instead made fun of them as they worked to constantly improve the defenses and patrol the outlying areas.

The Afghan Soldiers had created their own base inside our base. The point they were making to us was clear: they wanted no part of the operation or the Marines involved in it. They wanted to smoke opium and hash and just hang out while we did the work.

Just about every morning and evening, the Afghan Soldiers woke us up with a blanket of hash or opium smoke that covered our base. My Platoon Sergeant and I continually had to ensure the welfare of our Marines and keep them motivated while their partners were engaged in degenerate activities. These Soldiers smoked constantly and were always high when they interacted with my young warriors. Since they were high all the time, our initial partnered patrolling became very difficult and unproductive and eventually nonexistent.

Initially, when my Marines tried to partner with the Afghans, patrols were always late on their departures because the Afghan National Army Soldiers were stoned and took their sweet time getting ready. On dismounted security patrols, Marines constantly had to take tactical pauses and stops because their Afghan counterparts were out of shape, high on drugs, and unable to keep up with them. Constantly, these foreign Soldiers shed their flak jackets, bulletproof vests, Kevlar, and rifles, sometimes even leaving them on the deck of the desert as they patrolled, forcing my Marines and linguists to carry the weight back to the PB.

Why was my CO not doing anything to solve this situation? Why was this our problem? And why did my Marines have to deal with this unprofessional conduct?

Toward the end of our first week, I was on duty in the COC as the Watch Officer and noticed one of my Marine patrols entering friendly lines looking upset and angrier than usual.

"Lance Corporal James, Private First Class Sisca, Lance Corporal Hall, come in here. What's going on? Why do you all look angry as hell right now?" I asked them. I knew why they were mad and what they had to deal with, but I wanted to hear it from them so I could start building my case to get this unit removed.

"Well, sir, on our way out, the Soldiers would not listen to us, started cursing and spitting at us, and were making calls on their cell phones," said Lance Corporal James, obviously upset.

"Damn right, sir. These guys even started using their RPGs as water bottle holders and their magazine pouches to hold their chow," said Private First Class Sisca with his slight Boston accent.

"Even worse, sir, on the way back one of the Afghan Soldiers took off all of his gear because he was tired and hot and left it on the desert floor. Our interpreter had to pick up the Soldier's rifle and gear and then carried it back for him," said Lance Corporal Hall in a tone that clearly signaled he needed me to act on this.

"Roger. Grab me Staff Sergeant," I said to my three Marines.

Lance Corporal Hall yelled for his Squad Leader, who came running up to us in a hurry. His Squad Leader then informed our Platoon Sergeant, who came to the COC.

"Staff Sergeant, from now on pass the word that we are no longer taking Afghan Army Soldiers with us on any of our patrols. Let the other Squad Leaders know from now on we are not going partnered. As a matter of fact, get the Afghan Commander as well so I can inform him of the change too. I want him here in front of me," I said in an effort to rectify this situation. It was one thing to mess with me, but like a father protects his children, if anyone messed with my Marines, I would take it to a new level.

Little did I know, my resolve would soon be short-lived and take a complete 180-degree turn. I felt in my gut this was enough evidence to fry these incompetent "Soldiers" and that my CO would side with me 100 percent.

The next day, my CO returned to Razza, and I approached him with this information. Because he had the power like that of God out here in Shorsurak, I was certain he would agree with my decision and rectify this pestilence at the PB.

"Sir, I need to talk to you for a minute," I told him in a very calm manner.

"Bodrog, what going on?" he replied, knowing I was about to tell him some type of news he did not want to hear.

"Sir, I am not going to partner with the Afghan National Army anymore. I spoke to the Fourth Tolai Afghan Commander as well, and he even told me that he will do everything he can not to partner with the Marines, even sabotage. This is crazy.

"My reasons for this are because the Afghans are constantly smoking hash, falling out of patrols, discarding their gear and weapons on patrols, and putting my guys' lives at risk. They constantly curse and spit at Marines, continue to impede our evolution and progress, and above all do not have any respect for you, my Marines, or me. You need to do something, sir, or they need to go," I explained to him in a very tactful manner, making sure my mental revolver was locked and loaded before I spoke. My points were very valid, and I thought I made a great argument. To my dismay, the political realm of this war was itself a quagmire to comprehend.

"Lieutenant Bodrog, I understand you are frustrated. We all are. Trust me. I know, and I am with you. But we have to continue to work with these Afghan Soldiers no matter what the risk and cost. They will be the ones to take over and fight for this country when we leave. We need to be patient and understand their shortfalls. We need to help them and ensure we give them the capability and tools necessary to fight the enemy and protect the innocent lives of the people. I do not need any international incidences while we are here, or insubordination. We will continue to have patience with them and talk to their Commanders to get them to work for us, not against us," he replied, obviously feeling my anger and trying to calm me down.

"Sir, it is just not working out. My Marines and I will not patrol with them, and likewise is the case with the Fourth Tolai Soldiers and their Commanders. They are incompetent, and most, if not all, are on some type of drug, if not multiple. The next step is them shooting one of my men or allowing the Taliban to infiltrate this PB. I am not letting my Marines patrol with them, sir, and I informed the Afghan Commander if this continues I will arrest him and his Soldiers, especially if they try to sell my Marines drugs again," I replied, obviously in a more defiant and sterner tone, one that could potentially be seen as borderline belligerent.

I was not trying to disobey an order or undermine my chain of command, but I was going out on combat patrols and witnessing this, and my men were in the dirt every day living this nightmare. The situation we constantly saw on the ground was definitely different than the one inside the hooch of our forward combat operations center at Razza.

"Lieutenant Bodrog, this needs to work, and we are going to make this work. I cannot discipline them because I am not in charge of them. I would get rid of them if I could, but this goes higher than me. Their Commanders have promised me they will talk to their Soldiers and correct their problems and deficiencies. Like I told you, we are partnered on everything we do, and if you or your Marines cannot do the job, there are other platoons in the AO who would die to be in the position you all are in right now," said my Captain, obviously reinforcing the intent given to him by his higher chain of command.

Honestly, I had not seen this coming, and this was twice now that I had been indirectly told I was going to be removed. But now other people would die to be in this position? I did not like to fight for political gain or favor and was humbled that my Marines were the main effort in the south, but where was the logic? Talk to their Soldiers? Yeah, we would see how that one would work out. No matter how much my CO talked to the Afghan Commanders or Soldiers to help them out, they would just gaff him off. They would take the compassion and understanding my Commander gave them and throw it right back in our faces.

Like animals, they started to lawlessly live among the Marines, destroying everything they touched. Every morning and evening the PB smelled of opium and hashish. During our combat patrols, when our PB operated on low strength or a majority of Marines were on missions, the Afghan Soldiers stole our cammie netting, notebooks, writing utensils, food, and water. Some even tried to steal our issued military gear. When Marines and Corpsmen walked by them, the Soldiers raised their hands like guns and made sound effects like they were firing it at them. Uncivilized in their manner of speaking, they ridiculed us when they could, always starting conflicts. If it were not for my Squad Leaders and Platoon Sergeant constantly mitigating these situations, a fight to the death would probably have occurred.

My Marines were the professionals, always on a high state of alert and on edge, raised by Staff Sergeant Lebron and myself to be aggressive and win at all costs. They had received battalion honors and numerous awards during all training exercises, including training at Mojave Viper Combined Arm Exercise in California. However, at this point I was about to be the one to lay down the law when no one else would.

The first week ended in Shorsurak with the Marines and the Afghan Soldiers of the Fourth Tolai literally at each other's throats. We were being as tolerant and as patient as possible with them, but they were being impossible to work with. Every layer of civility and every standard the Marines were implementing toward the Afghan Soldiers was met with resistance and friction. This breakdown in good order and discipline could not last.

For my Marines, it was like trying to domesticate people who have the mentality of a Cro-Magnon man and live in the second century BC. These people have not evolved like the rest of the world and just did not understand our modernized and civilized concepts of military order and discipline.

It is hard to believe, but these people find it completely normal to defecate in the same water canals in which they bathe and from which they drink. It reminded me of the movie *Borat*, when Borat is urinating in the same water his friend is using to wash his face. The Afghans in this particular region use their hands to wipe themselves after they go to the bathroom, and then they eat food using the same fingers, which they did not wash or clean. They do not even know what germs and bacteria are or even believe they exist. They are primitive in everything they do and cannot even grasp the simplest concepts by which we as Americans and Marines live.

CHAPTER 21

The start of the second week at PB Razza was no better. As I was on duty in the COC with my Radio Operator, a call came in to us from Lance Corporal Evola, my Marine on Guard Post watch.

"Watch-O, be advised, an Afghan Soldier is breaking through the concertina wire and leaving the PB without permission. He cut the wire with a tool and now is walking down to the village below us to the west. Should I let him go?" he said in a very distressed manner, keeping his finger straight and off the trigger of his medium machine gun, patiently waiting to be given the command to fire.

Our biggest threat up to this point was infiltration by the Taliban into our PB at the hands of our drug-addicted Afghan partners. Now these Soldiers were deliberately breaking through our concertina wire with absolute disregard for the safety of my men inside the base.

Out of everything I have learned and read from the many engagements and operations fought throughout history, any individual who has ever tried to get in or out of a defense position without clearance or proper authority would have been shot. No questions asked!

My CO, once informed of the situation, refused to give the order to fire and instead opted for asking the Afghan National Army Commander at the PB what was going on and why his Soldier had left our defensive wire. It was not like the Soldier had mistakenly left or it was easy to leave, so there should have been no discussion or double standard. He had deliberately refused to obey the general orders we had established, and he had destroyed government property.

Leaving our wire took a deliberate act of vandalism, as he needed to cut through our defense with tools. This was a complete disregard for military law, regulation, and order. Rules were in place to save lives. They were not guiding tools for leadership; they were the laws of the land because the reality was that people could die.

Once again, sensitivity and double standards in the war zone prevailed, and we had to cater to their dimwitted third-world decisions like parents afraid to discipline their children. These Soldiers were getting away with murder, and they were not being held accountable to the same standards my Marines were being held. Why were we, a first-world military, being taken down to the level of these third-world pricks and being held accountable and responsible for their conduct?

As a leader, I have always applied Darwinian principals to the evolution and training of my platoon and Marines, telling them to never settle for second and always strive to be first in everything. Darwin applied the theory of survival of the fittest and natural selection to animals in nature; I applied this supposition to my Marines. After all, competition drives Marines, and we want to be the finest at everything we do. Before arriving to Afghanistan, my Platoon Sergeant and I had successfully eliminated every weak element that would have caused friction or catastrophe from my platoon after receiving the green light from our Battalion Commander to do so. It was great, allowed competition, and bettered the platoon.

Second Platoon was my own personally hand-selected best of the best, and it was killing me that these Afghan Soldiers were bringing the standards down and that my Marines would receive nonjudicial punishments or brig time if they stood up for the principles of the Corps they had joined to be a part of, fought for, and believed in.

My Platoon Sergeant and I were in charge of our entire defense perimeter, and we had ensured that our PB borders were lined with triple-strand concertina wire with clear entry and exit areas complemented by serpentines. To get out of our patrol base would have taken a deliberate act of planning and ingenuity. Even more disturbing was the fact that if the enemy was watching, which he was, he could now utilize these gaps in our defense to attack us.

Before I received any other traffic from my post over the radio, I called my fellow Platoon Commander and friend, First Lieutenant Hartsell, and my Corporal of the Guard, Corporal Garst, into the COC to brief them on the current situation. Lieutenant Hartsell owned Weapons Platoon and had the heavy guns. He needed to up the posture of his Marines during this time. Once his Marines were put on alert, all three of us ran to the southwest guard post to interdict and block any attempt at entry by this unknown Afghan Army Soldier who had left our defensive lines.

As soon as we got there, the Afghan Soldier who had left our defensive perimeter was walking toward us, trying to get back in. Acting on instinct and under the premise that not one Marine knew the faces or names of our Afghan counterparts and that this could potentially be an infiltration attempt by the Taliban, Corporal Garst put his hand out and physically stopped the forward progression of the Soldier trying to breach our defense and get back inside friendly lines. The bloodshot eyes and slurred jargon of this Afghan Soldier were enough for all three of us to know he was stoned out of his mind.

All hell started to break loose at this point, and the three of us stood on ground zero. The entire Afghan platoon on Razza, who had been watching our actions and efforts to keep this unknown Soldier out of the patrol base, went crazy, to say the least. Every one of the Afghan Soldiers grabbed their AK-47s and RPGs and ran toward us at full speed, muzzles pointed at our faces and fingers on the triggers. It was not until I turned around to see the commotion behind me that I realized the seriousness of the situation. There were twenty-seven AK-47s and three RPGs pointed directly at the faces of First Lieutenant Hartsell, Corporal Garst, and me. Each one of these weapons was set on "fire" and was being held by itchy and unstable Afghan trigger fingers. To escalate the situation, Mortarmen from Lieutenant Hartsell's platoon and Marines from my platoon had also been watching the situation and were now standing in an on-line formation behind these

Afghan Soldiers with their rifles raised, thirsty and hungry to squeeze their triggers and send all these Afghan Soldiers to the afterlife to meet their maker.

I remember First Lieutenant Hartsell, a very family oriented and religious man, curse for the first time ever in my presence.

"Bodrog, turn the hell around! ANA, drop your weapons now! I said *drop your weapons now*! Sergeant Smith, tell your Marines to hold their fire," he said as he sized up the platoon of Afghan Soldiers running toward us.

"Hartsell, if these hypocrites so much as inch for the triggers of their weapons, I will gladly toast to their death. You can join me in the celebration," I said to him.

In an effort to gain control of what little ground we had left, I turned to my Corporal and then my fellow Platoon Commander and said, "Garst, you have the left. I will take the right. Hartsell get ready for anything that comes down the middle. Each of you take a third of the sectors in your direct front," I replied, trying to remain cocky, confident, and calm before the impending wall of lead and rockets that was about to come spraying and flying at us.

"Put your weapons down! I will take out every one of you! Drop 'em now! Marines, hold your fire," yelled Hartsell, clearly trying to de-escalate the situation while making sure the Marines who were still standing on line behind the Afghans with their rifles raised knew what to do.

At precisely this moment, the Afghan Commanders and the embedded Marines who worked with the Fourth Tolai at PB Razza came running over to us to prevent this situation from igniting further. After a few minutes that seemed like an eternity, the Afghan Soldiers finally dropped their weapons. These Soldiers had tried to kill us, and now tensions were higher than ever.

From what I was told by our Marine counterparts who were embedded with the Afghans, the Soldier who destroyed and broke through our defenses wanted to go for a swim in the canal because he was hot. When the Afghan Soldier asked my Marine to let him leave the base to go for a swim, my Marine did not grant him permission. After all, we knew our general orders, and we were in a combat zone, not a swim club.

Furthermore, as with all units that enter or exit friendly lines, mission cards and accountability needed to be conducted. This was not done, and if the Soldier's mission was to swim in a canal, I would have personally denied the request. After all, Marine leaders in my AO were being fired for their junior Marines cooling off in a canal even with security posted. The Afghan leadership was nowhere to be found, and I allowed no double standards on my PB.

Comfort comes second to the security of a base. That said, the Afghan Soldier had become angry and disobeyed my Marine's orders when he was not allowed to leave. He had then gone back to his side of the base, deliberately cut through our concertina wire defense perimeter, and went for a bath in the canal anyway as a way to spite us and our military rules.

The embedded Marines eventually identified the Afghan Soldier, and we let him back inside friendly lines at the base. Nothing for nothing, but at any other PB this guy would have been shot. The Afghan Soldier should have been relieved, fired, and charged for destruction of United States government property at the very least.

In any base, if people are allowed to come and go freely without any recourse or lack the responsibility to execute their duties in a safe manner, the defense perimeter becomes nonexistent. Just like a country that refuses to enforce its very own borders is no longer a country, such is the same with a PB; it is no longer secure, and the lives of the men inside are at risk. What really frustrated me was that no matter how badly these Afghan Soldiers performed or messed up, there were no repercussions from my CO or theirs.

If we look at history, either the English-speaking Germans at the Battle of the Bulge or the recent attempts by al-Qaeda in Iraq to dress up in Iraqi uniforms and sneak into United States bases to kill our forces, the possibility of the Taliban killing an Afghan Soldier going for his daily swim, dressing in his military uniform, and then sneaking into our patrol base to kill Marines was not far-fetched at all.

Acts like this were happening all over Afghanistan at coalition bases. Afghan infiltrators were constantly entering bases in attempts to kill our Marines and partners, yet we still allowed the Soldiers to behave recklessly. Like a broken record, this thought kept playing over and over in my head, and I could feel the pain of these now-routine circumstances stabbing the back of my brain.

Many nights both before and after this event occurred, I could not sleep. My Platoon Sergeant and I stayed awake ninety-six hours straight after this initial event because of the uncertainty and fog associated with this madness. The Taliban did not keep us up at night; the Afghan Soldiers we shared the base with did. For all we knew, we could have Taliban at the PB dressed in an ANA uniform or an Afghan Soldier paid off by the Taliban waiting for the right moment to strike.

We had to come to the reality that either the Taliban had already slipped into our defensive lines disguised as Afghan Soldiers or they would attempt to breach our wire when a majority of the Marines were executing their rest plans. After all, my Marines and I had no idea who our Afghan counterparts were. They had no identification, wore their uniforms when they felt like it, and came and went out of the patrol base as they pleased. Even the embedded Marines who were there to educate and train these men were exhausted and admitted that most of them were lost causes. Any tactically savvy enemy with a brain and a pair of eyes could have exploited us, especially if they had knowledge that the Soldiers were stoned on drugs the majority of the time.

What reinforced my paranoia was that even though my CO spoke to their leadership numerous times, the Afghans continually tried to sneak in and out of our base whenever they thought we were not watching, like it was a game. We should have shot each and every one of them who broke our defensive lines and put my Marines' safety and security at risk. Believe me, my Marines and I had to do everything we could to restrain ourselves.

Eventually, the solution of stopping the destruction of our defense perimeter came in the form of a remedy my Platoon Sergeant came up with, and I approved. We ended up reinforcing all the concertina wire with incendiary trip flares to finally get the Soldiers to stop destroying our defensive perimeter. The visual image of a six-foot-seven Marine from New York City emplacing incendiary devices ten feet from where you live, pulling the safety pins, and smiling as he handed them to you was enough to convince any man we were not playing around. If they tried to break the wire now and jeopardized the safety and security of my PB, they would wind up with a face full of fire. The intent was clear: no one in or out without the permission and authority of my Marines.

The days flew by after we showed the Afghan Army Soldiers how far we were willing to go to prove a point. Sure, every now and then Afghan Soldiers still stole camouflage netting, sandbags, chow, and water from my Marines, but like uncivilized-thinking beasts, they were slowly starting to learn through repetition and muscle memory, just like Pavlov's dogs. The Afghan Soldiers soon did not breach my wire anymore and asked permission from the Watch Officer in my forward combat operations center every time they wanted to leave.

Litter and trash still filled the Afghans' berthing areas everywhere we walked. They defecated where they slept, and they constantly smoked hash and went swimming (with Marine approval). But some in the patrols were getting a little better. The majority only interacted with my Marines when it came to integrated patrolling. The ANA were not as late as they usually were and stopped complaining as much as they had before.

The Marines got revenge and had their fun too, whether it was by throwing full water bottles at the Afghans' heads while they slept or patrolling hard routes through the desert and in corn fields, muddy farm fields, and canals. Unbeknownst to me at the time, my Marines made these guys suffer when they could for the constant friction they dealt with each day of the operation.

Sergeant Olds, my physical fitness stud and senior Squad Leader, was mentally and physically at war with these Afghans by now. The pride of the platoon was on the line every day, and the Marines were watching. Sergeants Brown and Guthrie, although fed up as well, ensured that no one messed with their Marines, and any Afghan who did had to go through them first.

CHAPTER 22

By the close of the second week of Operation New Dawn, my Marines and I faced probably the worst situation anyone could face. As my Platoon Sergeant and I were sitting with our men, giving them a military lecture, we received a call over the radio that one of our Marines, Corporal Garst, had just been blown up by an IED approximately five to six kilometers southeast of our position.

Instinctively, my Platoon Sergeant and I, for fear that our Marine was either injured or killed, put our mental and physical wheels in motion and immediately launched our quick reaction force (QRF) to go get our Marine.

"First Squad QRF, gear up. You're going with the Lieutenant! Garst just got hit! Double-time it! Olds, you got it," yelled my Platoon Sergeant.

"Good to go. Roger that, Staff Sergeant. Lance Corporal Vancamp, stand by for the grid. Lance Corporal Morris, you're taking point. James, Hall, Sisca, we are stepping off now with the LT. Get your gear on and let's go. Garst just got hit," said Sergeant Olds as he task delegated his squad to prevent any wasted time in the support of our Marine who got blown up.

With a team of EOD Marines directly attached to his squad, Sergeant Olds immediately did a quick accountability check, and we left the wire. Our movement carried the squad reinforced with EOD more than five kilometers in temperatures that were as high as 125 degrees Fahrenheit. It was almost noon when we left friendly lines at the PB, and the sun in Shorsurak was unforgiving and lethal. It took us thirty minutes and all of our adrenaline, water, and chow to double-time the five kilometers with all our combat load and gear, but we hustled and arrived to the site of the compound where my Marine had been blown up.

By the time my squad and I arrived on the scene, our biggest fears were abated. Out of water, dehydrated, and borderline heat casualties, my Marines and I were rejuvenated when we saw Corporal Garst walking in front of us. Chills ran all through us, cooling our sunburned and sweat-covered bodies at the sight of our Marine.

After speaking with Corporal Garst to find out how he was blown up, he informed us that he had set off an IED when he exited an abandoned former compound he was utilizing to reestablish communication with the PB. This compound happened to be the same abandoned compound my platoon and ANA had discovered IEDs in twice prior to this incident. We all knew the threats it posed, and no matter how careful we tried to be, these threats always faced us, no matter where we went in the Helmand Province.

Corporal Garst informed me that the pressure plate IED he had stepped on was located in the doorway of the compound and that he missed it going in and hit it full-on coming out. Talking with Corporal Mount and Lance Corporals Rivera and Taylor, who were on scene with him, I was informed that once the explosion happened, all they saw was Garst get launched about six feet into the air and then come crashing down to the ground in a rain of mud, dirt, and smoke.

When our EOD attachments conducted an assessment of the area, they soon discovered a secondary directional firing charge (DFC) inside a room in the same compound. This was another IED that had not gone off yet. Through careful examination of both explosive devices, our EOD technicians came to the conclusion that the ammonium nitrate and fertilizer used to make the bombs had still been wet when the enemy emplaced them, and the explosive device only partially went off. This meant that the full force of the explosion had not occurred, and less than a quarter of the bomb materials exploded. This was the direct reason my Marine was alive and had kept both his legs. The lack of education by the enemy in designing, building, and emplacing the explosives had saved the life of my Marine. I disliked the Taliban with a passion but thanked God for their lack of education in this IED's design.

It was very common for a Marine to witness the stupidity of our Taliban enemy. During operations or downtime at our PB, we would hear nearby explosions late at night or early in the morning and wonder what they were. Then when we investigated, local nationals in the area of the explosions would tell us the Taliban had been emplacing bombs in the field and had blown themselves up. We confirmed this when we did our battle damage assessments (BDA) and discovered pieces of body parts and clothing around a huge crater in the ground. We also heard news of the Taliban blowing themselves up in their vehicles after mistakenly pulling the trigger of their RPGs. Some of it was actually comical for us, but we always knew in the back of our minds that only a minority of a very motivated enemy was performing these foolish acts.

The day Corporal Garst was blown up, our EOD Marines concluded that because the TTPs of IED emplacement by the Taliban were constantly changing and evolving, they usually discovered ways to use low metallic components in their construction, which our mine detectors could not pick up. This meant the enemy was now building IEDs our mine detectors would not be able to identify. This is why Corporal Garst was blown up. The metal and mine detectors he and his ANA used to sweep the compound before he entered were essentially useless against the low metallic IEDs. The enemy was getting good at hiding them from our advanced machinery.

After a quick assessment of my "Unbreakable Marine" by my Corpsman, Corporal Garst told us he was good to go and then led his squad on the five-plus-kilometer walk back to the PB. There was no room for weakness in my platoon, and Garst embodied this way of thought, especially in front of his Marines.

I could not believe he had just been blown up and was now leading his patrol back. Pissed off that my Marine got blown up in a compound in which we had found IEDs two times earlier in the week, I devised a plan to solve the problem once and for all. With the support of EOD and their C-4 demolitions, I was granted permission by my Company COC to completely blow up and destroy the abandoned compound.

One way or another, my platoon was going to get a win on this day and ensure no Marines would ever get blown up at that compound again. Once confirmation checks were complete, deconfliction was in order, and final approval conditions were met, EOD set the six-minute timing fuse for close to twenty pounds of C-4. From a safe distance, we watched anxiously for the compound's subsequent destruction. With a huge shockwave and subsequent sound from the explosion that caused our ears to ring, the compound was laid to rubble. It would never again be used to kill a Marine or friendly unit.

Once my platoon reentered friendly lines at PB Razza, Corporal Garst was checked out and examined again, this time by both of my Naval Corpsmen, Doc Williams and Doc Greenough. Suffering only from a minor headache, he took a day off to rest and recover, refusing to leave his Marines and the platoon for medical evaluation at FOB Geronimo under any and all circumstances.

Instantaneously, word of his story spread throughout the battalion and regiment. Like wildfire, he soon became an inspiration for units in the Helmand. He had stepped on an IED and lived. Everyone needed good news from time to time, and what could be better than news like this? The event quickly earned him the nickname "The Unbreakable Marine." News of this event and media attention were soon to follow.

CHAPTER 23

The last two weeks of Operation New Dawn went by as quickly as they could for my Marines in the Shorsurak desert. The days were filled with triple-digit temperatures and sandstorms. It was too hot to rest during the day, and at night our PB was infested by camel spiders, snakes, and scorpions, which made it impossible to sleep.

We kept the complaints to a minimum and learned to love this new "playground" we were now a part of. My platoon was definitely going to be a more hardened unit by the time we walked out of this scorching desert.

On one particular evening in the COC of PB Razza, my Radio Watch named Lance Corporal Dagr, a Marine from Weapons Platoon, found out the hard way why it is particularly important to always be aware of one's surroundings. Situational awareness was a term preached to all Marines by their leaders because it kept them on their toes and from getting killed.

While engaged in radio checks with our Marines on guard post, he failed to notice a spiderlike creature walking on the tent rods directly above him. When I sat next to him as the Watch Officer, I felt something moving above me and looked up to see what it was. I noticed the creature was an eight-inch-long camel spider, and it had its sights set on my Radio Watch as it crawled ever closer, perfectly positioning its body over his head.

Once the camel spider was directly over Lance Corporal Dagr's head, I silently gave my Marine the hand and arm signal to look up. No sooner did he look up than this camel spider launched itself off the tent rods and came flying down with perfect accuracy onto his face. While I laughed hysterically, Lance Corporal Dagr swatted and hit his face until he eventually killed the camel spider. It was like a scene out of the movie *Alien vs. Predator* when the spiderlike creatures latch on to the faces of their victims. For the rest of the night, both he and I stayed alert and focused, especially for kamikaze camel spiders. From what the Marines told me, Lance Corporal Dagr did not sleep for three days after that event.

Patrols during the last two weeks centered on areas near canals and clusters of village compounds where life was present. This was done to enhance our COIN capabilities of interacting with locals, and it offered my men the opportunity to purchase needed water or food to sustain them on long patrols. It also afforded us the opportunity to actively and passively gather critical intelligence on the enemy in the vicinity, the villages, and local people of the surrounding area.

With no way to cool our body temperatures at our PB, my Marines consumed hot bottles of water and utilized primitive refrigeration techniques such as stuffing water bottles in socks soaked with water and allowing the air to evaporate the heat from the bottles, thus cooling the water. When MREs became too much to bear for our appetites, my Marines stuffed these hot bottles of water with Ramen noodles and mixed in items such as sugar, salt, baked beans, and tuna to change up their nutritional intake.

As tactical Commander, I was left in charge of the PB most of the time while my CO and XO attended daily meetings with the battalion at FOB Geronimo. The Afghan Soldiers in Shorsurak continued to be a problem for Marines, but against all our complaints to our higher command, they stayed.

The Marines were still in the process of acclimating to the above 130-degree daily temperatures and performed admirably considering all the internal and external friction they encountered from the Afghan Soldiers and the terrain. Every week the Marines averaged at least three or more IED finds and one to two weapons cache finds and destroyed a few IED-making facilities. The Marines patrolled more than

150 kilometers and conducted around thirty patrols every seven days according to our honesty traces and graphic map data.

Finding IEDs or bomb-making materials did not even daunt my Marines by the end of the third week in Shorsurak. To them it became just another day of patrolling, and my guys exerted zero inhibitions toward them because they keenly knew precisely what to look for when searching. They all knew they were making a difference and potentially saving the lives of future units that would operate in this area once we left.

One of our last tactical discoveries was in the fourth and final week of the battalion operation. Out of nowhere, a local Afghan man came to our base and asked to speak to the Commanders in charge because he wanted to be an informant against the Taliban. He said he knew the location of local Taliban members named Zendani and Mullah Razi, who were responsible for the drug trade in the area and had links to a terror cell leader in the north of our AO named Mullah Abash. (Mullah Abash would later be responsible for the terrorist cell that killed my colleague and friend First Lieutenant Scott Fleming.)

After I had a long discussion with my CO about how I thought this guy was a liar and opportunist who wanted nothing more than money, the local Afghan convinced him to go on a foot patrol to the homes of the enemies he claimed he knew. I was immediately ordered to grab half of my platoon and half of the Afghan platoon to lead a joint patrol south of our PB to find these terrorists.

The local Afghan who claimed he knew where these men lived took us on a five-hour patrol just north of the Garmsir District, which is the Nawa District's southern border. We patrolled nineteen kilometers and crossed over three adjacent unit battlespaces with this individual before he claimed he did not know where he was going.

Thoughts of an ambush filled my mind the entire time. Once again, our Commander had made another great tactical decision at the behest of another lying local national over one of his Lieutenants. What was worse was that we all thought this was an obvious trap. To mitigate the risk, I separated my patrolling squads by time in order to cover our flanks in case of an ambush.

Once we reached our limit of advance, our closest friendly position was FOB Delhi, the main base in northern Garmsir District, five kilometers to our south. Out of food and using local well water for hydration, we approached a nearby village for a tactical pause. After arguing with the local national through our linguists, we were informed that the man just wanted money and did not know the two individuals he claimed to know.

We ended up utilizing our Afghan counterparts to search all the compounds in the village to look for any illegal materials such as bombs, weapons, chemicals, and drugs. To our relief, our Afghan partners discovered more than two hundred pounds of poppy, twenty yellow jugs that could potentially be utilized to make IEDs, numerous wires, lithium batteries, and small amounts of ammonium nitrate. Realizing we could not bring all of these materials on our seventeen-kilometer patrol back to base, we dumped and burned this small amount of materials in a nearby field so they could not be used against Marines.

Having no use for this "informant" anymore, my platoon and I began the long patrol back to the PB. On the way back, my Marines started to notice our Afghan Soldiers fall out and collapse onto the desert floor one by one. This forced my Marines to pick them up and carry them on their shoulders or backs like babies. It was one of the most serious and funniest moments I remember. Some of the other ANA Soldiers who did not pass out broke rank to find shade to cool off in, smoke hashish, or swim in the nearby canals because of the extreme heat. Many of the other Afghan Soldiers who were not cut out for long patrols began to literally cry because of their severe hunger and dehydration.

After ensuring all Marines and Afghans who had left on the patrol returned to friendly lines, I remember my fellow Platoon Commander Lieutenant Hartsell waiting for me in the COC with the coldest bottle of water I had ever drank. The water lowered my high core temperature, which was a result of being in the direct desert sunlight all day.

"Bodrog, that was some intense patrolling. You did close to forty kilometers in about eight hours. I was coordinating with Geronimo, the Garmsir District, and the MEF [Marine expeditionary force] to relay your position and grid locations because I was losing contact with your guys. You even crossed into LAR's [Light Armor Reconnaissance] AO. The Marines at Geronimo were amazed at how far your platoon went. I requested both rotary and fixed wing aircraft for standby missions in case you came into a troops in contact [TIC] situation that far down south. I was watching y'all and was ready for anything. You guys found a lot of things too. Higher wanted you to carry it back, but I told them negative. I informed them that you would burn it because it was too much to carry in these temperatures without support," he said to me, excited my platoon had returned.

Exhausted and dehydrated, I thanked him and conducted a patrol debrief with my Marines, going over the conduct of the patrol. This was a continual process that occurred after every patrol and enhanced our efforts to fight the enemy. If it were not for Lieutenant Hartsell's commonsense approach to things, I know the mission would have been a failure. Thank God he was watching out for my platoon during the conduct of this mission.

Our last big find came in the closing days of the operation. Two days after the previous event, while on a routine local security patrol that coincided with retrograde preparation, my Third Squad Leader, Sergeant Guthrie, noticed two shady-looking Afghan individuals wearing all black (a usual color of Taliban fighters in the area) and running in and out of a compound, carrying a large black plastic bag.

When my Marines and Afghan Army Soldiers approached the local nationals, they soon discovered the local had in his possession twenty-five pounds of raw opium that was going to be used to make heroin once it was sold to dealers in Pakistan. In American dollars, this bag equated to more than $240,000 worth of potential drugs.

I still remember the faces of the Afghan National Army Soldiers as plain as day when my Squad Leader brought the twenty-five-pound bag into the PB to be stored as evidence. The ANA behaved unprofessionally and were like little children in a candy store. Just as a fat child loves cake, these guys swarmed around Guthrie, trying to grab and lick the bag he held tightly in his arms. If these Afghans had had straws, I am positive they would have tried to figure out a way to suck the opium out of the round plastic bag.

It was a hard thing as a Commander to have deal with and explain to my Marines the unprofessional conduct and childish nature of our Afghan counterparts, who were supposed to enforce zero tolerance against drugs, especially for the fact that if any one of them had gotten their hands on the opium, they would have either smoked it or sold it for profit.

While all this was going on, the other Marines who had conducted the patrol placed the two drug-wielding individuals in our detainee facility at PB Razza to be questioned for intelligence collection purposes. They were treated very humanely by my Marines. I knew they would be. After all, my Marine named Corporal Berry was outstanding at tactical site exploitation (TSE), tactical questioning, detainee handling, and evidence collection. If any of my Marines were to have a future career in forensic science or evidence gathering, it was him. He was our go-to guy, sought after by all the leadership in Lima Company whenever we needed to process suspected Taliban or collect data. He was our own little platoon CSI agent.

After we searched and tactically exploited the two individuals, our Corpsman gave them medical examinations. My Marines made sure they had plenty of chow and water and were not being deprived of their basic necessities. At the guidance of my detainee handlers, the two drug dealers were even given prayer time and extra clothing to wear at night when it became cold outside.

My Marines would not have been treated as nicely or as fairly as these criminals were being treated if their roles were reversed. I guarantee it! The Taliban don't even treat the Afghan population as well as we treat Afghan criminals. Even in a war zone, these drug dealers had more rights than Marines did under certain circumstances.

CHAPTER 24

When one of their tribal members is arrested or detained, village elders have an obligation under a code called *Pashtunwali* to try to negotiate or bargain for that detainee's release. Usually a few people tend to show up on their behalf, but this was not the case for the Marines of Second Platoon. By morning, I received calls over the radio from all of my Marine Guards on post.

"Sir, this is post one. I am informing you that there are more than sixty local nationals outside the wire gathering by the compounds fifty meters to the west. They look unarmed," said Lance Corporal White, my M249 SAW gunner standing post.

"Watch-O, this is post two. I also count about sixty, maybe seventy, local nationals. I don't see any weapons either," confirmed my other Marine on post, Lance Corporal Ludwick.

"Sir, this is post three, I do not have eyes on the compound, but the entry control point [ECP] is clear. No one at my position, sir," confirmed Lance Corporal Lamoreaux.

"This is post four. I have eyes on, sir. All sixty are gathering fifty meters southwest of the patrol base around a pair of compounds on the low ground below. I do not see any vehicles, only tractors. Zero positive ID on weapons as well," said Lance Corporal Choi, reconfirming the words of my other three Marines guarding the PB.

"Roger. All posts be advised, stay vigilant and be cognizant of the area. Up your security posture and be ready for anything. Let me know of any changes to the situation," I reported back over the radio to my four guard posts.

I then called my Corporal and Sergeant of the Guard to brief them on the situation. I had my Platoon Sergeant stand up a QRF and informed my CO that a shura was imminent.

Out of all the patrols the Marines of Second Platoon conducted and all the people they interacted with up to this point, no one we encountered, not one local national, ever knew the names or the location of the Taliban (or were willing to tell us, in any event). It amazed me that within hours there were now sixty people outside my base, protesting for the release of these two drug dealers, especially considering the fact that these locals had very little means of communication and transportation.

Other than at a bazaar, I had never seen this many local nationals gathered in one place at one time, especially in such a short amount of time. Not even at local shuras or tribal meetings did this many individuals show up. How had these locals found out these two individuals were in our custody so quickly, I wondered. That's when my Marines and I knew that the two Afghan men we had detained were high-value individuals, and it confirmed our suspicion that they were bad guys. Why else would this many local nationals be rallying for and trying to negotiate their release if they were not highly valued and important?

My Marines were ready for anything, especially if these protesters decided to grow a pair and start firing at us or tried to conduct suicide bombings. The protesters reminded me of the protesters back home in America. *Great. Because we arrested these two individuals, now we have jobless "Afghan hippies" smoking hash and having a nonviolent march at our doorstep.*

My CO initiated a shura with the tribal elders of the group to calm the situation. The elders tried very hard to get the two men released and even threatened not to leave until they were let go. They were yelling and screaming at my Captain to let them go but to no avail. He meant business and would not budge. To their dismay, my Marines had enough evidence to hold the two Afghan drug dealers and felt very confident that these bad guys had valuable information on the Taliban in the area. There was even a good possibility that they were Taliban.

My platoon coordinated with the local Afghan Police on the issue of holding these two men. We ended up compromising a transfer of authority to extract the two individuals later that day and hand them over to the Afghan Police for processing. Behind the scenes, we needed to get these two Afghan drug dealers out of our PB quickly before more protesters showed up and a riot ensued.

That night, the situation with the Afghans outside our PB was resolved once we told them the two men were no longer at our base and were now in the custody of the Afghan Police. We gave the local nationals the new location where they were being held and then informed them to leave and take up the matter with the Afghan Uniformed Police. All sixty or more protesters left a short while later, very understanding and perceptive as to why the two men were arrested and why we transferred them to the authority of the Afghan Uniformed Police. Strangely, they even thanked us for doing our duty, arresting the men, and working with the local Afghan Police on the issue.

CHAPTER 25

By the end of the fourth week, on 15 July 2010 the operation successfully culminated and retrograde had begun. Second Platoon made the five-kilometer walk back to Brannon after PB Razza was completely broken down. We disappeared without a trace and made the PB vanish into the desert sand like a mirage. During the conduct of Operation New Dawn, the performance of my platoon of Marines and Corpsmen was outstanding.

In a period of one month, we had conducted close to two hundred dismounted security and ambush patrols covering over five hundred kilometers of enemy terrain. My Marines discovered eighteen IEDs, five weapons caches, and more than ten sites with explosive materials used to make IEDs; captured two drug dealers; confiscated more than 220 pounds of opium seeds; and took possession of about twenty-five pounds of raw opium.

I could not help but wonder how many lives of their fellow Marines my men had saved by discovering and confiscating all these materials. I mentally asked myself, *Out of all the adversity we encountered and through all the explosive materials we found, was Corporal Garst's brush with death worth it? Did we make a difference in Shorsurak at all by finding all these enemy materials?* From my intuitions and instincts as a Commander of Marines, I have to believe my platoon did save lives and that it was worth it in the end.

Once we arrived back at PB Brannon, which was now in the hands of First Lieutenant Vali and a squad of his Marines, the stay for the Marines of Second Platoon was very short-lived. During the entire month-long operation, Lieutenant Vali and his Marines had drastically improved the Brannon building. The patrol base now also had a well for water, and power generators had been sent in to improve the PB's electrical grid. He brought me up to speed on the complaints and overall atmospherics of my previous AO, informing me that he had encountered mostly nonkinetic "white noise."

He and his Marines only witnessed one significant kinetic act of violence between four Afghan men. As Lieutenant Vali was explaining the story, what I was able to gather was that four Afghan men came to the PB a few days ago with multiple stab wounds and needed immediate medical treatment.

When Lieutenant Vali asked the men their *modus operandi*, or reason for the stabbings, the local men were quick to quote Koranic verse and Pashtunwali code as justification. What had happened was that two pairs of brothers became involved in a stabbing match against each other over a minor dispute. First, two rivaling men initiated the stabbing match, but because of the Afghan code of Pashtunwali, each of the men's brothers became involved as well. A huge knife fight and stabbing match then ensued, the endstate of which was that each pair of brothers had restored honor to their families because they were stabbed by an "enemy." I listened in amazement as Lieutenant Vali explained this story to me, awestruck that none of the men had died in the knife fight. This was the same Afghan logic that constantly impeded operations.

CHAPTER 26

Just prior to retrograding at Shorsurak, my CO had informed me that both my platoon and the platoon of Lieutenant Miller (who was still at Toor Gar) were going to detach from Lima Company on 17 July 2010 and attach directly to Headquarters and Service Company (H&S), which was located at FOB Geronimo, that same day. The reason the Marines of both First and Second Platoons were to be detached was because we were going to be responsible for creating an integrated operational maneuver element, consisting of both Marines and ANA Soldiers, to conduct kinetic actions for our Battalion Commander throughout the battalion's AO. The operational maneuver element would come to be known as the combined action company.

My platoon and First Platoon were going to undertake the mission of forming the first combined action platoons and combined action company in Afghanistan. We were going to be our Battalion Commander's right-hand punch. It was a task, to my knowledge, that had not been conceived or even accomplished since the days of the United States Marines in Vietnam more than forty years ago.

As far as the big picture was concerned, once we teamed up with Lieutenant Miller's platoon, we would form and construct the first integrated Marine and Afghanistan platoon and company in history. This was not a military transition team, and we were not embedding. We were fully integrating. I personally had never read or learned about this ever being done before.

The hard work of my men had paid off and had been recognized by the higher powers. My guys were being chosen for a bigger purpose, and now we were going to be undertaking a mission that no United States Forces had been able to accomplish up to this point in the war.

From the night of 15 July 2010 until the morning of 16 July 2010, Second Platoon spent their entire time packing all of their personal and serialized gear, conducted accountability, hygiened, and refitted at Brannon. By morning, with all our bags packed, staged, and ready to go, my Marines gathered all their combat gear and conducted the seven-kilometer dismounted movement northeast back to COB Toor Gar.

We left PB Brannon in the able hands of Third Platoon's First Lieutenant Vali, a squad of his Marines, and the platoon of Afghan National Army Soldiers still under the Command of Baz Mohammed. It was hard to leave Brannon for me and most of my Marines. After all, it was our home and a part of us all. All the Marines in my platoon had tirelessly worked their tails off to create it. It was a masterpiece, representative of all our best qualities as Marines, and now we had to let it go. At least we were leaving it better than we inherited it.

From our first day at PB Brannon, throughout Operation New Dawn, and until our last day at Brannon, my Marines' outstanding record spoke for itself. My platoon patrolled a total of eleven hundred kilometers, conducted more than five hundred patrols, discovered eighteen IEDs, uncovered six weapons caches, found thirteen sites with explosive materials used to make bombs, detained two drug dealers, confiscated twenty-five pounds of opium, and destroyed more than 320 pounds of poppy seeds.

By the afternoon of 16 July 2010, all of my men had arrived at COB Toor Gar, eager for their next follow-on mission. I informed my Platoon Sergeant to make sure our men were well rested and to start working on our mission cards for the movement to FOB Geronimo the following morning. Up to this point, every mission my platoon encountered, both at PB Brannon and in Shorsurak, had culminated in mission success. Now we were going to be given our chance to make history. All of our hard work and aggressive behavior was being recognized.

On the morning of 17 July 2010, the Marines of Second Platoon said their farewells to the rest of Lima Company and departed friendly lines at COB Toor Gar for FOB Geronimo. Twenty-five of us left, while seven of my Marines stayed behind to reinforce COB Toor Gar's defensive lines. Corporal Garst, Corporal Keuther, Lance Corporal Ford, Lance Corporal Hammock, Lance Corporal Evola, Lance Corporal Roland, and Lance Corporal Ludwick were not going to be coming with the Marines of Second Platoon on their next mission. It pained me to leave them behind because no one liked to lose Marines, but it was an order I had to obey for the good of the company.

Every one of my Marines was informed of what we were about to take part in and its significance. They remained humble though and enthusiastically wondered about the details of our next mission. As I mentioned earlier, to all of our recollections, the last time a combined action platoon had ever been achieved was in Vietnam by the United States Marines and the South Vietnamese. We were not only going to be responsible for the creation of a platoon but also an entire company. No one knew if it was going to be possible or if it would even work. The Afghan Soldiers, after all, were not the South Vietnamese. This was a different war, a different time period, a different enemy, and a different set of rules and partners.

This photo was taken in January 2010 on the Big Island of Hawaii four months prior to my platoon's deployment in support of Operation Enduring Freedom (OEF) 10.1, Helmand Province, Afghanistan. Taken during Pohakuloa training (PTA), this picture depicts the Marines of Second Platoon standing in front of the volcano named Mauna Kea. Opposite Mauna Kea is the active volcano named Mauna Loa. At the completion of PTA training, Second Platoon and the rest of Lima Company conducted a twelve-mile conditioning hike on the volcano of Mauna Loa.

This photo was taken in January 2010 on the Big Island of Hawaii four months prior to our deployment to Operation Enduring Freedom (OEF) 10.1, Helmand Province, Afghanistan. This picture was taken during Pohakuloa training (PTA) and depicts Second Platoon and Weapons Platoon (Company L) after successfully completing range 10.

This photo was taken in January 2010 on the Big Island of Hawaii during PTA training. It depicts the leadership of Second Platoon, Lima Company. From left to right are First Lieutenant Bodrog, Sergeant Brown, Sergeant Olds, Sergeant Fladseth, Corporal Reynolds, and Staff Sergeant Lebron.

This photo was taken in March 2010 in Twentynine Palms, California, during enhanced Mojave Viper training. My Marines of Second Platoon, Lima Company, Third Battalion, Third Marines are wrapping up their successful training exercise.

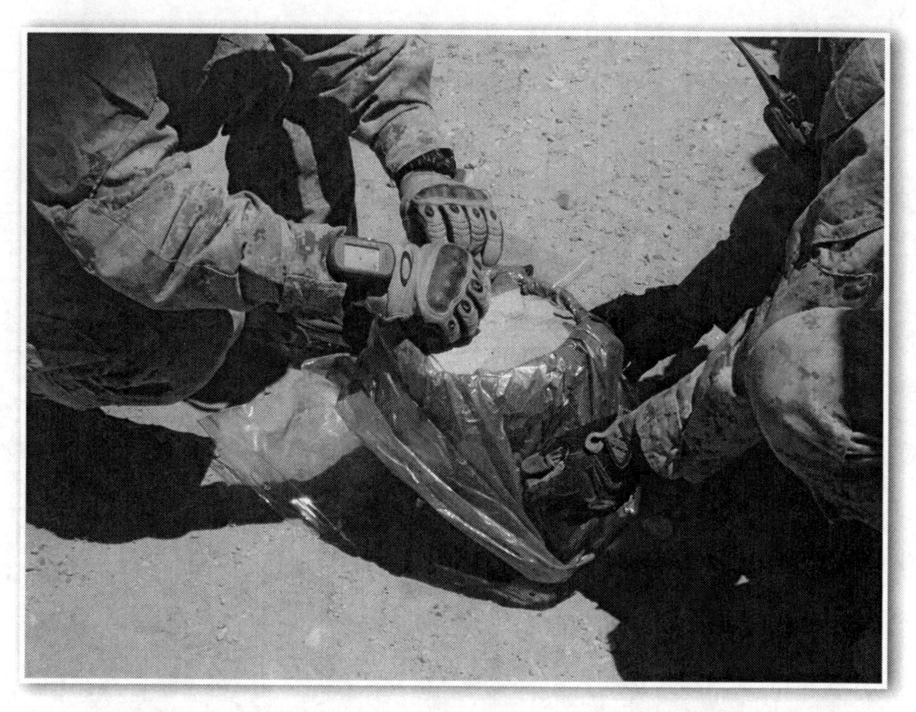

This photo was taken on 25 May 2010 after our first dismounted security patrol in country. First Squad, led by Sergeant Olds, acting on a tip from Sergeant Brown, discovered an IED during a security patrol south of PB Brannon. The IED was hidden behind a bush next to a compound wall. In this picture, EOD had disarmed and removed the IED and brought it back to PB Brannon for exploitation.

EOD shows my Marines the items used in the IED to kill or injure those caught in the blast radius. This particular IED was a forty- to fifty-pound mix of ammonium nitrate, fertilizer, and motorcycle parts.

On a routine dismounted security patrol on 26 May 2010, my squad witnessed three Afghan military-aged fighting males fleeing the scene where another IED was discovered. My squad trailed the men because our ROEs prevented them from firing at potential enemies who were fleeing. After following the three men to a compound, we conducted a search with Afghan Soldiers. During the search, we discovered more IED-making materials that could have potentially been used to kill Marines or innocent civilians. In this picture, we have a part of a mortar, wires, batteries, power sources, and blasting caps. These are all the ingredients necessary to build an IED. The compound was burned down and destroyed after we exploited it for evidence.

This photo was taken on 1 June 2010 at PB Brannon. Lance Corporal James (right) and Lance Corporal White (left) are cleaning and preparing chicken for chow. Not in this picture is Lance Corporal Evola preparing the glaze and seasoning for the meal. My Marines bought eggs, rice, chickens, sheep, and goats—among other things—from the local market to cook and eat when they did not want to eat MREs. As you can see from the picture, the chickens were just cleaned in a vat of water before they were skinned and cooked on our HESCO grill.

This photo was taken on 1 June 2010. Second Squad is crossing a canal as part of their dismounted security patrol. It was not uncommon for Marines to get wet on every patrol; it was expected. A common TTP of my platoon was to make the patrols hard by staying off main roads and trails. Instead, patrolling through farm fields, muddy areas, and canals was the main way of patrolling to eliminate the risk of stepping on IEDs. Canals in the Nawa District of the Helmand Province, like the one shown in this photo, were built by American contractors in the 1950s to improve quality of life for the people in Afghanistan. Shown here are Sergeant Brown (front), Corporal Truehaft (rear), and Nassir, our platoon linguist.

This photo was taken on 4 June 2010. Marijuana plants and opium fields were found everywhere in our area of operations. Drugs and drug use by the local population and Afghan forces were constant problems my Marines faced on a daily basis.

This photo was taken on 5 June 2010. It was not uncommon for local nationals to come to PB Brannon and request medical assistance. In this picture, an Afghan local national boy of about two years old has suffered third-degree burns to his legs and feet. In the Afghan culture, if children cry too much and do not stop, parents will throw boiling water or chai tea on their bodies or feet as punishment. This two-year-old boy was brought to us by his parents after they threw boiling water on his feet and torso. Our Platoon Corpsmen, Doc Greenough and Doc Williams, are making the initial assessment and prognosis of treatment.

This photo was taken on 5 June 2010. After determining the prognosis, Doc Greenough applies a burn cream to the two-year-old local national boy's feet. It was the only treatment the Marines at PB Brannon could give to this young boy short of sending him to an Afghan hospital in Lashkar Gah.

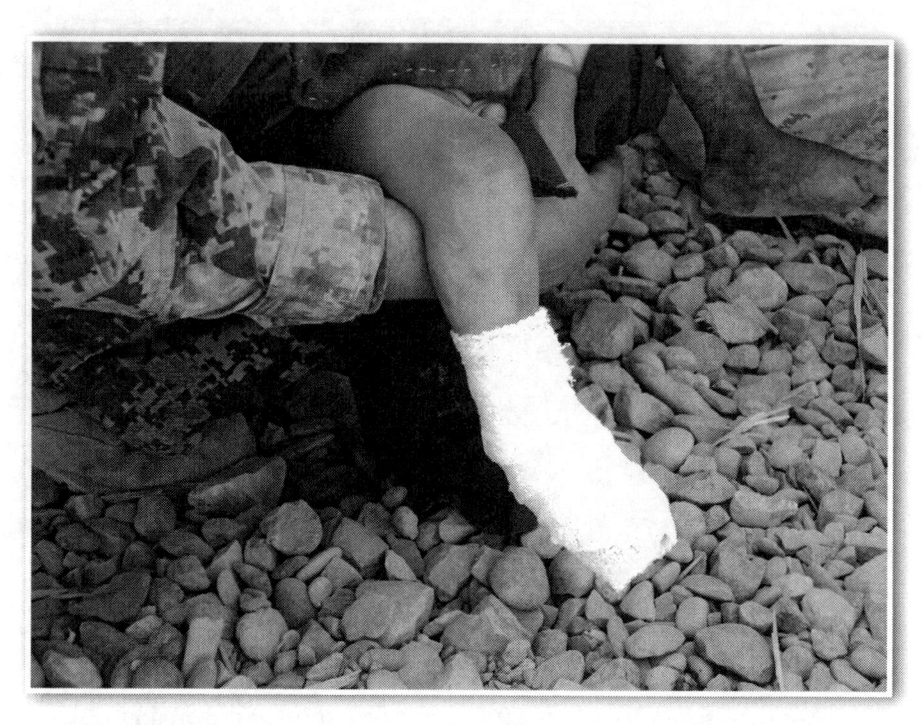

This photo was taken on 5 June 2010. Our Platoon Corpsman applies a burn dressing to the two-year-old local national boy's right foot and then prepares to treat his left foot for third-degree burns.

This photo was taken on 1 July 2010 during Operation New Dawn in the Shorsurak region of the Helmand Province. Lance Corporal Evola reads a letter from home. Receiving mail and care packages was always a morale booster for my Marines and Corpsmen. This was especially true during the 140-degree weather and sandstorms we faced in the desert every day during this month-long operation.

This photo was taken on 15 July 2010 and depicts the Marines of Second Platoon, Lima Company, Third Battalion, Third Marines at PB Brannon in the Nawa District of the Helmand Province, Afghanistan.

Front row (left to right): Sergeant Olds, Corporal Garst, Corporal Morris, Private First Class Sisca, Lance Corporal James, Lance Corporal Hall, Lance Corporal Vancamp, and Lance Corporal Hammock.

Second row (left to right): Staff Sergeant Lebron, Corporal Mount, Sergeant Brown, Corporal Berry, Lance Corporal Blomstran, Lance Corporal Evola, Lance Corporal Gerrity, Lance Corporal Castro, Corporal Truehaft, Lance Corporal Brown, Doc Williams, and First Lieutenant Bodrog.

Third row (left to right): Sergeant Guthrie, Lance Corporal White, Doc Greenough, Lance Corporal Ludwick, Lance Corporal Choi, Lance Corporal Taylor, Lance Corporal Rivera, Lance Corporal Lamoreaux, and Lance Corporal Ortiz.

Not pictured: Corporal Bass, Lance Corporal Ford, Corporal Keuther, and Private First Class Roland.

This photo was taken on 15 July 2010. Pictured is the leadership of Second Platoon gathered around the mortar pit at PB Brannon. A common TTP of my platoon was to sink the baseplates of our mortar systems during occupation of new PBs or when we were in new AOs. This was done to both deter and intimidate the enemy by establishing dominance in an unfamiliar area. From left to right are Sergeant Olds, Corporal Garst, Sergeant Brown, Staff Sergeant Lebron, Corporal Berry, Sergeant Guthrie, and Corporal Mount.

PART III

Forward Operating Base Geronimo ... Welcome to Hades ...

The Commander in combat is often an enigma to his men, a Sphinx-like being, seemingly placid amid the carnage of combat, immune to the heartrending scenes of destruction, the screams of the wounded, and cries of civilians who have just lost every possession and often the lives of their loved ones. The Commander appears to have a split personality; one moment being indifferent to the point of heartlessness and the next moment being caring and self-sacrificing.
—Colonel B. P. McCoy, *The Passion of Command* (USMC)

Marines die. That's what we're here for. But the Marine Corps lives forever. And that means you live forever.
—Gunnery Sergeant R. Lee Ermey (USMC) as Gunnery Sergeant Hartman in *Full Metal Jacket*

There is a path to the top of even the highest of mountain.
—Afghan Proverb

CHAPTER 27

The Marines of Second Platoon arrived at FOB Geronimo at 1000 on 17 July 2010. The mounted movement from COB Toor Gar to FOB Geronimo was twenty kilometers and took about sixty minutes to drive. We had all been through so much in the last few months that the thought of hitting an IED on the convoy to Geronimo was the last thing we were concerned with.

As we sat strapped into our heavily armored convoy of Medium Tactical Vehicle Replacement (MTVR) vehicles and Mine-Resistant Ambush Protected (MRAP) vehicles, every one of us was excited and anxious for the uncertainty that lay ahead. My Marines and I had a plethora of questions and ideas regarding our immediate futures as we watched COB Toor Gar grow smaller out our rear bulletproof windows. These questions ranged from as small as what our living quarters would be like to as big as what our missions would entail. There were so many things unanswered for us, and our biggest fear was looking unprepared on day one of this new assignment.

There were many rumors circulating throughout the Marines in the battalion as to how we were going to be utilized. After all, it was not every day that two rifle platoons were plucked out of their company and told they were going to be a shock force for their Battalion Commander. It would have been like someone taking two of my squads and telling me they work for a different Platoon Commander and Platoon Sergeant. This just did not happen too often.

According to my Platoon Sergeant and senior enlisted Marines, this sort of thing never occurred. Not one of them had any idea how this was going to work. Neither had they ever witnessed this type of action before in their Marine Corps careers. The only way I could reason our detachment from Lima Company was by two methods of thought.

The first was that my CO in Lima must have messed up thus far in the deployment and this was the punishment. After all, he had been investigated during our time in Shorsurak. The second was that both Lieutenant Miller and my platoon really were doing something right, and since the AO in the south where we were located was generally not kinetic, this would be the perfect time for our Battalion Commander to put together something special and flex his muscles.

Regardless of either of the two justifications, my Marines and I chose the latter. We knew that certain elements in our command had issues, but we remained loyal to them until the end. We knew how well we as a platoon operated together and how high we set the bar for the other platoons in the battalion. We were honored to be part of the company chosen for this mission.

As all devil dogs know, in the Corps, walls talk, vibrate, and breathe with rumors and gouge from the hearsay and conversations that occur between Marines. Everything comes out in the wash because the United States Marine Corps is a very small community. There are always people watching and listening to everything that goes on, and secrets are very hard to hide. Both the Lieutenant and Lance Corporal rumor mills flowed with information, most of which was false, but they circulated many of the rumors the Marines had been hearing regarding how our two platoons were going to be utilized.

Some Marines heard rumors that we were going to be a quick reaction force for the battalion. Others assumed we would be a transition or mentor platoon and company for the Afghan National Army Soldiers (our least favorite course of action). The rest assumed we would assist the Marines at Geronimo on post and patrols by reinforcing the Guard Force Platoon. Regardless of the chatter from the rumor mills, it was on the Marines to choose to listen to the words from the underground.

The only fact that remained true was that once my Marines and I reached Geronimo, off-loaded our gear, and checked in, we would receive our mission statement from the mouth of our new Commanding Officer. The rumors would be squashed, and our Marines would be informed.

Confident and hungry for our next fight, my Marines and I rolled into FOB Geronimo ready and willing to take on anything thrown at us. As soon as the Marines jumped out of the vehicles onto the sandy, moondust-like ground, the realization of being detached from Lima Company for the remainder of the deployment finally set in. We were now the bastard offspring of our battalion, much like children from a divorced family, caught between their fighting parents.

CHAPTER 28

FOB Geronimo was an expeditionary base built in 2009 by First Battalion, Fifth Marines. Eventually it transformed into a mini city and could hold a battalion or more of Marines and military servicemen. Geronimo was located east of the Helmand River and was in the district of Nawa. It served as a major transition point and nucleus for various units coming from Camp Leatherneck, Camp Bastion, and Camp Dwyer.

For Marines living at patrol bases, it was a good place to rest and refit when given the opportunity. Marines were allowed to use the morale, welfare, and recreation center (MWR) to refit, rest, or call home to family or loved ones. It was complete with a dining facility (DFAC), gym, running track, air-conditioning, and showers. It was the kind of place that could bring out the inner nastiness of hardened grunts if left unfettered, because of how comfortable and fat they could get with all the material items that made them think of and wish for home.

Once my Marines and I put our combat boots on the moondust-like dirt that covered the ground at FOB Geronimo, it was almost as if planning had not occurred between my Gunnery Sergeant in Lima Company and the men at Geronimo. We exited the vehicles only to find ourselves standing in limbo, waiting for a liaison to tell us what was next. Our Lima Company Gunnery Sergeant, Gunnery Sergeant Locovez, who had come with us for the movement to Geronimo, had no idea what was going on and couldn't even point us in a direction or inform us where we were staying. After I exited my vehicle, I walked up to my Marines, who were all huddled together in a circle with their gear, looking at me for answers.

"Hey, sir, what's next? Where is Gunny? Do you know where we are staying? Where should we put our gear?" said Sergeant Guthrie, clearly catching on to the fact that I knew about as much as he did at this point.

"Stand by for now. Get with Olds and Brown and locate the Camp Commandant. I am going to find our new Executive Officer and Commanding Officer so I can check in. Once you find the Camp Commandant, see where we can stage our gear. Give me ten minutes and I will be back. Keep the Marines busy until I do," I said to him.

I was hiding my frustration behind the gaze of my stern sphinxlike warrior face over the fact that our Company Gunny had done very little coordination on our behalf. What was worse was that my Platoon Sergeant had been pulled from our movement ten minutes prior to departure to take care of business at Toor Gar. He would not arrive for a few hours; therefore, my Squad Leaders needed to step up and act for him until he arrived.

I walked away from my Marines and headed straight for the Headquarters and Service Company Command Post (CP) to figure out the best course of action for the platoon. As I walked into the H&Q CP, I was greeted by my new Commanding Officer, his Executive Officer, his Company First Sergeant, and his Company Gunnery Sergeant.

I had met our new CO before when my platoon conducted operations in Shorsurak during Operation New Dawn, but I'd had no idea he was going to be my new Company Commander. Having averaged about three to four hours of sleep every other day during that operation, my memory was a little jaded and sluggish when it came to recalling much about him. However, the visual of him standing over a map of the AO with his Marines in the CP brought back vivid memories. All I really remembered was his personable attitude, demeanor, and no-nonsense reputation for getting things done right. To say the least, when my Platoon Sergeant and I figured out we were going to work directly for him, we were pleased to know our men would be in good hands.

Our new CO was a very amiable man, and he had a manner about him that made a Marine wonder if he was a prior enlisted grunt. He was not like some of the typical senior Officers I had encountered in my limited time in the Corps who got off on talking down to their Lieutenants or enlisted Marines with an elitist ruling-class attitude. He had a unique persona and way about him, almost as if he had never forgotten where he came from as he rose up through the ranks. He had the ability to identify with the lowest Private First Class all the way up to the most senior Lieutenant—a rare trait for some career men.

Before he was with H&S Company, he was a Reconnaissance Company Commander and was known for being squared away and locked on. He had earned a reputation for putting a ton of faith and confidence in his subordinate leaders and never micromanaged Marines, which was one of his greatest qualities as a leader. His reputation was very well-known throughout the battalion. My platoon knew he would make us a better operating unit.

His Company First Sergeant, First Sergeant Olea, had a great reputation and a hard work ethic as well, much like my Lima Company First Sergeant. They both always put the welfare of Marines above themselves and took commonsense approaches to solving issues or concerns. The H&S Company First Sergeant was a very tall and confident man who knew the ins and outs of the Marine Corps system. He was the go-to guy who could make things happen and get things done when it came to the enlisted Marines. What made our situation even better was the fact that Staff Sergeant Lebron and Sergeant Olds were on the last deployment with him in Trebil, Iraq, and had developed a personal working relationship. This man knew what my Marines brought to the table and was in a position to make sure they were taken care of and utilized to the best of their abilities on and off Geronimo. A little positive politics could go a long way, especially on a deployment.

I anxiously approached our new CO to check in and find out the course of action for my men. Standing over a table that had a map of our battalion AO on it, our new CO was in the process of finishing up with a backbrief by one of his Guard Force Patrol Leaders who had just gotten back inside the wire.

Once he finished, I introduced myself formally so as not to set a bad example and ruin my reputation with my new command.

"Good morning, sir. First Lieutenant Bodrog checking in. I was wondering where my platoon is going to be staying. Right now I have not received too much information on our purpose here at Geronimo. Can you tell me what our mission is?" I said to him.

"Absolutely, Lieutenant Bodrog. Right now my Company Gunnery Sergeant, Gunny Heimdall, is out at the vehicle lot with your Marines showing them where to stow their gear. He will help your Marines to get set up here at Geronimo and see to their living arrangements now that you have all made it here. We are all glad to have you and your Marines here.

"As far as my intent goes, it is simple. Your platoon and Lieutenant Miller's platoon were selected to come to Geronimo because your platoons have a stellar reputation and are the best in the battalion. I expect your conduct and character to reflect your reputation. I expect both of your platoons to work hard, constantly train your men, and never let them get too comfortable or complacent. Set the highest example at all times. As of right now, your two platoons are on standby for any mission the Battalion Commander sees fit to use you for. With that being said, your platoons have to be ready for missions at any given time, and I expect you to execute a mission within one hour or less of receiving your order.

"Your platoon mission from Operations is as follows. The Marines of First and Second Platoons, who are now part of H&S Company, are going to train, mentor, and lead the Afghan National Army Soldiers in sustained combat operations in order to create a combined action task force and integrated maneuver element in support of the battalion's operations. In saying that, it is on you and your men to come up with a training plan and set an operational standard for this new unit. My endstate is that your platoon and First Platoon will create the first Afghan and Marine combined action platoon and combined action company up to this point in the war. This will effectively enable the successful transition of lead security from the Marines to the Afghan forces. In essence, once your platoons are fully integrated, you will be an integrated maneuver element capable of conducting high-speed operations in our battalion AO, hitting areas hard, and getting out just as quickly before the enemy even has time to react.

"What your Marines and the Marines of First Platoon are going to create is something that, to my knowledge, has never been done up to this point in this war, especially not to this extent. Have you read the book *The Village* by Bing West? If you have, that will give you an idea of what I am talking about and what we are going to create," he said to me.

"Yes, sir, a few times. It was required reading for my platoon prior to deployment. In the Lima Company AO, I was in charge of Patrol Base Brannon. It was named in honor of Corporal Philip Brannon, who was killed in action during Vietnam," I replied.

"Good to go. Then you know about the actions the Marines did with the South Vietnamese and how they fully integrated them into their platoons and created CAPs when they were fighting the North Vietnamese. I expect us to create and execute roughly the same concept. You will receive your Afghan Army platoon in a few days, and my Headquarters and Service Marines will arrange an area for your Marines and Afghanistan Soldiers to live at together.

"The Afghan unit is currently rebuilding at this time, and many of the Soldiers are getting back from their vacations and time off. It will be a challenge for you and your Marines. It will be a challenge for you to work with your counterpart Afghan Platoon Commander. It will be a challenge for your Platoon Sergeant to work side by side with his Afghan Platoon Sergeant, and so on. Both Lieutenant Miller and you will make it happen, and I have the highest confidence in you both.

"My ultimate goal is a one-for-one ratio, Marine to Afghan Soldier, and the complete forced integration of Marines and Afghan Soldiers in both of your platoons, thus creating a combined platoon and ultimately a combined company. With that being said, everything you do once you receive your Afghan platoon will be joint and partnered.

"The Taliban will be caught off guard and will not know what to think when they see a completely combined unit, both Marine and Afghan, firing rounds downrange at them. As of right now, I want you and your platoon to get your living arrangements set up. Once that is finished, I want your Squad Leaders and yourself to meet me back in this hooch at 1700 for your official brief. Do you have any questions?" he said to me, giving me the extent of his intent and command vision for the rest of the deployment. Extremely efficient, in only a few paragraphs, I had an intent and command vision. It was now up to me and my Marines to figure out the details.

"Nothing too major right now, sir. I will let you know when we get set up. My only question right now is as far as the Afghan platoons go, what units are we getting?" I responded to him. I would have more questions later that day once I backbriefed my Platoon Sergeant and Squad Leaders on our new mission statement and received their input.

I couldn't believe my ears as I listened to the words I was hearing. I was elated, to say the least. Not only had I finally been given a mission and intent, but I had also been given responsibility and trust to execute that same mission and intent. Up until this point, my Marines and I always had been given half of an intent and a bunch of what-ifs and "I don't knows" from our previous CO. For the individual Riflemen, that was par for the course, but for a Platoon Commander it was not. Now we had direction and vision and clear-cut orders and expectations. We had been given a rope to either dangle and hang from or hang ourselves with.

"On or about 27 July, the Third and Fourth Tolai will be directly attached to your platoons. You did some work with the Fourth Tolai out at Shorsurak if I remember right," replied my CO, half-serious and slightly smirking as he asked me the question.

"Yes, sir. We had a little trouble with them. They gave us some problems here and there. If I could make a recommendation on behalf of my platoon to work with the Third Tolai, that would be outstanding. We have not worked with them yet. First Platoon may have a better experience with the Fourth Tolai since they do not have a history with them at this time," I responded to him, now a little concerned that my platoon might end up bearing the burden and responsibility for training those uncivilized, unprofessional, and drug-addicted Soldiers yet again. Nothing for nothing, but if these Afghan Soldiers were going to be directly attached to my platoon, I knew our mission would be a failure from the start.

There was too much negativity and bias from my Marines toward the Fourth Tolai and the reverse. My boys would kill these Afghan Soldiers if they were forced to work with them again, and practicing tolerance would be dreamworld nonsense in this case. At least if they were attached to First Platoon, both units would have a clean slate with each other.

"Not a problem, Lieutenant Bodrog. I will make sure that happens. No worries. I have heard some stories about them and remember during Operation New Dawn when they were with you guys in southern Nawa. Most of the dope-smoking Afghan National Army Soldiers have been fired, and the guys in the platoon are new for the most part. I don't see why it would be a problem giving you their Third Tolai to work with," said my new CO. He was obviously aware of the negative reputation of the Fourth Tolai and their subsequent lack of adequate performance during Operation New Dawn with respect to my platoon and Lima Company.

"I appreciate it, sir. I have nothing else. By your leave, I am going to see how my Marines are doing getting set up," I replied, still in formal manner. Obviously, I was now a little more comforted knowing he was tracking on my views toward the Fourth Tolai and was taking my request into account.

"All right. Let me know if you have any problems moving in and finding a hooch. See you back here at 1700 for the evening situation report," he said to me as I made my way out of the H&S Company CP.

With the introductions in order, I left the CP and went back to the area where my Marines had been dropped off. I could already see the men in my platoon walking back and forth like ants in a marching line from the vehicles to the hooches with all of their gear and packs.

"Hey, sir, we found the Camp Commandant and coordinated our living area. It is not far. I will show you where to put your gear. What's the word from the CO?" said Sergeant Olds to me as I walked up to him.

"I will sit down with all the Squad Leaders and leadership in a bit, once we get settled. Everything sounds good so far. Make sure the boys don't get too comfortable. We will probably be moving again soon," I replied.

At this point, moving around for my Marines was a normal and expected event. After all, within the two months of us touching ground in Afghanistan, we had moved six times. We had lived and moved from COB Toor Gar to PB Brannon, from PB Brannon to Shorsurak, from Shorsurak back to PB Brannon, from PB Brannon back to COB Toor Gar, and then from COB Toor Gar to FOB Geronimo. Now we were going to be conducting high-speed missions, which would mean lots of traveling. It was going to be a great and memorable opportunity.

Chapter 29

The Marines of Second Platoon got to drink their first dose of the reality of our new purpose within four hours of being at FOB Geronimo. Just when we thought we would have some time to get settled into our living area and reap the spoils of our dining facility, air conditioners, shower units, and Alaskan Shelters, our first mission came across the net. As the battalion's QRF, we had to be ready at a moment's notice for any and all missions.

"Lima Two Actual, this is Hades Six. Report to the battalion COC," said my CO, sounding intense and anxious to put us to the test as he said my call sign over the net. Lima Two Actual was my call sign, and Hades Six was the call sign for my new CO.

"Hades Six, this is Lima Two. Roger. En route," I said back to him, confirming receipt of his message.

I grabbed Sergeant Olds, who was now my acting Platoon Sergeant, and he and I double-timed it from our hooch over to the COC to find out what was going on. As we entered the room, we saw our new CO hovered over a map of our AO with the senior Officers and enlisted Marines in the battalion. This did not look good.

"Gentleman, take out your notebooks and writing material and stand by to copy. The situation right now is that Kilo Company is reporting that one of their Marines on a routine dismounted security patrol jumped into the Helmand River to save the life of a drowning Afghan Uniformed Police Officer who fell in. As of right now, the two are missing. The last time that the platoon of Kilo Marines on scene had eyes on was at a position in the river about seventy-five meters from where they went in, located right here on the map.

"We do not have the name of the Afghan Uniformed Police Officer at this time, but the Marine who fell in is named Corporal Joe Wrightsman. He is a Squad Leader with Kilo Company. Get your platoon stood up, grab two Communications Marines and all the communication gear you require, and stage over by the helicopter landing zone!

"Gentlemen, make sure your Corpsmen bring body bags in case the worst occurs. We are going to insert via air as soon as possible next to the Helmand River and aid in the conduct of searching for the two who fell in. Kilo Company has a platoon out there right now, and we are going in to reinforce their search. Right now the entire Marine expeditionary force [MEF] is throwing in every available asset to recover the two bodies. Our latest intelligence reports indicate that the Taliban are aware of the situation and are on their way to the location to recover Wrightsman's body in order to make it a trophy.

"This will be at minimum a one-day operation, but prepare to sustain for at least a week out of temporary PBs along the mountains adjacent to the Helmand as the situation changes. Lieutenant Bodrog, I want your platoon staged at the HLZ and ready to depart one hour from right now," my Commanding Officer said. He had a hard gaze, and his body language reflected the extreme seriousness of the situation. Direct and to the point, he was telling me he was ready to put my guys to the test, entrusting them with the most important mission the battalion had faced thus far into our deployment.

"Roger that, sir. We will get it done. My boys will be ready," I said back to him.

I was honored that my platoon was being entrusted with the mission and at the same time humbled by the prospect of saving a fellow Marine and Afghan Uniformed Police Officer before the enemy got to them. Within five hours of arriving at FOB Geronimo, the Marines of Second Platoon had their first mission: a helicopter insert along the Helmand River to assist in the regimental search and recovery mission for our missing Marine and an Afghan Uniformed Police Officer.

With great haste and professionalism, I returned to my platoon area, informed my Squad Leaders, and gave my tasks. My Platoon Sergeant had shown up to Geronimo at precisely this moment as well, and now my platoon was 100 percent operationally capable again. Sergeant Olds grabbed all of the communication assets, Sergeant Brown prepared our mission card, and Sergeant Guthrie—along with all of the Fire Team Leaders—got the Marines and Corpsmen briefed up and ready to go. At exactly 1500, the Marines of Second Platoon were staged and ready to depart from the HLZ. They were ready, anxious, and humbled to find one of our brothers who may have possibly drowned while trying to save the life of one of our Afghan counterparts.

One hour later, two CH-53 Stallion helicopters arrived, and my platoon and I quickly loaded. I handed the helicopter pilot a manifest with my platoon's personal information, which included blood types, serialized equipment, and the last four digits of their Social Security numbers, and we flew off. Flight manifests were necessary and always conducted in case the worst were to happen to my Marines or me and information was needed to identify or triage us.

At this point, all of us had faces like that of a Roman Janus coin. On the one side we all had dark faces, ones that resembled tragedy because we knew Corporal Wrightsman had probably drowned trying to save the life of an Afghan Uniformed Police Officer. On the other side, we were honored that we had been entrusted with the mission to bring Wrightsman home and to safety.

We truly felt like high-speed Infantry Marines going hundreds of miles per hour, executing orders quickly, and given the responsibility to live out in the wilderness, surrounded by enemies, for an undetermined amount of time. We appreciated the fact that we were not sitting at a PB, routinely patrolling the same area day in and out like many of the platoons in the battalion.

CHAPTER 30

While in the air, flying through the Afghan clouds and en route to the objective, our primary mission suddenly changed, and my Marines and I received a new set of orders from our pilot as the situation unfolded on the ground. Our new mission at hand became a tactical recovery of aircraft personnel (TRAP) mission, a task my platoon had not conducted up to this point.

A Navy HH-60 (Pave Hawk) search and rescue helicopter carrying Parajumpers that was being utilized to search the Helmand River for the bodies of the Kilo Company Squad Leader and Afghan Uniformed Police Officer had reported a critical mechanical failure and had to make a landing along the shoreline of the Helmand River in an area adjacent to where the Kilo Marine and Afghan Uniformed Police Officer were reported to have been last seen. The helicopter pilot, whose call sign was Pedro, made a hard landing on the shoreline of the river and was in urgent need of security so he could conduct repairs and get his helo back in the air and off the ground.

My platoon was spun up on the situation during our flight to the objective site, and when we landed, we quickly departed the CH-53 helicopters to set up a defense around the downed Pave Hawk and its Sailors and Airmen. In this unfamiliar area, all of my Marines badly wanted to find Corporal Wrightsman, but securing the downed helicopter so it could be fixed and flying again was our new mission priority for the overall success of their recovery. If the Taliban blew the helo up, it would be a huge propaganda and media win for them. Not to mention destroying this helicopter would be a critical loss to the possible success of this mission and finding our Marine and the Afghan Uniformed Police Officer trapped beneath the river. It was an action we could not let happen or afford to the Taliban.

After about two hours of my platoon holding a 360-degree security perimeter, the helicopter received the maintenance it needed, lifted off, and departed the area to continue the search and recovery effort. Once the dust cleared, my platoon broke down our defensive position and patrolled southeast for high ground to set up a temporary PB for the night.

My Marines found an old goat path on the side of a mountain to our southeast and made the two-thousand-foot climb for the summit to establish our temporary patrol base. From this temporary patrol base, we would then be able to have security and send out our Marine units to search the riverbed for Corporal Wrightsman and the Afghan Uniformed Police Officer who had fallen into the Helmand. The PB would give us the high ground and crucial overwatch positions to provide guardian angel security positions for my Marines searching the body of water below.

My Marines established the PB right next to a small village, along the precipice of a cliff that overlooked the east side of the Helmand River, which we now called the River Styx. Carrying our gear load and all of our logistical items up the steep and jagged cliffs was very time-consuming. However, my entire platoon reached the top after only a few hours.

At the top, we discovered a small village of a few compounds and very friendly local nationals. We made sure we informed the local nationals of the village of our intentions and explained to them that we would be using some of their land for a few days during the conduct of our mission. This time, unlike Shorsurak, our intentions were not a request. We were taking the ground at all costs whether they liked our presence or not. We were careful not to divulge the nature of our mission. Suffice it to say, Pandora's box could have been opened, and the Taliban, through indirect resources, could have been informed of the status of our defensive position, our missing Marine, and our intentions.

The area of the patrol base we chose was on a easily defendable hilltop and had clear visibility in all directions with good avenues of approach for our machine guns, which effectively allowed us to put any of our potential enemies in a kill zone. Taking the high ground was very vital for our situation because the area we were in was no-man's-land and had almost zero United States and NATO presence. In other words, the region we were in was a breeding ground and hotbed for the Taliban.

We immediately set up our COC, communication lines, and a 360-degree defense to maintain our security posture. The Marines of Second Platoon spent all day and part of the night in two- to four-man teams searching from north to south along the Helmand River, between our helicopter insertion point and the location of our temporary PB.

The area we covered was roughly six thousand meters long and covered multiple grid squares on our maps of the AO. It consisted of very unforgiving rocky and steep terrain, hills, and mountains. Mud was knee high along the shorelines, rocks would fall from the mountaintops, and the jagged precipices and cliffs made for very strenuous climbs up and down.

A Marine named Staff Sergeant Jeremy Austin, in a television show titled *Marine Force Recon*, described the terrain in Afghanistan as if "Satan himself took his hand and just drug it through there," referring to the landscape of the country. This provides the best description I can think of for the terrain my platoon constantly encountered and fought through, especially during this mission.

Although we tirelessly searched and patrolled the crests of the riverbeds and combed the river that entire day and night, our efforts resulted in negative findings of either Corporal Wrightsman or the Afghan Uniformed Police Officer.

CHAPTER 31

Bright and early the next morning, about an hour before sunrise when the air was still cool, my Marines broke down the temporary PB and continued their search south along the riverbanks of the Helmand. Setting up overwatch positions and guardian angels for security, my Platoon Sergeant and I sent small units consisting of two- to four-man teams along the bottom of the cliffs we stood on to start searching for any evidence or signs pointing to the whereabouts of our two warriors. We moved slowly and carefully along the river, looking for gear, pieces of clothing, shadows, or anything that could hint at the location of our Marine or the Afghan Uniformed Police Officer.

My Marines physically combed the river with grappling hooks, securing themselves to each other with rope lines so as not to get sucked into the murky Helmand and drown. My platoon kept tight security on all possible areas where the Taliban would most likely try to take some shots at us while we patrolled the floor of the riverbed.

It was risky to send Marines in and out of the water considering the fact that the Helmand River had just swallowed one of our own. I knew all my Marines could swim, and I closely monitored them with the help of my NCOs to mitigate the risk factors. The currents were very strong, which meant Marines would have to be secured by a rope and understand that they could go no farther in than waist-deep. All morning and afternoon we moved south along the river, again finding no traces of life or evidence of our Marine.

Late that afternoon, we set up our next temporary patrol base approximately two thousand meters to the south of the original PB, on the highest mountaintop in the area. It was a grueling, punishing, and exhausting patrol and climb to the summit of the mountain, but it was also a key piece of ground we had to claim to deny the enemy the ability to use the terrain and surrounding area against us. It took about five hours for the entire platoon to reach the apex of the miniature mountain and start establishing the conduct of the defense for the night.

Climbing the mountains along the Helmand made me think about Offensive Redwing and the stories in a book titled *Victory Point*. The Marines in the book were located in the Korangal Valley and patrolled over terrain and climbed mountains worse than what we encountered. I used the stories to motivate myself and my men during our movement up and down the surrounding environment.

One particular part of the story my Marines liked and found hysterical was the account about the mules and donkeys the Marines used to transport their gear and combat loads jumping off cliffs and committing suicide because the terrain was strenuous and the mountains were a brutal climb, even for the animals. I could only imagine what those Marines were thinking when their animals, which were carrying their gear loads, said enough was enough and took to jumping off cliffs rather than continuing to patrol up and down the mountains of the Korangal.

Sitting on top of the mountainside overlooking the Helmand River was a very beautiful sight, to say the least. This was especially true at night when stars, planets, and the moon, all too many to count, lit up the sky. Everything looked so peaceful thousands of feet up. All of Nawa District looked tiny in the distance below. People looked like ants, small villages were sectored off by mud walls, and everything looked calm and serene. Mentally, looking down at the Nawa District from the mountaintops made me realize that the villages below would have looked exactly the same more than two thousand years ago when Alexander the Great led his military through this region.

It was on these mountaintops over the Helmand River that my platoon shed their "Lima" name and received the call sign Hades, solidifying our place as the battalion's maneuver element.

Now that my Marines were a part of H&S Company, I felt my platoon needed a new identity. After all, we were officially detached from Lima Company and were not a part of it anymore. Very humbly and out of respect for my new Commanding Officer, I made the suggestion (with the backing of my Platoon Sergeant and Squad Leaders) that my platoon shed the "Lima" call sign to eliminate any and all confusion with my Marines and Corpsmen in order to assume the call sign of Hades 2. "Hades" came from the call sign for H&S Company, and the "2" would designate Second Platoon.

Sarcastically faking tears in his eyes and laughing at me for trying to make this an emotional moment way up high on the mountaintop overlooking the Nawa District and Helmand River, Captain Armas gladly granted my request. My platoon had evolved, and now symbolically we were unstoppable minions of Hades, the Greek god of the underworld.

Chapter 32

My Marines continued to search the river all afternoon and part of the night once again, but sadly we came up short in finding Corporal Wrightsman and the Afghan Uniformed Police Officer. At this point we started to wonder if our efforts were in vain. The Helmand River is a large river, and it has a very strong current, much like the Tigris and Euphrates Rivers in Iraq. There was a definite possibility that the river could have carried them miles downstream and we would never find them.

During the third day of our search and recovery operation, not much changed with the conduct of my platoon. At this point, many of us came to the realization that Corporal Wrightsman and the Afghan Uniformed Police Officer had drowned. Every one of my Marines were averaging about two to four hours of sleep a night if they were lucky. They tirelessly searched the river for about twenty hours each day in the 125-degree or higher heat.

Many of us were getting frustrated and wanted to find Corporal Wrightsman before the Taliban did, especially because of the fact that we kept receiving intelligence updates over our communications net informing us that the Taliban knew about the situation and were conducting a search and recovery mission of their own. We all feared that if they recovered his body before the Marines did, they would mutilate it or use it as a war prize and display it over the Internet and television for viewers around the world. My Marines promised themselves that they would not let that happen and would stay as long as it took to find him.

We searched the river to our most southern limit and then concentrated our efforts back up north to our original helicopter insert grid once again. Halfway through the third day of our operation, our Parajumpers, carried by Pedro, recovered the submerged and drowned body of the missing Afghan Uniformed Police Officer about eight hundred meters north of our PB. Equipped with scuba gear and survival equipment, the Parajumpers had tirelessly searched the depths of the Helmand under our protection during the daylight hours over the last three days.

We knew at this point that the body of Corporal Wrightsman had to be close and its discovery was not far behind. The only solace that made us believe his body was in our vicinity was the fact my Marines were randomly finding his personal military issued gear and belongings along the riverbed. Every now and then as my Marines searched the riverbed, objects like cigarette packs, utility gloves, writing materials, and cigarette lighters were found floating along the shallow parts of the river, which signaled to us that his body was not far away and possibly trapped underneath the water. Logically, these items were a sign telling us to keep searching because his body was nearby.

The evening was no better for the Marines of the now Hades Second Platoon. All of us were tired and anxious to recover the body, even more so because the Afghan Uniformed Police Officer had been recovered and our Marine was still out there somewhere, underneath the river. Internally, the situation became even more personal when the Afghan Uniformed Police Officers who were also part of the search called off their rescue efforts after their fellow Afghan Uniformed Police Officer was discovered by our Parajumpers.

All their personnel and assets soon left the banks of the Helmand once they had attained the body of *their* drowned Officer. It was not enough that one of our own had risked his life to save a drug-addicted Afghan Uniformed Police Officer, but this clearly demonstrated the lack of respect and the indifference the Afghans had toward our Marine and the Marine Corps.

The Afghan Uniformed Police and Afghans in general obviously did not care about our Marine or the fact that he had sacrificed his life to save one of theirs. How could they though? Life was meaningless to these people, and they did not put value behind the efforts that went into trying to save the life of their fallen comrade. To them, it was just two more deaths and nothing else. These Afghan Uniformed Police Officers were only involved in the operation because behind the scenes, our command told them they had to help in the search and forced their hand in the process. If we were not forcing them to participate, they would have left their Officer there in the river and would have continued to go about their daily business of smoking hashish and harassing the local population like nothing had happened.

The situation on the ground at our temporary patrol base grew very tense that evening, and my Platoon Sergeant and I felt obligated to have a talk with our Marines to calm them down. They were all angry, and we as their leaders did our best to mitigate it, but they were not ignorant. Coupled with this inherent hatred we all felt toward our Afghan partners for calling off their search once they received the body of their own, out of nowhere a sandstorm hit our PB like it was from the pits of Hades itself.

The sandstorm clogged all our weapons and radio assets, making it almost impossible to see, hear, and breathe because of its thickness. We all banded together in our defensive trenches and covered each other from the skin-blistering wind, dust, rocks, and particles. The storm lasted all night, with my Marines constantly redigging their skirmisher trenches and covering their gear so the sand did not damage it. It was a very miserable time. In those miserable times, however, Marines usually find their greatest memories.

By the morning, all of the Marines of Hades, Second Platoon, were tired, dehydrated, and covered from head to toe with sand, but even more hungry to find our missing Marine. Out of our hatred for our allied partners and through the misery of the night's sandstorm, we soon found a resurgence of limitless motivation.

My Marines were and are a very aggressive bunch of men. They will go a hundred miles an hour to complete any mission at hand. If during an endeavor they hit a wall, they simply regrouped and then went a hundred miles an hour again to complete it. They lived for mission success and fought for each other every day. Our minds were made up, and not one of us would give up or quit the search for our Marine. We would have searched for him until we reached the ends of the Earth if that was what it took.

CHAPTER 33

We set out once again at 0400 that morning, splitting our platoon into three sections. One section would search the river from south to north, and the other would search from north to south. Their limit of advance would be when they met in the middle. The third section, comprised of a small reinforced fire team, stayed behind to guard our temporary PB. They would maintain security and overwatch, guard our communications link with the COC at FOB Geronimo, and continually transmit updates on the situation and our progress to the battalion. Over the radio, our Battalion Intelligence Officer constantly sent us information updates of possible heat signatures discovered by our aircraft assets. Many of these signatures were not far from our current position and even possibly indicated the location of the Corporal Wrightsman's body submerged beneath the Helmand.

At approximately 0700 on 21 July 2010, the Marines of Hades, Second Platoon, along with the leadership our new company, discovered the floating body of Corporal Joe Wrightsman on the riverbank, two thousand feet directly beneath the cliff of the mountain where our PB was located. This put Corporal Joe Wrightsman's official death on the date of 18 July 2010. At this point, the feeling of relief that swept through us all was unexplainable and reinvigorating. It didn't matter at this point if we took enemy contact or not. We had found the body of one of our own, and that was worth more to us than killing Taliban. Every one of my Marines and Corpsmen in the immediate vicinity ran toward the body of our fallen brother and immediately set up security around him, protecting the corpse like a mother protects her children from a predator.

It was a sad picture, seeing the drowned body of our fellow Marine. Rigor mortis had set in, and the animal and aquatic life in the river had all taken a toll on his body over the last four days as he lay trapped beneath the surface of the water. The only comfort we found was that at least the family of Corporal Wrightsman would be at ease knowing we found their son's body, brought him home, and denied the Taliban the chance to take it and use it as a war trophy.

Over the last four days, Marine Super Cobras and Navy HH-60 Search and Recovery Helicopters had been constantly flying over our position and sweeping the river as we conducted our operation. It was finally a Predator drone that had found the heat signature of his body in the waters of the Helmand.

It took less than five minutes for us to coordinate a linkup and extraction plan with our air assets when we found Corporal Wrightsman, but overall, extracting his body came very quickly and timely because air was constantly on station. If the Taliban were watching us, they would still be a potential threat and could try to engage us or the helicopters as a last effort to take our dead brother from us. We needed to remain vigilant and keep our guard up at all times during this handover process.

Providing security around Corporal Wrightsman, my Marines and I carried him roughly three hundred meters to the hasty HLZ we had established on the shoreline of the Helmand River. Once we handed him over to the Naval flight crew, our mission came to a slow close. After the helicopter departed, the threat of Taliban trying to conduct a mass attack on our forces slowly dissipated.

My Marines and I regrouped, patrolled up the mountain to our PB, and established a hasty HLZ for our extraction. My platoon extracted about an hour after the body of Corporal Wrightsman was recovered and airlifted out. We could all sleep better now knowing we had done our job and brought one of our Marines home to eternal rest. We hated losing one of our own but were grateful that we had the honor to bring him back and prevent the Taliban from taking his body from us. Forever, my Marines can look back on that day with humility and be proud of what they did.

CHAPTER 34

My platoon arrived back at Geronimo around 0900 that same day and finally had a chance to rest and refit. The Marines had been working tirelessly and had been on the go since day one in Afghanistan. At this point, time to relax was a request my Platoon Sergeant and I gladly afforded them. It didn't matter to my Marines at this point whether they would have the chance to kill Taliban or not. They had found the body of one of their own, and if the deployment were to end on that day, it would have been worthwhile. It was a tangible act they all earned and will carry with them until the day they die.

Over the next few days at FOB Geronimo, the Marines of Hades Second Platoon had a chance to move into their living sustainment area (LSA) and settle in. Now that we were going to create a combined action company, we had to begin setting up our LSA. Our new Company Commander drew up the plans and gave us his intent on how the LSA would be set up.

By his efforts, our CO was able to get an area of FOB Geronimo sectioned off for both Hades First and Second Platoons away from the rest of the battalion. The area the Marines and our Afghan National Army Soldiers would be living in was going to have living quarters, a training area, a spot designated for a mobile section, a mosque, and a chow area for the Afghan Soldiers to cook their food.

The LSA was to be surrounded by HESCO barrier walls on three sides and a sand berm on the west side to section us off from the other units at Geronimo. This would create and maintain the mystical illusion for everyone watching at Geronimo that no one other than the Marines and Afghan National Army Soldiers involved were allowed to see what was being created "behind the curtain." Both First and Second Platoons were ensured that we were going to have the full support of the battalion and that anything we needed was only an arm's length away.

The Marines of both Hades First Platoon and Hades Second Platoon worked diligently day and night to establish the new combined action company living area. By 20 July 2010, our LSA started to come to form. The only thing my Marines and I did not set up was an area for the mosque. If our ANA Soldiers wanted one that badly, they could do the work themselves.

Our Afghan National Army Soldiers were scheduled to move in with us on 27 July 2010. This meant my Marines had a few more days to get their priorities in order, and Lieutenant Miller and I could have time to work together on a training plan for our combined unit. The great thing about living in our new home was the fact that my Marines did not have enough time to become spoiled with the creature comforts afforded to us at FOB Geronimo.

Living in triple-digit temperatures outside in the desert under the hot arid sun was the norm for them. These conditions had hardened my Marines, and now they were addicted to them. Of course, they all complained at first, but losing creature comforts (air-conditioning, bed racks with mattresses, showers) allowed them to focus on their mission and the task at hand. We were there to work, not play. Creature comforts have the ability to distract Marines and make them complacent of their surroundings.

Anytime a Marine gets too comfortable, he or she becomes complacent and goes internal. When a Marine goes internal, he or she loses focus on his or her surroundings and starts making selfish comfort-based decisions. Marines need to be treated like hellhounds. They need just the right amount of chow, water, and tough love to always keep them hungry, pissed off, and on edge at all times. This keeps their warrior spirit and fighting mentality finely tuned, alive, and ready for the fight. If Marines are treated too well, they will not want to fight and will become lazy, complacent, and get killed. Sweet, sweet misery and adversity brings Marines closer! We are always around each other, and if we all have something to whine and complain about, it fosters cohesion and brings us closer together.

CHAPTER 35

Our work came to a sudden pause on 22 July 2010 when First Lieutenant Miller and I were tasked with our next mission from our CO. Staff Sergeant Lebron and I looked at each other, thinking to ourselves, *Already two missions in our first week, one regimental level and one battalion level, and we do not even have our Afghan National Army Soldiers yet.*

As Lieutenant Miller and I, along with our Platoon Sergeants, approached our CO in the H&S COC, we were immediately briefed on our next mission. The facts were still uncertain, but from what we were told, a Marine AH-1W Super Cobra had just crashed north of our position in India Company's AO. Our platoons were to respond as the battalion's QRF and conduct another TRAP mission. We were to stay in the hostile and unfamiliar territory until the helicopter, all sensitive material, and the bodies of the fallen Marines were recovered.

The information we were fed was that the AH-1W Super Cobra had been hit by an enemy RPG rocket and subsequently crashed three kilometers north of COB Spin Gar, which was India Company's main operating base. The terrorist cell said to be responsible for the attack was led by a gentlemen named Mullah Abash. He was a notorious terrorist in this area and usually operated with his Subcommanders Mullahs Razi and Zendani. My Marines had been on the hunt for Mullah Razi and Zendani since the beginning of our deployment. Now we added one more name to our target list.

Marines from India Company were the first responders on scene, and they were currently setting up security around the helicopter and the two Marines killed in the crash. They were receiving fire, and the enemy situation was hostile.

After a quick backbrief to our Squad Leaders from our Platoon Sergeants, the men from Hades First and Second Platoons loaded up in our armored vehicle convoy and departed friendly lines for a one-hour movement north to COB Spin Gar.

Upon arriving at Spin Gar, Lieutenant Miller and I were given fragmentary orders (FRAGOs) by the India Company Commanding Officer, Captain Magni. Their Air Officer, whose call sign was Geico, briefed us on our air assets and informed us that if we were to declare a troops in contact (TIC) situation, air assets were only ten minutes away. We were informed that a platoon reinforced with India Company's Marines were providing security around the downed helicopter and had been taking sporadic enemy fire throughout most of the day. Our mission was going to take place the following day on the morning of 23 July 2010. Hades First and Second Platoons would relieve the India Company Marines currently on scene and hold security around the helicopter until it could be recovered by friendly forces.

On the ground, the enemy situation was hostile, with the India Company Marines on scene receiving small arms fire (SAF) every hour on the hour. The enemy wanted to take the ground and kill all the Marines defending it. We were informed that the downed helicopter had multiple crash sites, and it was in three separate pieces, all of which were being secured by India Company Marines. Our last bit of information before the end of the night was that the bodies of the two fallen Marine pilots had been successfully recovered and transported back to friendly lines by Pedro. As bad as this news was, we were all relieved that the Taliban had not been able to retrieve their bodies and use them as trophies for their propaganda campaign. India Company had done an outstanding job getting to and securing the crash site before the enemy even had a chance.

Hades First and Second Platoons planned and prepped all night at Spin Gar, going over the scheme of maneuver for our platoons to make the three-kilometer movement north the next day to the crash site. By the time the sun rose the following morning, we were going to patrol from Spin Gar to relieve the Marines at the crash site.

At 0800 the next morning, my platoon took the lead security and patrolled more than three kilometers north from COB Spin Gar toward the vicinity of the crash site. Short of running, we double-timed it to the crash site to assist in securing the area and reinforce the Marines there.

Within twenty minutes, my forward squad conducted a linkup with the India Company Marines who were providing a cordon, and then my platoon got set in, taking the northern 180-degree security sector around the downed helicopter. In doing so, my Marines had a defense around both the main body and tail of the helicopter, which had been separated from each other when the Cobra crashed into the ground. Roughly half an hour later, Hades First Platoon arrived on scene and established themselves on the southern half of our 180-degree security perimeter, which locked our defensive cordon into place. They took the responsibility of guarding the third crash site in addition to the two my platoon guarded.

We then officially relieved India Company in place and received no more details than what was already briefed to us. They had done a stellar job providing quick response to the site, repelling the enemy assault, and defending the two fallen Marines with their lives. The on-scene Commander, Lieutenant Thorson, informed us that he knew little of what had caused the helicopter to crash and that the situation on the ground was still very hostile. He was uneasy as well because the ammunition and rounds from the helicopter crash had landed in the center of the field we were guarding, and the possibility of them "cooking off" and firing still loomed. While at the site, he and his Marines had heard an increasing amount of small arms fire in the surrounding area, and they had taken fire earlier that day. They constantly remained vigilant and in a high state of alert, making sure to let our Marines know the ever-increasing enemy threat around us even as they prepared to depart.

The Marines of India Company had been originally tasked to conduct a company-sized operation known as Operation Thresher prior to the helo going down. For obvious reasons, the mission had to be postponed one day because of this incident. It was an operation designed to be a systematic search and clearing of unique areas of interest in their battlespace. Now it was also going to include the capture or kills of the men responsible for taking the lives of two of our own.

Our battle handover took about thirty minutes to complete and resulted in the departure of our sister platoon and company so they could execute their company operation. The Marines of Hades First and Second Platoons executed a TRAP around the downed helicopter and secured the general area.

Within a few hours of maintaining the defense and getting our bearings, First Lieutenant Miller and I started sending out patrols to the north and south to have the Marines establish security in the immediate surrounding area. We could not afford to allow the enemy to backlay or set up ambushes against our positions and gain the advantage. Even though India Company had recovered the bodies of the two fallen Marines, there were still valuable intelligence assets and weapons they could use against us if they had the opportunity.

Many of the locals in the immediate area came off very friendly to us. When asked about the enemy that had conducted this act, however, not one of them apparently knew or had seen any enemy forces shoot down the helicopter with an RPG or rocket. *Big surprise. A helicopter crashes and none of the local nationals saw anything or can give us any information. Counterinsurgency is really paying off,* I thought. *Maybe if we give them money or offer them projects they might remember something,* I said to myself.

Although my Marines and I received sporadic fire, the area we were in did not seem hostile to us at all, regardless of the fact that a helicopter had just been shot down. Local Afghan children were trying to walk with us on local security patrols, and elders were offering us food and chai tea when we set up security in the village to our north. Not feeling very friendly at all toward the locals, who had possibly participated in aiding or abetting the enemy, we declined their chai and did not allow them anywhere near the patrol or the crash site.

It just didn't make any sense to my Marines and me. The area seemed quite peaceful and serene, and we felt protected more than anything. If the locals were hiding something or the enemies responsible for this act were still in the area, they were doing a very good job of concealing it.

Hades First and Second Platoons held security around the helicopter for the next two days. The area was not kinetic aside from a firefight that broke out about two kilometers to our south between Taliban and an Afghanistan National Police Station and their Uniformed Policemen. With respect to this incident, our platoons heard a few rounds of mortars and gunfire being shot in the distance but not enough to gain positive identification or even declare it a hostile act or intent. Our primary mission was still to guard the crash site at all costs until recovery was made.

CHAPTER 36

For the final two days of this TRAP mission, Lieutenant Miller and I had our platoons conduct four to five patrols a day and two at night. They were constantly looking for any enemy in the area, but they found nothing. It was like we were chasing a ghost we wanted to believe existed but could not find. So much for COIN. Where were all of the good and decent Afghans wanting to help the Marines and take their country back from the evil Taliban?

By the morning of 25 July 2010, our Regimental Combat Logistics Battalion (CLB) arrived on scene to pick up the remaining wreckage and conduct a battle damage assessment of the AH-1W Super Cobra crash. It took CLB about ten hours from start to finish to remove all the pieces from the crash, consolidate the sensitive materials, and clean up the wreckage. The pieces of the wreckage that CLB could not take back or did not need for evidence were blown up in place with charges of C-4 demolition.

By 1700 that night, my Marines set up security and escorted CLB as they left our area. Once this was complete and the area was cleaned up and secured, the Marines of First and Second Platoons patrolled back to COB Spin Gar, where we were to be trucked back to FOB Geronimo early the next morning. As we were leaving, the local national who owned the field where the helo had crashed demanded reparations and money for the damage. Without hesitation, my CO took charge and refused to pay the local for any damage to his field out of respect and honor for the two Marines who had lost their lives in the line of duty.

The result of the mission was that two United States Marine Corps Officers, Major James M. Weis and Lieutenant Colonel Mario D. Carazo, were killed, and their helicopter was destroyed. However, it is with humility and honor that I can proudly say that when the event occurred, every Marine in the battalion and regiment (especially India Company) came to their call to ensure they were recovered and brought home to their families. Although many local nationals were questioned, there was zero evidence to hold or detain any of them. The only bit of information we knew was that a Taliban leader named Mullah Abash was the coward behind the killing of our Marines.

During CLBs assessment, their on-scene investigator unofficially determined that the helicopter propeller had separated from the body as it was crashing and showed no signs of damage or impact from a rocket or gunfire to his knowledge. The Marines from Combat Logistics Battalion deduced that if a rocket was the cause of the downed helicopter, there should had been some damage to the propeller because it separated, but there was none. Therefore, all evidence pointed to mechanical failure, which in turn led to a failure in its maintenance. This was good to hear, not because two Marines were killed but because we did not want any news of an enemy victory.

This meant that if this were true and a mechanical failure had been the cause of the crash, the enemy could not claim responsibility for the two dead Marines or receive recognition to fuel their propaganda against us. (These claims were later refuted, and it was officially determined that the enemy had in fact shot down the helicopter with one or multiple RPG volley fires.)

With two TRAP missions conducted and the recoveries of now three fallen United States Marines, two helicopters, and an Afghan Uniformed Police Officer, the Marines of Hades First and Second Platoons arrived back at COB Spin Gar at 2000 that same night, anxious to return to Geronimo the next morning. At this point, my Marines and I all wanted the same thing now more than ever: to kill Taliban.

This photo was taken on 18 July 2010 on the mountains above the Helmand River during the regimental search and recovery operation for Corporal Joe Wrightsman and an Afghan Uniformed Police Officer. Sergeant Brown, Second Squad Leader, is observing the general area while keeping an eye on his Marines, who are searching the shoreline of the Helmand River for the bodies. The mountain in the background is where Second Platoon set up their patrol base over the course of the next four days.

This photo was taken on 19 July 2010 on the Helmand River. Sergeant Brown, Second Squad Leader for Hades 2, utilizes a grappling hook to drag the bottom of the river in an attempt to find Corporal Wrightsman and the Afghan Uniformed Police Officer.

This photo was taken on 19 July 2010 on the banks of the Helmand River. Corporal Berry utilizes his Kevlar to lower his body temperature and cool off during the search for Corporal Wrightsman and the Afghan Uniformed Police Officer. Temperatures were around 130 degrees Fahrenheit during the four days of our regimental search and recovery mission. Marines were under guardian angel overwatch security at all times and were allowed to drop gear momentarily in an effort to cool their body temperatures while they searched the river.

This photo was taken on 20 July 2010. Corporal Mount is in his fighting hole as part of the conduct of the defense. My Marines manned these fighting holes at night to prevent the enemy from infiltrating our positions during the regimental search and recovery mission.

This photo was taken by Sergeant Mark Fayloga (Combat Cameraman). First Lieutenant Bodrog and Sergeant Brown are observing areas along the Helmand River that could possibly be used by the Taliban to attack the Marines of Hades Second Platoon. Here Lieutenant Bodrog and Sergeant Brown get “eyes on” a vehicle reported to be illegally carrying AK-47s and IEDs.

This photo was taken by Sergeant Mark Fayloga (Combat Cameraman). The Marines of Hades Second Platoon are on the top of a mountain overlooking the Helmand River and surrounding areas from a temporary patrol base. My Marines can now rest knowing they recovered their fallen brother and the Afghan Uniformed Police Officer. They are watching the sunrise to the east while they wait for the inbound helicopter to land and extract us back to FOB Geronimo.

This is one of the many weapons caches the Marines of the combined action company were responsible for capturing. During a routine vehicle checkpoint and subsequent search of a vehicle, my Marines discovered the vehicle was carrying more than what the driver and passenger led us to believe. In the trunk of the vehicle, inside rice and fertilizer bags, these hidden items were discovered.

This photo was taken on 23 July 2010. This was the second tactical recovery of aircraft personnel (TRAP) mission for the Marines of Hades Second Platoon. In this picture, a United States Marine Corps AH-1W Super Cobra was reportedly shot down by enemy RPG fire. The two Marine Corps helicopter pilots killed were Lieutenant Colonel Mario D. Carazo and Major James M. Weis. In the picture, the Marines of Hades Second Platoon have security around the helicopter.

This photo was taken on 23 July 2010. This is the tailpiece of the AH-1W Super Cobra that came apart when it crashed into the ground. My Marines were tasked with securing this piece of the aircraft and denying the enemy the ability to recover it until friendly forces could safely extract it.

COLONEL RANDALL P. NEWMAN
COMMANDING OFFICER, RCT-7

July 22, 2010

To those who aided in the recovery of Corporal Wrightsman,

On behalf of the Marines and Sailors of Regimental Combat Team 7, I would like to commend all who assisted in the search for and ultimate recovery of Corporal Wrightsman of 3rd Battalion 3rd Marines and Wahidullah Fida Mohammad of the Afghan National Police. The immediate and sustained actions by all involved led to the recovery of men lost in the line of duty and serves as the embodiment of our motto Semper Fidelis – Always Faithful. Nobody returned from the battlefield until all returned reinforcing a pact amongst warfighters that allows all to take the actions necessary to accomplish the mission here in Afghanistan confident of the full support of all resources and units if needed.

On July 18, 2010 Corporal Wrightsman was leading a combat patrol that included a crossing of the Helmand River. After scouting a fording site, Corporal Wrightsman proceeded to lead the patrol across the river when Patrolman Wahidullah lost his footing and was being swept away by the river current. Corporal Wrightsman unhesitatingly jumped into the river despite wearing full combat gear in order to attempt to save his comrade in arms. The remainder of the patrol sprung into action to try and assist in their recovery from the river. The strength of the current and depth of the water ultimately defeated immediate recovery efforts and both Corporal Wrightsman and Patrolman Wahidullah were swept downriver beyond sight of the patrol. The patrol immediately notified higher headquarters and a massive search and recovery effort was launched that ultimately led to the recovery of Patrolman Wahidullah on July 19 when he was spotted by a supporting Pedro flight and recovered by rescue divers and of Corporal Wrightsman on July 20 when he was spotted by a U.K. predator flight and recovered by Marines of 3rd Battalion, 3rd Marines. The recovery of these men would not have been possible were it not for the swift and sustained response by headquarters and units throughout the Afghanistan theater of operation.

Those who played a part in this successful recovery are legion but I would like to specifically commend the following:

66th Emergency Rescue Squadron
- LtCol Tom Dorl
- Lt Graham
- Lt Viani
- SMSgt Atkins
- SSgt Adams

3rd Battalion, 3rd Marines
- H&S Company
  - Operational Maneuver Force led by Capt Jason Armas
  - Jump Platoon led by Gunner Law
  - Combat Operations Center directed by Major Joseph and Capt Zjawin
- Kilo Company – 3 squads led by Capt Belcher
- Lima Company – 3 squads led by Capt Pernotto
- Weapons Company – 6 squads led by Capt Hunt

Afghan National Security Forces
- Nawa District Police commanded by Nafas Khan and Ahmed Shah
- 1-1-215 Kandak of the Afghan National Army commanded by LtCol Gul Ahmad

Theater Level Aviation Support
- Voodoo 17, Savage 57, Cody 11 and 17 – Reaper
- Henchman 61 – U.K. Predator
- Vapor 33 – Scan Eagle
- DeepSea 52 – EP-3
- Pedro – USAF HH-60 MEDEVAC
- Hawg 55 and 61 – USAF A-10
- Stoic 34 – USMC F-18 from KAF
- Uproar 43 – USMC carrier based F-18
- Dealer 24 and 54 – HMLA-167

R.P. NEWMAN
COLONEL, USMC

PART IV

Forming the Combined Action Company

Now this is the law of the jungle—as old and as true as the sky; and the wolf that shall keep it may prosper, but the wolf that shall break it must die. As the creeper that girdles the tree-trunk, the law runneth forward and back; for the strength of the pack is the wolf, and the strength of the wolf is the pack.
—Rudyard Kipling, poem from *The Second Jungle Book*

We must remember that one man is much the same as another, and that he is best who is trained in the severest school.
—Thucydides

A person must build each step before they have a staircase.
—Afghan Proverb

CHAPTER 37

The morning of 27 July 2010 was the official start and spawn of the mission that was going to facilitate the creation of the first United States Marine and Afghan National Army Soldier CAC since the inception of the war in Afghanistan.

There was still much work to be done to establish the LSA to support both the Marines and Afghan Army Soldiers. With the tents and living quarters in place, Staff Sergeant Lebron and I now needed to sit down with our Squad Leaders and select a training area for professional military classes, an area for our mobile section, and a place to set up a mosque for the Afghan Soldiers to pray in.

The only thing that bothered my Marines and me was the mosque. It had been the experience of the Marines of Second Platoon that many of the Afghan Soldiers used their religion as a way to get out of operations and missions rather than for spiritual means. Besides, we were not there to promote their religion, even though we were forced to be as tolerant as possible to their needs and feelings, especially during their holy months. Regardless of any preconceptions we had about the Muslim religion, the only time Afghans were religious zealots was when it benefited them or got them out of manual labor.

By the time we returned from our second TRAP mission, HESCO barrier fortifications and concertina wire were in place around the Hades Company LSA. The illusion that the Marines were going to create a masterpiece behind the sand-filled walls had now been initiated.

There were no plans, no training schedules, and no syllabi to construct our unit. There were no after-action reports or data left behind from previous units during the last nine years of the Afghan War on how to establish this combined action company. FOB Geronimo did not even have formal classrooms with computers and Internet, aside from our morale, welfare, and recreation center (MWR). Creating a plan was all on the Marines of Hades First and Second Platoons. We had to figure out what courses of action and methods would work.

The line we were going to be walking was going to be fragile and ready to break at any minute. The Afghan National Army Soldiers we were going to train were known to give up and quit at any time. Many of the Afghan Soldiers joined because it was an opportunity to receive a better chance to immigrate to America and leave the desolate wasteland of Afghanistan far behind them.

Regardless of what people think, many Afghan Soldiers did not fight for their country or for their brothers and sisters. Many did not even understand what a country was, let alone what Afghanistan was. Many of the Soldiers in the Afghan National Army were not even Afghan by birth. Most were from Uzbekistan and other northern countries that bordered Afghanistan.

The notion and understanding of creating a joint partnered American and Afghanistan unit did little to faze the Afghan Army or make them proud of what they were doing. Patriotism is a virtue inherent in American democracy and a word associated with freedom. The Afghans knew little of freedom and thus little of patriotism. After all, what did they have to be patriotic about? On the surface, they fought for a paycheck and the opportunity to leave their country in hopes of one day coming to America.

The majority of Afghan Soldiers my Marines encountered had no concept of patriotism or nationalism, just a greedy and selfish understanding of the fact that getting out of Afghanistan meant either killing or being killed. Each Soldier would do what it took to better himself at the expense of the man to his left or his right to increase his chances of getting to the United States of America. Displaying a genuine mind-set and other weak virtues such as generosity or kindness was not prevalent in these men, who for years had been indoctrinated in the harshness and brutality of their previous communist and radical Islamic Muslim rulers.

The majority of Afghans live in a society in which there is zero trust. Almost everyone is a manipulator and liar, and greed propels most, if not all, of their decisions. Most Afghans care only for themselves and look to only better themselves. These people will sell out their own family members if the deal is good enough.

My Marines, who were tasked to mentor and lead them, were very uncertain and skeptical that the Afghan Soldiers would have what it took both mentally and physically to fight alongside them. After all, not one Afghan Soldier could be trusted because their lives were based on selling each other out in order to survive. I constantly asked myself questions like, *Will this happen to my platoon if we are engaged in a firefight? Will the Afghan Army sell us out to the Taliban and lead us into an ambush while we are on a security patrol? Will our new partners make a deal with the Taliban and infiltrate our LSA?*

This was the reality of life in Afghanistan, and preparations had to be made to prevent a foreseeable future such as this. We knew these partners of ours had the potential to sell us out to the enemy if the deal was good enough, and we had to be on guard at all times.

Everyone involved in this experiment, from our Battalion Commander on down to the lowest Private, were very unsure if the combined action company would work, but they still had the confidence to put their faith in my Marines to at least try. In my mind and in the mind of my Platoon Sergeant, our men had what it took to train, mentor, and lead our new partners, and we were going to accomplish this mission for our battalion at all costs.

CHAPTER 38

My Marines and Corpsmen are the embodiment of the American dream and spirit. They continuously exhibited an unfaltering work ethic coupled with unstoppable desire to win in order to be the best at everything they did. Their personalities and the camaraderie they exhibited on a daily basis were reminiscent of men in the movie titled *Memphis Belle*.

Although my men are Marines and not Airmen, the closeness the men in the movie shared reminded me of the closeness and loyalty my platoon shared at all times. They took care of one another and had a connection that is only found in a close family. Mentally and physically, each of my Marines was a top earner and the picturesque image of the "American working man." Morally and ethically, they were top earners. They all embraced the realization that they were not individuals but a group—an unbreakable tribe that could accomplish and achieve all they put their minds to.

They took great interest in each other's lives, and the bond they shared was one only a Marine or one who has been in combat can understand. They were motivated, carnivorous, bloodthirsty warriors—unfaltering, unwavering, and never hesitating. My Platoon Sergeant and I knew that our men lived and held themselves to the high standards we set for them. To lower our standards meant mediocrity and weakness. Staff Sergeant Lebron and I had shaped them into pieces of steel and given them a higher purpose they could believe in and work toward together.

In our minds, the Afghan Soldiers were going to become the best operating Afghan unit in the entire country if they could survive the training my Marines of Hades Second Platoon were going to give them. By the time my Marines were finished with them, these Afghan Soldiers would believe they were the best too. Hope, cowardice, and mediocrity were not a course of action.

We were not going to make the same mistake many units do when they arrive to Afghanistan. We were not going to make the Afghans our equals, because no matter how hard they worked, they would never achieve the same mental, physical, or civil standard we as United States Marines possessed. America had entrusted us with the mission to be the best fighting force in the world, one that was second to none. The simple fact was that they were a third-world military. From an evolutionary standpoint, my Marines were the stronger animal and had a responsibility not to devolve to a weaker level. We instead had to help our foreign partners sustain themselves in their combat operations and bring them up to a level capable of defending their country against the enemy Taliban.

We were not going to make these Afghan Soldiers into Marines, because not one Afghan Soldier could possess the potential it took to become a United States Marine. We were going to make them better Soldiers and fighters who would eventually be capable of operating independently without the help or assistance of other United States forces. My Marines were playing a tiny but vital role in the facilitation of the Afghan Soldiers' transition to slowly begin taking back and fighting for their country.

In essence, my Platoon Sergeant and I applied our own neo-American Civil Rights Act with respect to the conduct of forcible integration and training of both our Marines and Afghan National Army Soldiers. The Marines and the Afghans were going to be given no choice in the matter and were going to forcibly integrate. They were going to live, eat, drink, sleep, piss, and shower as one platoon and company until they did not know any better and it became muscle memory.

The only difference in the "Civil Rights Act" that the Marines of Hades Second Platoon were going to enforce was that there would be a method of competition and a system of rewards based on content of character and merit. Nothing was going to be given to our genetically less fortunate and ill-prepared counterparts to level this playing field. Everything was going to be earned and fought for through hard work, hardship, trial, and pain.

This may not seem like a difficult task, but living among third-world men who speak a different language and have values of right and wrong that differ from American values is no walk in the park. We must remember that the culture of Afghanistan presents a huge friction point in the most primordial aspect. This is a culture in many respects that has been unchanged for more than two millennia. These are people who bathe where they defecate or urinate and throw trash on the same piece of ground where they sleep. These are people who use their hands cupped with water to wipe their buttocks after they defecate and then use those same hands to eat food. From a first-world and civilized standpoint, having grown men learn to how to clean up after themselves was one of the most basic concepts my Marines had to teach these Soldiers before we could even start training for combat.

If there is one thing that is certain, it is this: people cannot be forced to like each other. Multiculturalism or diversity for the sake of multiculturalism and diversity will never work. There must be a goal and endstate to get people of different cultures and nationalities to work together, or else it will be like the Tower of Babel. Marines are expert professionals in this respect because as long as they are given a mission, task, purpose, and endstate, it will be executed. If not, they will just start throwing rocks and breaking things.

CHAPTER 39

As my new Afghan National Army Soldiers from the Third Tolai formed up on the morning of 27 June 2010, it was almost like a scene out of a comedy film. I say *my* Afghan Soldiers because even though they had a Platoon Commander and chain of command, both Lieutenant Miller and me, along with our Marines, were the ones really responsible for their training, conduct, and actions.

If they succeeded or failed, it was going to be because of us. If the Soldiers quit or committed a crime, the responsibility would be ours alone. It was a double-edged sword to know that mission success or failure was going to be the burden of my Marines and that all responsibility for the conduct of the Afghan Soldiers was forfeited to us. They were our like our puppets; we held the strings, and it was our responsibility to put on the show for everyone watching.

Staff Sergeant Lebron and I were not only in charge of the conduct of our combined platoon but also the conduct of the integrated weapons section that was going to be attached to our platoon for combat missions. This weapons section was led by Mortarman Sergeant Smith. Organic to his combined weapons section were the M240B medium machine gun and 60mm mortar weapon systems.

The Afghan Soldiers who showed up on the first morning of training wore different uniforms and different covers. Some were wearing sandals. Many used their RPGs as water bottle holders. A few pointed their AK-47s or M16-A2 service rifles at their own faces, picked their noses, had their boots unlaced, and wore their pants unbloused as they stood in their initial formation. They were clearly disorganized and lacked essential leadership.

These Afghan Soldiers formed up vertically in four columns, not horizontally in three columns like the Marines. Within the formation itself, many were talking on their cellular phones or listening to music, smoking cigarettes, and joking while their Platoon Commanders and Platoon Sergeants gave them orders and acted like they were able to take charge of their men. My Platoon Sergeant and I looked at each other in amazement at this chaotic mess standing in front of us.

The first day of training was merely introductory. My platoon looked at the Afghans like they were our mentally handicapped step-brothers who had no business even wearing a military uniform. The Afghans looked at my Marines and wondered why these warriors looked so serious, disciplined, and focused. It was an awkward first impression and an even more awkward silence as the two units stood side by side as partners, representing the future prospect of security and safety for Afghanistan.

Our counterpart Afghan Platoon Commander and Platoon Sergeant were initially not too bad of men. They seemed ready and willing to partner and integrate with my Marines and humbled to be learning from us. They understood from the inception that my Marines were in charge of making them a better fighting unit and that it would behoove them to listen to us and learn our TTPs.

The Afghanistan Platoon Commander and Platoon Sergeant liked to play the fool, always trying to see how much they could get over on us, testing us to see if we would give into their demands. They liked to complain about the problems their Soldiers faced, such as a lack of military gear and education, and they used every attempt to get free military items from our battalion.

This way of thought was the same for any Afghan units Marines came into contact with. The Afghan Soldiers knew Marine units rotated in and out every seven months and were fed the same cultural sensitivity crap during months of training prior to deploying. When the new units came in and the old rotated out, the Afghan leadership would play dumb and see how strong or weak new leaders were by testing the waters. They would ask for free gear, weapons, or other logistical items, which aloof Marine leaders who did not know any better would give in to under the false pretense of counterinsurgency and cultural sensitivity. These items usually never made it to the Afghan Soldiers because their own leadership would sell them on the black market for personal cash.

What was worse was that new leaders didn't really understand counterinsurgency and confused giving the Afghans money and free items with winning their trust and confidence. Many commands even forced their leaders into believing that not giving the Afghan Military or local population projects, jobs, or money would in effect create more Taliban and enemy forces. This was not counterinsurgency in the David Galula sense of the word; this was welfare and a false conclusion. This became a justifiable way to fund both sides of the war and prolong the fight against the Taliban.

It was greed, which is not an uncommon trait in American society, that propelled the Afghan units. No matter how much progress a Marine unit made, by the time the next unit rolled in, they always started back at square one. Good leaders were able to see this happening, and if they were smart, they could identify the honest Afghan National Army Soldiers who were trained by Marines and place them in positions of leadership to mitigate the friction a new unit faced or encountered. A majority of the time though, generosity and an underlying sense of guilt for the plight of the "poor" Afghans compromised great leadership decisions because many leaders felt they would create an enemy if they did not give in to Afghan demands.

CHAPTER 40

The main goal, or endstate, my Platoon Sergeant and I set out to accomplish on the first day was to integrate our two platoons together in a single formation, introduce ourselves, lay down the ground rules for the LSA, and get the Afghan National Army Soldiers in their billeting areas. For now, Lieutenant Miller was going to organize his platoon separately from my own until both our platoons were at a level to conduct combat missions as a combined company. However, we both utilized the same training plan and TTPs during this training process.

Putting a face on the image of the CAP was the first step in our process. We had to see what we were dealing with before we could even get to work. Integrating the two platoons together was tough because Marines have a lot of pride and honor. To force each of them to stand next to a lesser man in a formation is almost insulting. Marines just cannot turn off years of training to be the best and kill, by being manipulated into believing they are equal to Afghan Soldiers.

I did not blame them. Many times I questioned my own raison d'être as a Marine Officer. I did not go to military school and conduct hundreds, if not thousands, of hours of infantry training to become a project manager and political-social tool in Afghanistan. Many times I thought, *Why is the Marine Corps being utilized as a second land Army, and why are we doing the Army's job?* We were trained from day one to be warriors and killers, not bureaucrats of a global welfare socialist Keynesian society. It was very hard for us to turn off this mind-set and look at ourselves in the mirror. Many of us felt as if somehow we were destroying our Corps principals for the sake of a purely political-social agenda.

When not given a choice, partnering was forced upon my Marines because it was the mission, and that was the only thing that mattered, regardless of personal opinion. My Marines were required during every formation to stand next to the same ANA Soldier they stood next to on day one. Once the formation was accomplished and both the Marines and Afghan Soldiers knew their places, my platoon leadership and I introduced ourselves and laid down the ground rules for the conduct of training and subsequent integrated operations.

As is the case with many foreign and domestic linguists, as my Platoon Sergeant and I gave our Commander's intent and tasking statements, we had to rely heavily on the skill of our interpreters to transmit our words to the Afghan Soldiers. Many times our linguists spoke too softly, conducted themselves in an overly sensitive manner, and could not understand or translate military verbiage in to comprehensible dialogue. Sometimes even the simplest translation caused great difficulty. In the back of our minds, my Platoon Sergeant and I were always suspicious that our linguists were putting their own twist and spin on the words or sentences we wanted translated to the ANA.

The only advice I can give to eliminate this uncertainty is two things. The first is to have two linguists present—one you trust and one you don't. In this manner you know if what you are saying is being relayed. Afghans' body language and responses to a linguist's statements were always a visual indicator that whatever the linguist said caused a change to their status quo.

The second piece of advice is that if at any time you feel your point is being misinterpreted, make sure to ask the linguist if they understand what you are asking them to interpret. Many linguists are only doing the job because it helps their chances of immigrating to America. Their biggest fear is getting fired or letting Marines down because that could ruin their chances to come to the United States. That said, linguists must be treated as civilians and dealt with delicately in this respect. Time is always against Marines in terms of training. In an effort to not waste time, make sure the linguist knows it is all right to tell you as the leader that he does not understand and needs the statement or question rephrased.

With all these thoughts repeating in the back of my mind, Staff Sergeant Lebron and I approached the integrated formation consisting of our Marines and new Afghan partners.

"Gentleman, at ease. I am First Lieutenant Bodrog, and this is my Platoon Sergeant, Staff Sergeant Lebron. I will keep this short and to the point, as I hate to waste time. I expect great things from this combined action platoon in the months to follow. We are tasked and entrusted with being an integrated maneuver element for my battalion. You mission is as follows. The Marines from Hades First and Second Platoons will fully develop, partner, mentor, and train the Third and Fourth Tolai Afghan National Army Soldiers in zone in order to conduct integrated combat operations throughout Task Force Third Battalion, Third Marines battlespace and adjacent battlespaces." I repeated the mission one more time, as is doctrine for giving a mission statement, and then I continued to speak to the men.

"For my Marines, listen up. This is nothing new for us as a Corps. Historically, CAPs were achieved in our own past by Marines during the war in Vietnam. This is not against our doctrine as Marines. To my knowledge, this will be the first combined action platoon since the start of this war nine years ago. I expect you all to set the standard, be professional, and uphold the principles of our doctrine and Corps at all times.

"For the Afghan National Army Soldiers, these are my ground rules that are to be obeyed at all times. I expect two things out of each and every one of you. I expect you all first and foremost to be professionals. There are numerous things that divide us both as a culture and as a military, but there are also many things that unite us. I value your opinions and prejudices; however, this is not the time or the place for either. We need to believe in and ensure that our focus is on the traits that unite us in order to enable us to successfully partner together.

"The obvious hurdle we have to get through first is the language barrier. We speak English, and you all speak Dari or Pashtu. There will be a lot of frustration between both the Marines and Soldiers when it comes to carrying out simple commands. All I ask is patience because your frustration shows me an unmistakable attempt at trying to make this partnered unit work. I expect you all to learn some English, and I expect my Marines to learn some Dari and Pashtu.

"A majority of Marines share a Christian background while you are all of the Muslim faith. Religion is a great thing; however, it must not be a course of action to fight over in this respect. We all must respect each other's faith but not let it divide us. We must hold true to our values but not let them fuel our own personal hatred and discontent of one another.

"We are all here for the same reason regardless of our differences, and this should be the only thing that is relative. The reason is to kill Taliban. Regardless of what method we use to achieve this goal, the endstate will be the same: the enemy will be dead. The Taliban were responsible for training the cowards who attacked my country. They are also responsible for training the same cowards who are currently destroying yours. At the end of the day, let whatever motivates you be the desire to kill the cowards who have taken so much away from our nations and innocent families.

"My Marines of Hades Second Platoon will make you better. I expect you all to listen to my Marines and give them your 100 percent at everything you do as an individual and as an integrated unit.

"The other thing I expect out of you all is accountability. By accountability I mean be accountable for yourselves, your issued gear, your actions and inaction. I want you to be accountable for the man to your left and to your right as well as your own actions. Correct what needs to be corrected and discipline who needs to be disciplined according to the rules of our LSA.

"There will be no drug use. There will be no quitting. And there will be no questioning of the intent of me, my Platoon Sergeant, and my Marines. Furthermore, your Afghan Commanders were selected to participate in this combined unit, as were each and every one of you. For this reason, I ask you to give your loyalty and trust to them.

"I expect you to take care of the area where we are living. If you see trash, pick it up. If you see a Soldier sleeping on the guard post, correct him. Accountability encompasses all of our actions, and safety is at the forefront of everything we do. Safety is paramount, and we all need to protect each other.

"Does everyone understand?" I said to my new integrated unit, obviously unsure if the Afghan Soldiers understood or even comprehended our linguist, the ground rules I had laid down, or the mission for that matter.

With head nods and smiles on their faces, the Afghan Soldiers replied, "Nay," the word for yes in Dari.

I then turned to Staff Sergeant Lebron, and with a head nod, he started to speak. "I am Staff Sergeant Lebron, your new Platoon Sergeant. Like my Lieutenant said, we will not tolerate laziness or weakness. We have a saying in my platoon, and my Marines who are standing next to each and every one of you can attest to it. The saying is as follows: *Trample the weak, bury the dead, kill all that is different. Only the strong survive.* I will work hard for you and never quit on this unit as long as you all put out and work hard for me.

"My Marines will make you better. We will set the bar high, and then when you reach it, we will set it even higher. You will be the best, and you will know you are the best. Being the best is a standard I hold myself to and one that I will hold each and every one of you to. If you do not agree with something me or my Marines say or if you want to quit, the doorway is right behind me, gentlemen. My Marines are in this country fighting for your freedom and your way of life, so give them the respect and courtesy they deserve.

"After this formation, I want to see all of the Marine Squad Leaders and the Afghan Squad Leaders to discuss overall expectations and gear or uniform discrepancies. Gentleman, what we are creating here is something never achieved or accomplished in Afghanistan, and we are the only ones doing it now. Does anyone have any questions?" said my Platoon Sergeant confidently and with an underlying desire for an Afghan Soldier to test or question his method of thought just so he could kick him out of the formation and set the standard early on. Not one Afghan National Army Soldier questioned him.

"Very well then. I need all of the Squad Leaders on me. Olds, Brown, Guthrie, find your Afghan Squad Leader counterparts. Don't hold their hands but show them where they will be living and show them how they will be living in the tents our Marines put up for them. If they give you any problems or if issues arise, let me know. Also, I need gear or weapons discrepancies so we can knock it out early and ensure we are looking out for their troop welfare," he said, giving our Squad Leaders a huge responsibility to make sure their counterparts were good to go and ready for business.

"Roger that, Staff Sergeant," replied my three Squad Leaders.

Like clockwork the Marines started to interact with their counterparts while the Squad Leaders showed their new partners where they would be staying. This process was slow and uncomfortable at first, but once routine set in, so did interaction and a small layer of trust.

Discrepancies with the Afghan National Army Soldiers in terms of their personal gear and uniforms needed to be rectified first and foremost. The Soldiers had to look the part to play the part. For the Marines, interaction was truly professional in nature. I did not expect my men to get along with the Afghans and like each other like friends do. Neither did I expect them to tolerate, sympathize, and demonstrate compassion to mitigate our differences. We were not going to go out of our way to accommodate them. After all, we were all grown men and military professionals. There was no room for weakness or friendship in this respect.

I appreciated the fact that initially my men and the Afghans did not really like each other. Starting on an even plain had good potential to build strong camaraderie, competition, and a desire to get rid of all the weakness and mediocrity that could slow us down in battle. Sensitivity and socialism in a war zone does not breed the best; it breeds weakness and victimization. This was not going to be one big happy family but a functioning, highly skilled, and trained combined action platoon and eventually company. United States Marines, down to their core, are true professionals.

CHAPTER 41

Trial by error was the key methodology and course of action my platoon used to develop a solid training schedule based off our training and readiness (T&R) standards and Block I-IV training requirements. There were many cultural factors we had to take into account during training. In our training schedule, we had to build in time for routine breaks, prayer, chow, religious days off, etc. Little do people know that the Afghans' religion limits and controls even their military's daily conduct, especially in terms of their combat operations and capabilities.

The Afghan Soldiers always made it a point to make sure our combined training encompassed and facilitated their five daily prayer times, their two-hour chow breaks that occurred three times a day, and their Thursday night and Friday time off. This was a big deal for our new Soldiers and for my Marines. *With all this time off, how did the Afghans ever get anything done?*

As far as my Marines went, they did not believe in or understand what a day off was during a deployment. The only time they had off was when my Squad Leaders, Platoon Sergeant, and me stood post for them at a patrol base as a reward for hard work or during holidays such as the Fourth of July, Thanksgiving, or Christmas. As Marines, we improvise, adapt, and overcome, but this definitely fueled our contempt for them even more because these Soldiers had more time off than they did time working during certain weeks.

The majority of the Afghan Soldiers and local Afghans nationals we encountered were very mentally sensitive, unlike United States Marines. This is not to say that the majority are not hardened warriors. All in all, they are the best warriors I have ever encountered. However, they do not like to be yelled at and hate manual labor and anything that has to do with working hard. The majority of them do not fare well with criticism either, and they will whine if they are corrected for doing something wrong or incorrectly.

Early on, the biggest mistake my Marines and I committed was treating the Afghan Soldiers like recruits in boot camp when conducting our training. With little guidance on the proper way to instruct men with a third-world mind-set, we resorted to personal experiences in our method of training. As Marines, all of our initial training had come from boot camp or Officer Candidate School, so we stuck with what we knew worked best. The Afghan people and the Soldiers exist in a culture that learns by hardship and punishment. During the course of our initial training, many of my Marines yelled and screamed at them like drill instructors in boot camp in an attempt to capture their Afghan way of learning.

This way of instruction was a good stimuli and method initially for a few reasons. It definitely worked for some of the Afghan Soldiers and brought out their killer instinct, but at the same time it alienated a majority of the other Afghan Soldiers and made them feel resentment toward the Marines. After all, they were grown men and did not appreciate or respond well to being yelled at, especially by younger beardless men. Initially, this was a good method for the fact that we now knew what was not going to work. The drill instructor mentality was a good training method to build Marines but not to build the Afghan National Army Soldiers.

After a few days, my Marines and I finally resorted to a much slower, trial-and-error approach, taking small baby steps to achieve small goals. We eliminated treating them like boot camp recruits unless they really messed up and deserved a good vocal reaming. A majority of the time, Marines would not even waste their breath on the ignorance of the Afghan Soldiers and would go directly to their Squad Leaders to let them conduct the reprimand.

Many of the Afghan Soldiers became very responsive when they felt like they were equal to the Marines. When Marines conducted the training alongside the Afghan Soldiers, the group mentality set in, as did the sense of belonging to the group. After a few days of trial and error, the combined action platoon and company's training plan was developed, as well as the methodology behind its instruction. Much of this was created through our initial failures of instruction and pushing past these failures until we attained solutions.

Out of our trials and tribulations, my platoon agreed on utilizing a crawl, walk, run approach to our partnered training. We would legitimize the Afghan leadership and bring them to the same table as the Marine leadership to prove this was a joint effort. It would be frustrating and test every ounce of patience we had, but it was the course of action we had to choose.

The Japanese have a saying that goes, "The nail that stands up must be hammered down." We needed to make sure we used the group mentality approach to our training in order to bring every Soldier and Marine to a standard, thereby keeping the good Afghan Soldiers while identifying and eliminating the other Soldiers who did not fit the mold.

We initially conducted basic infantry tactic classes, sustainment training, and simple physical training exercise events to build cohesion and make our counterparts effective in combat. This training enabled our selection process of Afghan Soldiers to commence.

Chapter 42

The key to making the Afghan National Army Soldiers train and execute orders like we wanted them to be executed was not an easy task, but my platoon soon discovered the secret. There was a plethora of behind-the-scenes work that had to take place to facilitate the plan and mission.

The first thing that had to occur was that both Marine and Afghan Commanding Officers and Executive Officers had to be on board with the training and execution. This had to be achieved. At no time should Marines be allowed to give in to the Afghans' demands unless they conducted a cost-benefit analysis. Afghan Commanders were very greedy and corrupt leaders, and they had to know from the start that the Marines were in charge and that we were training their Soldiers to make them better fighters.

That said, living arrangements and intent for training had to be clearly discussed and formulated into action. In our case, both our units had to live with each other and see one another every day in order to forcibly integrate our platoons. Every night our Commanding Officer and usually First Lieutenant Miller or I would eat dinner with their leadership counterparts, conducting the face-to-face aspect and solidifying our partnership, training schedules, and focus of our newly integrated platoons.

We knew that by winning the trust and confidence of the Afghan leadership and taking time out of our day to make an attempt at partnering, our combined action platoons and company would be a success. Bringing the leadership to the table, discussing intent, and making them feel as if they were a part of the planning gave the Afghan leadership a sense of purpose and responsibility.

For the Marines of Hades Second Platoon, our Commanding Officer had put his reputation on the line to create the CAC for Task Force Third Battalion, Third Marines. Every night he sacrificed sleep and the opportunity to call his family at home in order to eat dinner and drink chai tea with a majority of the Afghan Commanders because he knew how effective a combined Marine and Afghan force could be against our enemy and for the future of Afghanistan.

A combined unit was able to cross more lines and break more cultural boundaries in combat than a Marine-only unit because this was the Afghans' country, not ours. They were not under the same ROEs that Marines were. They knew the customs, culture, and traditions much better than we did. They could look at an individual and know if he or she was Taliban or not.

Another secret in creating this unit was to legitimize their chain of command and give the illusion that the Afghan Platoon Commander and Platoon Sergeant were in control. What I mean by this is even though the Marines were in charge, we developed ways to show the Afghan Soldiers that their leadership was effective and capable of making decisions. Whether this was done by giving them credit for our work or honoring them with a job well done, we had to give the appearance that the Afghan leaders were involved in the decision-making process, not just the Marines, even though this was primarily the case.

At the end of the day, the Afghan Soldiers needed to trust and believe that their leadership was there to take care of them and mitigate the problems they faced. After all, Marines are not babysitters, and we had to teach them how to go about fixing their deficiencies, even more so without our help. My Platoon Sergeant and I mentored our counterparts and gave them all the answers on how to win and be successful by providing them all of the tools necessary to be effective leaders for their men.

However, we had to make sure the individual Afghan Soldiers would never know this. They could never know this. They could not be allowed to see the weakness of their leadership because it would delegitimize them. Trust in leadership comes from competency, loyalty, and troop welfare, among other things. There are no bad Soldiers, only bad leaders. My Platoon Sergeant and I knew we had to produce capable and effective Afghan counterparts who were legitimized in the eyes of their men and who at the same time followed the orders we gave them without question. Even though he and I provided the Afghans with logistical items such as boots, uniforms, and various military gear, we ensured that when the Afghan Soldiers received the items, they came from their Platoon Commander and Platoon Sergeant.

The one great thing about the Afghan Soldiers that worked in favor of my platoon was their loyalty to their command and their ability to follow orders from their leadership. No matter what the issue, when the Afghan Officers and senior enlisted Marines laid down the law, their subordinates did not question or cross them for literal fear of death or corporal punishment.

Platoon Sergeants and Platoon Commanders must play politics with each other. They have to know one another's strengths and weaknesses in depth and play on both when the time calls for it. They have to have a perfect balance with one another. Both must know the endstate as well and know who is in charge. They need to identify early on who the best and most effective leaders are and place them in positions of responsibility that will facilitate growth and understanding. Much of this is done by listening to their subordinate leaders.

In our case, early on my Platoon Sergeant and I made it clear to our Afghan counterparts that we were calling the shots and our Marines were in charge of the training of their men. We decentralized command to the lowest levels, allowing our Marine Squad Leaders to select their counterpart Afghan Squad Leaders so the integrated squads would be more effective in training and combat. We stacked the deck in our favor, sure, but when lives depend on critical decision-making skills, who wouldn't?

The next secret to our mission success rested in identifying any Afghan National Army Soldiers who could speak any English and had a positive attitude toward Marines and America. Once we discovered this, we then put those Soldiers in positions of leadership to mitigate any friction or backlash from the less responsive Afghan Soldiers. It was politics 101, but it was the only way to make the mission work. Positions of leadership were a great tool for power, and putting Afghan Soldiers who were sympathetic to our causes into leadership billets was essential to the success of the newly formed CAP and CAC.

The last course of action that had to occur for the CAC to work was forcibly integrating my United States Marines and Afghan National Army Soldiers to the point that they saw each other every day and were forced to interact. Both the Marines and Afghan Soldiers had to constantly interact with each other and learn one another's behavioral patterns in order to know what type of training worked and what type did not.

Chapter 43

Our Commanding Officer gave the Marines of Hades First and Second Platoons a timetable of two weeks to mentor, prepare, and train the Afghan National Army Soldiers for the conduct of integrated combat operations in our AO and adjacent battlespaces. It was a difficult task but not one that couldn't be executed.

Communication was the biggest hindrance on the combat training. My Marines and I did not know if the linguists understood or could much less describe the infantry TTPs that would be required of the Afghan Soldiers during the conduct of battle with the Taliban. We relied heavily on our linguists early on to conduct training, but once rounds started flying on the battlefield, linguists would be useless to us, and implicit communication through hand and arm signals would be the common language.

My Platoon Sergeant and I knew that if we relied less on linguists as time progressed in order to develop our hand and arm signals and sign language skills, it would build trust and camaraderie, especially when engaging with the enemy. When speaking through a linguist, conversations seemed more third person, and the tendency was to speak to the interpreter rather than the person you were communicating with. It was also one more layer of friction and uncertainty that could be peeled off, thereby reducing the fog we would encounter in a combat situation.

Another big setback for the Marines was the inability of the ANA Soldiers to understand the concept of time and space. Our Afghan Soldiers were consistently late for formations, training, and meetings.

Even worse, their leadership allowed this to occur and did not even hold themselves to the standard of being on time. They could not hold their own Soldiers to the same standard or else they would be seen as hypocrites. A military person with integrity cannot stand on the Holy Bible while they preach from it.

When my platoon formed up for accountability, the Afghan National Army Soldiers would constantly arrive late, change their personnel numbers, and add or drop Soldiers from their counts. Other times, an Afghan Soldier might be sick from drugs or be out doing a random task and would forgo their military obligations for a day or two. Accountability issues were a daily occurrence and a leadership failure on the part of my ANA Platoon Commander. Like I said, there are no bad Soldiers, only bad leaders. Not being on time or following orders had the potential to get my men killed. The leadership just did not emphasize the importance of being on time, and they did not understand the problems associated with not knowing where their Soldiers were during the course of a day's events.

As is the case with much of the Afghanistan military, most leadership is generally weak because the Afghan Army is generally weak. After all, the Afghan National Army is relatively new and has only been around for a few years. Regardless, I will argue that the Afghan Soldiers, for all of their many deficiencies, were quick learners and put out for Marines when their leadership was won over.

For Marines, improper accountability and being late is a no-go and makes a Marine look nasty and intolerable. If Marines do not make time lines, people can die. This is the reality and a standard to which we hold ourselves, whether life or death is in the balance or not. It goes back to having simple trust and confidence in one another. In the Marine Corps, if you say you are going to do something, you execute. If you are given a time line, you meet it. There is a saying in the Marine Corps that if you are on time, you are late, and if you are early, you are on time. Marines are never late, are always on time, and know the consequences if they fail to execute a task in a timely manner.

To the Marines, seeing their Afghan Soldiers consistently being late demonstrated a nonchalant attitude, one of disrespect and dishonor toward our efforts to make them a better fighting unit. It portrayed a sense of weakness and a lack of commitment, and it bred distaste for partnering. I can honestly say that early on in our training, frustration plagued my Marines and Corpsmen, but it was good because it proved to me that they cared enough to train the ANA Soldiers.

The responsibility on my small unit leaders was huge, and it had to be fostered and allowed to grow for the CAC to work. Individual Marines had to pick up the slack on numerous occasions and take charge of their Afghan Soldier counterparts to point them in the right direction. My men were the mental spark needed to up the evolutionary progress of the Afghan Soldiers. These small unit leadership acts directly resulted in the high level of success the Marines of Hades Second Platoon attained, especially as part of a fully integrated combined action platoon.

CHAPTER 44

The first two days of combined Marine and Afghan training were merely introductory trial-and-error days. My Marines and Afghan Soldiers faced many trials and tribulations. The hours of instruction were painful and produced few results. Frustration levels on both sides of the sphere were intense. This was good though, because in the process, my Marines and I were eliminating what did not work and building on what did. As I said earlier, approaching training with the boot camp mentality was not the best approach because we were not building Marines. We had to go with an easier approach to training because we were building Soldiers.

The third day of our training was the first actual day of no-nonsense training. By the third day, my Marines and I were able to correct the deficiencies of the ANA Soldiers in terms of their conduct during formations and their military appearance and conduct. They started to look like a professional military, which was half the battle. We started with the basic disciplines and built off them. We focused immediately on the demeanor they were expected to uphold when they were in our LSA as a way to make them part of the "herd" instinct.

With constant assistance and guidance from Hades 6, my Platoon Sergeant and I were able to work with the Afghan Army's supply unit and acquire all the essential military gear they required to conduct missions. What we could not acquire from the Afghans was supported by my battalion and Battalion Commander. These supplies included new uniforms, pyro, boots, NATO rifles, ammunition, camelbacks, rucksacks, etc.

The biggest problem for the ANA Soldiers was that their military was corrupt, which meant gear was hard to come by. Their military Commanders would steal money, gear, and weapons and then sell them on the black market, leaving their Soldiers with nothing. Their leadership sold water, gasoline, and JP-8 fuel to the local nationals for profit. This caused a big problem for our mobile combat power because the Afghans continually ran out of gas or had none at all to fuel their vehicles.

The local nationals eventually started to complain as well because the quality of gasoline kept degrading when they bought it from the Afghan Soldiers. Locals started to notice that the gasoline was becoming more and more diluted with water. This was done so that the Afghan Army could reap more profit off the free gasoline the United States Military provided to them to conduct military operations. If it was not for our CO and XO realizing this and devising ways to help out the local nationals and combat the corruption from the Afghan Soldiers and Afghan leadership, we would have been a failure from the beginning.

By the third day, the CAC had risen from the abyss, and my Marines and I had a training schedule set and ready for execution. Every morning at 0600 we conducted a fully integrated formation during which we accounted for the combined action company's two platoons reinforced of sixty Marines and sixty Afghan Soldiers and all of their serialized weapons and military gear. Accountability for our integrated weapons section, which consisted of nineteen Marines and Afghan Soldiers, was also conducted at this time.

Formation was conducted at 0600 because prior to this time, the ANA Soldiers conducted prayer and chow. During the formation, my Platoon Sergeant continually instructed and critiqued his Afghan counterpart, stressing to him the importance of accountability and how to conduct formalized personnel and weapons counts during formations. He even went as far as teaching his Afghan Platoon Sergeant, who was named Tay-Jee-Dee, logistics and how to conserve water and chow for mission sustainment so that the Soldiers' welfare was always at the forefront. It was a painful process each morning, especially if the Afghan Soldiers decided to behave badly or unprofessionally.

It usually took my Platoon Sergeants roughly a half hour to an hour to conduct roll call, check the Afghan Soldiers for drugs, and mitigate any issues we had from the previous day. Usually by 0630, all the issues from the morning were taken care of. The Marines and ANA Soldiers would then immediately conduct a police call of the LSA. It was a task that was good for both my Marines and Afghan Soldiers because it was a simple task in which both units could complete on the same operational level while at the same time fostering teamwork and building discipline and cohesion. It was a task with a clear endstate and one that was easy to accomplish.

Police call and cleanup of the LSA built pride in both units because the LSA became a tangible body that my Marines and Afghan Soldiers worked together on making neat and clean, striving always toward perfection and defensive improvement. As with all successes with the Afghans, a Marine unit might take ten steps forward one day and eleven steps back the next day. It was always a mentally comical sight to see an Afghan Soldier, immediately after conducting police call, throw water bottles and trash on the deck, knowing full well camp cleanup was conducted every morning for that very reason. No matter how many ways my Marines tried to spark a sense of evolution, the Afghans always ended up resorting to their primordial ways.

Once police call culminated, the Marines turned to physical training (PT). PT consisted of stretching, calisthenics, and a run around the internal perimeter at FOB Geronimo. At first, achieving a physical standard for both my Marines and Afghan National Army Soldiers was difficult because my Marines destroyed any Afghan Soldier in terms of physical fitness. Numerous times within the first week, my Afghan counterpart complained that exercising was too difficult, singling out Sergeant Olds, Sergeant Brown, and Sergeant Guthrie as being too rough and aggressive toward his men. Many times the Platoon Commander threatened to quit. It was a game he constantly played to get out of work. The simple truth was that no matter how many times he threatened to quit, he was obligated by his chain of command to integrate with my Marines.

My three Squad Leaders were very competitive, cock-strong Marines who did not tolerate mediocrity or want to hear about a grown man's feelings being hurt. They were alpha males, and I expected them to act like it. To rectify the situation, my Marines and I came to the agreement that PT would be conducted twice a day. In the morning, it would be light to benefit the Afghan Soldiers, and in the afternoon or evening my Marines had the opportunity to conduct a harder workout if they chose to do so by themselves. PT in the morning would even be delegated by my Squad Leaders to their Fire Team Leaders to foster their own growth as future leaders of Marines.

Another obstacle my Platoon Sergeant and I had to hurdle was getting the Afghan Platoon Sergeant and Platoon Commander to take part in the physical fitness activities with their Soldiers. At first the Afghan leadership wanted nothing to do with their Soldiers, striving toward the Russian model of drinking tea all day while their Soldiers did the hard work. The Afghan leadership needed to understand that their men would fight and die for them even more if they were involved in their lives and demonstrated their merits in front of them.

Between 0730 and 0900, my ANA Soldiers conducted their prayer and chow time. Because our training partially involved taking into account the needs of the ANA, we were required to constantly improvise and adapt our training schedule to meet their requests while maintaining a fluid conducive training regimen. This was at times a bit frustrating, especially when at the last moment they would inform us that their religious rituals varied on that given day and we would have to shift or omit training to meet their time lines. We all knew this was an excuse to get out of training because they were working hard and wanted a break. However, in some of these cases when frustrations were running high and patience was about out, it was nice break for the Marines to cancel some parts of the daily training.

During these extended hours of replanning the conduct of training, my Squad Leaders were able to focus more on training their Marines in more advanced techniques and tactics that would not be covered while training the Afghan Soldiers. This allowed them to continually refine their own military occupational specialties (MOS) and stay sharp with their infantry skills and continuing actions.

At approximately 0900 on most days, classes would start, and Marines would begin to instruct their Afghan counterparts in the basic TTPs with respect to the conduct of the Infantry Training and Readiness (T&R) Manual and United States Marine Corps doctrine. The Marines utilized the cooler hours of the morning to conduct the lecture portion of the classes, leaving the hotter parts of the day to conduct practical application.

Classes usually ran until approximately 1200 with a few breaks in between. My Marines used a variety of areas to facilitate classroom instruction, including the chow hall, LSA, and various shops and areas around the FOB that were conducive to training for combat operations. Areas around the FOB conducive to combat training involved the HLZ, war rooms, the battalion aid station (BAS) and the Motor-T lot.

Between the hours of 1200 and 1400, our Afghan National Army Soldiers had break time to conduct prayer and chow. This gave my men a chance to refit, prepare for afternoon classes, and address any administrative issues they had with their Squad Leaders and my Platoon Sergeant. The norm for this period of time was usually a thirty to forty-five minute lunch break, and the rest of the time went to preparation for the upcoming classes and periods of instruction.

During this time, my Marines had the opportunity to complete Marine Corps Institute courses (MCIs) or various other professional military education (PME) classes tasked down to them by their Squad Leaders. The completion of MCIs became a personal mission for Staff Sergeant Lebron and me because it furthered their educational development, fostered discipline, and enhanced their career opportunities in the Corps and life. A Marine will not sit by idle if their leadership is constantly challenging them to make them better.

From approximately 1400 until 1700, my Marines conducted a brief overview of the classes covered in the morning and then rolled right into the practical application and sustainment of all that was taught. After their break, and depending on the mood of our ANA Soldiers, my Marines would dictate how smooth or chaotic the remainder of the training day would go. There were times we were able to cover every class we set out to conduct in our training schedule, but other times we could not.

The usual complaints for not completing class instruction or sustainment training were that it was either too hot for classes or that the Afghan Soldiers themselves were tired. Regardless of the reason they presented in an effort to end training early, they usually began gaffing off my Marines and Corpsmen by bringing about unneeded hostility. Usually, this indirectly ended up forcing my Marines to become frustrated and wanting to end instruction early for the day.

This shortfall in conjunction with the language barrier could bring even the most successful of days to a bitter end, filling it with anger, resentment, and frustration. My Marines always watched for these early warning signs and either tried to teach something different or offer the Afghan Soldiers a short break so they could refit. They also watched in case our ANA Soldiers decided to go rogue and shoot one of us.

CHAPTER 45

The first week ended with modest progress. The CAC's foundation had now been laid, and we started to see an improvement in our Afghan counterparts. By the end of week one, as my Marines maintained this schedule, a dramatic change in the demeanor and performance of the Afghan National Army Soldiers started to form. They had been the like the baseball team in the movie *The Bad News Bears* when we were first handed their platoon. At the end of the first week, they were slowly starting to become disciplined and retentive to our periods of classroom instruction.

The culmination of the first week was an awards ceremony for the Afghan Soldiers to boost morale and encourage productivity. Rewards were a great motivational tool. The awards ceremony consisted of one or two Soldiers being picked to receive either a letter of recognition or a Benchmade knife as a reward for hard work during the week. This was also an indirect way to incentivize lazy Soldiers to work hard, because rewards for merit always breed competition and pride.

The Afghan National Army Soldiers seemed more confident than they had on day one because they now saw their work paying off. They saw how hard my Marines were working for them to make them better Soldiers. Some, though not all, respected my Marines for this. It was funny to watch, and little by little our Afghan counterparts started to follow Marines around the LAS, go out of their way to eat with them, and try to emulate the way they walked and acted on a daily basis. They started to carry themselves like Marines too. Personally, I think the Soldiers started to realize that there was no way out. The Afghan

Soldiers and my men were now together in their agenda to form the CAC, and they knew this was now their mission.

Our Afghan Soldiers started to quickly pick up English words and phrases and would greet my Marines with "good morning," "good afternoon," and "good evening" as they walked through my LSA. They were slowly turning into civilized gentlemen and professional killers. They were no longer throwing their trash all over the ground as they pleased like uncivilized beasts. Instead, they started using the receptacle and actually took initiative in policing their own living area. They still did not understand the benefit of not living where they threw their trash, but just like Pavlov's experiment, the Afghan Soldiers understood (like a bell going off in their heads) that if they kept throwing trash on the ground, they were going to keep picking it up every morning. It was amazing to see, but they started to become products of the environment of living around my Marines.

What made my Marines and I really believe our training was paying off was that our Afghan Soldiers were no longer walking around the LSA with their fingers on the triggers of their rifles or with loaded magazines in them. This was a huge step in our training because the ANA had no concept of weapons safety, and they were infamous across our AO for repeated negligent discharges and self-inflicted gunshot wounds. They had also earned a dangerous reputation of becoming upset and subsequently conducting shooting rampages on coalition forces, in particular the French and the British, during our deployment.

In one particular case, when my platoon was conducting Operation New Dawn in Shorsurak, we heard of reports over our radio of Afghan National Army Soldiers in Northern Afghanistan opening fire and killing a few British Royal Marines at one of their operating bases.

With verbal utilization and strict enforcement of a simple brevity code of "click, click" developed by my Marines, the Afghan National Army Soldiers understood the condition four of the M16-A4 service rifle. Condition four is when the weapon is on "safe," the magazine is removed from the rifle, the round is removed from the chamber, the ejection port cover is closed, and the shooter's finger is straight and off the trigger. When they noticed Afghans walking around the FOB or our LSA with their fingers on the triggers of their rifles and magazines inserted, my Marines would simply utter these two brief words, and instinctively our ANA would clear their rifles and ensure they were in condition four.

Within the first week, my Marines and I had to decide which classes were most pertinent for our ANA Soldiers. By the end of third day of combined training we were able to judge from their performance and capabilities what should be priority on periods of instruction. We decided the selection of classes based on how much the classes would benefit both the Marines and Afghan Soldiers as an integrated unit, especially during sustained combat operations. My platoon ended up teaching a multitude of classes through the methods of lecture, video, PowerPoint, hip pocket, and practical application.

We conducted a variety of medical classes in which our Platoon Corpsmen provided lectures on combat lifesaving and medical employment in the event that our unit sustained a casualty. The primary focus was to prepare our Afghan Soldiers with workable knowledge of how to deal with incidences they would face, especially in the absence of my Marines. These incidences included but were not limited to basic combat medical treatment, heat-related injuries they could face in the 130-degree or higher temperatures, how to apply a tourniquet to stop massive bleeding from a gunshot wound, and how to conduct casualty evacuations via ground or air.

My Corpsmen incorporated PT in conjunction with medical knowledge in order to sustain the periods of instruction, which they taught through repetition and muscle memory. For example, combat lifesaving drills started with a fifty-meter run to a "casualty." Once the Afghan Soldier reached the casualty, he would have to apply a tourniquet to a "gunshot wound" and then buddy carry the casualty to the mock HLZ approximately one hundred meters away. We would then have the Afghan Soldiers practice radio procedures to call in helicopters in support of the drill being conducted.

It was combat conditioning at its finest, and it helped build the stamina our Afghan counterparts lacked, giving them confidence that if their counterparts were shot or bleeding, they would instinctively know what to do while still staying engaged with the enemy.

My Squad Leaders, aside from running PT sessions, conducted big-picture classes on Marine Corps doctrine, American history, and English to facilitate the Afghan Soldiers' understanding of our American culture and simple commands from my Marines. Contrary to popular belief, the Afghans ate these classes up and were hungry to learn about things like Christianity, the Marine Corps warrior code, the World Wars, and the involvement of Marines in those wars. They devoured English classes and continually went up to Marines to spark dialogue in an effort to improve their grammar in conversation.

Subsequently, the Afghan Squad Leaders taught a few periods of instruction on the role of America in Afghanistan and the Afghan military's chain of command. It was amazing to see and hear how much they appreciated Americans in their country. The only thing they made sure to mention was their disappointment in the fact that they thought our foreign policy was shortsighted. They were disappointed at America because anytime our political leaders made progress or promises to them, we would then leave the country and leave Afghanistan alone to fend against the wolves. However, they were smart enough to know that my Marines and the military in general were not the ones making these decisions; we were only the instruments carrying out the foreign policy of our leaders.

My Squad Leaders would instruct their Afghan counterparts on leadership and accountability, highlighting the duties and responsibilities of small unit leaders. They each set aside one-on-one time with their counterparts, instructing them on the value of decentralized command and how to lead their Soldiers in training and in battle. My three Squad Leaders tirelessly taught their Afghan Squad Leaders the duties inherent of an effective Squad Leader and how it was their responsibility to obey the orders of their highers and carry out their commands.

My Fire Team Leaders taught periods of instruction on a multitude of infantry subjects such as the conduct of the offense and defense, hand and arm signals, implicit communication, techniques to defeat IEDs, military operations in urban terrain (MOUT), formations, patrolling tactics, movement to contact, buddy rushes, buddy drills, room clearing, and tactical site exploitation. Basically, if it involved infantry tactics or Marine Corps doctrine, my Fire Team Leaders accomplished it. The endstate was essentially that each of my Marines was to create the Afghan version of himself as best he could.

The use and utilization of hand and arm signals and implicit communication was our biggest moneymaker and paid us dividends. If the Afghans could understand simple commands and signals, we did not need to rely on our linguists. Sign language would become a primary method of communication during tactical combat operations because it was easy to understand and eliminated the language barrier that divided us both. Sign language was universal, and applying it for operational conditions and movements was a way to unite the Marines and Afghans and break down the language barrier that caused division.

My individual riflemen were responsible for teaching classes to their counterparts on weapons maintenance, assembly, and disassembly. They were in charge of upholding the conduct of the Afghan Soldiers throughout the day and made any necessary spot or on-scene corrections when the Afghan National Army Soldiers messed up. They policed all the little infractions to prevent big infractions from building up and occurring.

CHAPTER 46

By the end of the first week, the major disadvantage in training was still the internal friction I received from my Marines in educating the ANA Soldiers. Marines are trained to quickly and obediently follow and carry out orders to achieve mission accomplishment. The ANA Soldiers continued to display problems with time and space and consistently arrived late for classes. No matter how many times they were given a time hack or told to be somewhere, they just did not have a concept or even grasp the repercussions of being late. But my Platoon Sergeant and I changed all of that. Under the mentorship and guidance of our Commanding Officer, we were able to develop a method for handling the situation.

When it came to discipline, because we were a fully integrated unit, we had to give the ANA Soldiers and their leadership the impression that treatment of my Marines and the Afghan Soldiers were equal. Like I said earlier, the Afghan people understand physical punishment and are ruled by the sword, not harsh words and etiquette. They fear the stick rather than the carrot. So when it came to punishment, we had to make it appear that my Marines were suffering with them (even though this was not true). It was going to be a head game but an effective one for the benefit of the CAC.

Whenever my Platoon Sergeant or myself saw our ANA losing their discipline or making mistakes, we would pull the Afghan Commander and his Platoon Sergeant to the side and address them one-on-one. Instead of singling out their Soldiers for committing an infraction such as talking on a cell phone or improperly handling a weapon, we would inform their Commanders that we saw both Marines and Afghan Soldiers committing an offense. This way, the appearance that the Marines were messing up was now a justification for the Afghan Commander to punish his own men.

In reality, the Afghan Soldiers were the ones messing up, but we had to make a clear attempt to make discipline seem fair even though my men were constantly displaying correct behavior. My leadership and I made sure our Marines knew this, and we explained it to them beforehand so they did not have the impression that what they were doing was wrong. Instead, it helped them understand that it was meant to develop the Afghan Soldiers so they would learn from their mistakes, which would enhance their overall partnering capabilities.

Marines are indifferent when it comes to corporal punishment. We simply do not instigate it or practice it probably as much as we should compared to the amount of paperwork we push for rule breaking. The ANA Soldiers, on the other hand, use corporal punishment as their main means of discipline. That said, when we presented our case to our Afghan counterparts, Staff Sergeant Lebron and I gave them appropriate solutions to rectify the offenses. Our solution was purely a suggestion in word only, but the appearance was all that mattered.

When the Afghan Commanders asked how the Marines would be punished, we informed them that they would have negative paperwork go in their military records and if it continued they would receive lashings or beatings by myself or Staff Sergeant Lebron. Like I said before and want to reinforce, these were only words. Staff Sergeant Lebron and I never beat our Marines. Words have meaning though, and if we would have said we gave our Marines a stern talking to, we would have looked like weak leaders in front of our Afghan counterparts.

However, this type of mentality is what the Afghan Soldiers understood. A good measure of leadership is knowing your environment and your friendly and enemy forces. My leadership knew our counterparts' mentality with regard to punishment. Being beaten by a senior leader, in the Afghan mind-set, was the ultimate form of disgraceful punishment for a dishonorable act. Being beaten resulted in shame or disgrace and for that reason was justified in their warrior culture.

This had a great effect on our Afghanistan counterparts because, like I said, they feared the whip. Rumors spread just as fast in the Afghan National Army as they did in the United States Marine Corps. When individual Afghan Soldiers found out that their Marine counterparts were being "beaten," they made a ferocious attempt at correcting their deficiencies and working for the Marines. They gave their own leaders zero excuse to punish them.

The Afghan Soldiers even started to feel partially responsible for Marines getting "beaten" by their superiors because deep down when they found out what offense was committed, they knew they were doing it also and could be "beaten" next. This made them work even harder for my Marines because now they cared enough to help them not get beaten. Sure, it was a mental game, but psychological warfare has its advantages, and mission accomplishment requires improvisation and adaptation to overcome obstacles.

These actions forced our Afghanistan Commanders to start stepping up to the plate. The Afghan Commander and Platoon Sergeant did not want to look weak in front of the Marines because like all good Commanders, they loved their men to death and wanted the best for them. Thus, whenever Staff Sergeant Lebron and I informed the Afghan Commander we were disciplining our Marines for messing up, he would also discipline his Soldiers in an effort to maintain the standard of the Marines and look strong in front of me and my Platoon Sergeant. It was in this manner and through careful manipulation that we were able to discipline the Afghan Soldiers who committed offenses. What their discipline turned out to be, I cannot say; however, I never witnessed the Afghan leadership abusing their Soldiers because of anything my leadership said or did.

Of course, mind games cannot be limited to just words. Once in a while actions must be visual to be believed. To get around this, Staff Sergeant Lebron and I enacted police calls two or three times a day. We justified this to the Afghanistan Commander by saying Marines and Afghan Soldiers were constantly messing up and needed to learn discipline. We used hygiene and cleanliness as our main reason and said that as long as Marines and Afghan Soldiers kept throwing trash on the ground of our LSA, we would conduct police calls.

For Marines, living clean and police calling are a way of life; it is built into them on day one when they step onto the yellow footprints. It is not punishment; it is expected and a part of them.

It is not the same for the Afghan Soldiers, who willingly chose to live in their own filth. For my Marines, police call was a normal routine conducted after every formation and looked at as a break from the hard work of the day. For the Afghan Soldiers, it was manual labor that was beneath them and shameful punishment for messing up.

CHAPTER 47

One of the biggest hurdles my platoon had to face was the fact that both the Afghan and Muslim culture severely limited the Afghan Soldiers' training abilities. The Afghan National Army Soldiers had to have three chow times a day and be allowed to pray five times a day because of their culture and religion. The Afghanistan Soldiers had to be given every Thursday night off to prepare for their Friday religious prayer day. It was very frustrating to build a schedule around these issues, but success lay in the frustrations my Marines encountered. Our opportunity in training the Afghan National Army led into planning for future missions and operations.

The Marines of Hades Second Platoon could not foresee every mission coming down the stovepipe, so we had to plan for every contingency. After all, we were our Battalion Commander's personal maneuver element and could be called into action as the battalion's QRF at any moment in support of myriad combat operations and situations. This did hinder the direction of training because not all missions allowed us to properly prepare for the friction and uncertainty common in warfare. However, certain operations scheduled for our CAP or CAC helped my platoon focus on certain training aspects.

If we were to conduct a deliberate clearing mission, my Marines would focus on the basics of room clearing, conducting cordons, searches, and detainee handling. Classes would be basic but enough for the ANA Soldiers to grasp and understand. My Marines would touch on tactical site exploitation and hit the wave tops on proper evidence handling and forensic collection. We taught the Afghans how to use electronic countermeasures to defeat IEDs and how to use compact metal detectors to locate pressure plate IEDs hidden underneath walkways in compounds. We even taught them how to use our IED detection dogs to defeat IEDs and showed them how to insert a catheter with IV fluids into their veins when they became overheated or dehydrated on long missions.

If we had an operation in which my integrated platoon was tasked to conduct a blocking position somewhere in the middle of a desert or on a road, my Marines would cover the TTPs of proper vehicle checkpoint searching procedures for vehicles and personnel. We would give the Afghan Soldiers combat hunter classes and teach them how to profile and identify possible suicide vehicles or suicide bombers. We would train them to observe vehicle anomalies such as new tires, missing floorboards, or extra compartments that could signal that a vehicle either possibly had a bomb or was hiding something illegal.

Since my combined action company had an organic mobile element and my CAP was tasked to be the battalion's helicopter assault platoon, my men constantly rehearsed loading and unloading procedures for our vehicle and helicopter assets. My Marines ran speed drills in which the focus was to enhance the time it took for the Afghan Army Soldiers to get ready from start to finish loading and unloading vehicles. We had to make them fast, and we constantly tried to improve their preparation time. We drove throughout the FOB or conducted mobile insert drills in the desert to help with mission preparedness, coordination, and execution.

We conducted helicopter landing zone drills with our Afghan Soldiers. We instructed our partners how to set security on and off a helicopter and why it was important to have security for an inbound or outbound helo at all times. We would practice loading in sticks, which was the manifest for loading a helicopter, and practiced mock security actions once we landed and dismounted the helicopter in a hostile area.

We executed these drills, particularly focusing on the time from when the order was issued to when the Squad Leaders were briefed and backbriefed their Marines and Soldiers, informing them of the situation. We then would time the individual Marines and Afghan Soldiers on how quickly they prepared their military gear and concordantly staged it in preparation for the mission at hand.

CHAPTER 48

Throughout the first week of training our ANA Soldiers, the focus was purely administrative and tactical, not operational. The Afghan Soldiers had to learn classes on military TTPs and earn the mental and physical confidence needed first before they could practically apply them in a combat situation. The first week of training was rigorous and frustrating but by far necessary to be effective in a combat against the Taliban.

The second week of training was devoted to sustainment and testing the skills that would enable my Afghan Soldiers to be both proficient killers in a firefight and gentleman in a COIN situation when dealing with local nationals. In other words, we were training them how to be "smiling killers."

The first two days of the second week of training started with fully integrating the fire teams and squads from our CAP without the constant assistance of linguists and senior leadership. We slowly evolved from integrated formations to an integrated platoon mind-set in which leadership was more hands-off and responsibilities were decentralized down to the lowest rifleman. We started conducting local security patrols inside FOB Geronimo and around its exterior. During these patrols, we focused on rehearsing various tactical formations, buddy drills of fire, movement to contact, maneuvers, and many other aspects inherent in the conduct of patrols. In our integrated patrols, we used a one-to-one Marine and Afghan Soldier ratio to facilitate speed and control.

Next to all of my Marines in the patrol formation was an Afghan Soldier. Each Afghan Soldier had specific instructions to mirror the movements and conduct of my Marines during this part of training. It was a simple concept known widely throughout the United States Marine Corps as the buddy system, and it was very easy for our foreign partners to grasp. This system brought the Marines and Afghans closer because the buddy system approach promoted reliance on each other and forced interaction.

From sunup to sundown, my Marines conducted rehearsals until movement inside each patrol became muscle memory. Our ANA Soldiers did not understand every concept we threw at them, but they did sustain many and knew the basic fundamentals necessary for patrolling. The Afghan Soldiers grasped the staggered tactical column and wedge formations, which we utilized many times during combat patrols.

Our intent was to have them learn echeloning, a type of patrol in which each Marine is positioned successively to the left or right of the rear unit to form an oblique line. However, it proved too difficult a concept for them to understand and utilize in a short period of time. The echelon formation was great against the enemy in our area, who constantly tried to flank Marine units in firefights and ambushes. The echelon formation, in Afghanistan, was the preferred method of my platoon because it was a perfect configuration to outflank the enemy in an array of combat situations.

My Platoon Sergeant and I employed Afghan Fire Team Leaders inside our Marine squads and allowed them to control the movement of both Marines and Afghan National Army Soldiers in a patrol formation. In reality, if rounds were to start flying downrange at us, my Marines would have to step in and lead the patrol. However, in practice, the Afghan Soldiers were starting to implement and utilize our concepts. The Afghan Soldiers we selected as Fire Team Leaders placed themselves at points of friction and in positions in which they could lead their team both in a wedge or column. The Afghan Fire Team Leaders learned to utilize the hand and arm signals my Marines used to control the direction and movement of their integrated fire teams.

The essence of time was always against my Marines when it came to training their ANA Soldiers. The emphasis for training always focused on what worked and building off of those successes. Since the Afghans could understand and employ the staggered tactical column and wedge formations, my Marines built on and employed it. Since they could not grasp echeloning, we threw it out.

My Marines took the basic concepts the Afghans sustained and then threw curveballs at them. They patrolled the wedge and then simulated taking contact and performing buddy rushes. They patrolled the column and simulated the conduct of time-sensitive missions, forcing their units to make time hacks at mock checkpoints. They enhanced their TTPs of patrolling by simulating getting hit by an IED or taking indirect fire and subsequently responding to it by taking the appropriate resolving actions.

Since the Afghans understood basic English coupled with tactical hand and arm signals, we sustained it and advanced their practical knowledge of it. Every day after class was conducted, we culminated our training with written and verbal examinations focusing on military tactics, American history, Afghanistan history, grammar, and hand and arm signals. This reinforced that what my Marines were teaching was being remembered and sustained, ensuring that the training was working because the Afghan Soldiers were cognitively learning. Surprisingly enough, these simple periods of instruction were the ones that made the CAC successful. In the absence of a linguist, these basic concepts enhanced both implicit and explicit communication between my Marines and Afghan Soldiers.

Everything that benefited the evolution of training was built upon, and everything that denigrated training was thrown out. The reality of it was that there was so much we needed to teach our Afghan Army partners in order to conduct successful operations, but we could teach only the little they could retain in such a short amount of time. The other half of our training focused on the "killology" aspect of military training, including the practical application and employment of our weapons systems.

On the one hand, my CAP had to master the techniques and tactics of the weapons systems, and on the other hand, the platoon had to have the utmost proficiency in the procedures of employing them against the enemy. Rehearsals and classes would only take a unit so far. If a unit could not effectively employ their weapons and kill the enemy, the enemy would win. In combat, it is said that one does not rise to the occasion; he or she falls back on the level of his or her training. The only way to measure the effectiveness of training was on the battlefield with the Taliban.

Marines are self-declared masters of marksmanship, and we pride ourselves on the phrase "Every Marine a Rifleman." Regardless of MOS, every Marine is a basic Rifleman and must be proficient on the service rifle. That said, the Afghan National Army was the antithesis of this mind-set.

During our time in Afghanistan, ANA Soldiers were probably the last people anyone wanted to trust, let alone fight alongside. Their reputation for negligent discharges and incidents of friendly fire solidified this way of thinking. They were notorious for shooting themselves with their own weapons and displayed zero understanding for weapon safety. Luckily, my Marines knew this and dedicated our first week and a half of training to instilling weapons handling and safety in their training.

The early part of the second week of training was devoted to actual practical application and sustainment on the weapons systems themselves. My Platoon Sergeant and I were both in charge of and responsible for the employment of the weapons for both our CAP and integrated weapons section.

My Squad Leaders constantly supervised and ensured their Marines were going over weapons safety and knew the conditions and employment of the M16-A4 service rifle, M203 grenade launcher, and M249 semiautomatic weapon, which were organic to the platoon.

While my platoon conducted their training, simultaneously Sergeant Smith, the integrated Weapons Section Leader, and Corporal Bennett, the Assistant Section Leader, conducted classes and gun drills for on the M240B medium machine gun and 60mm mortar system with the Marines and Afghans.

Sergeant Smith and his Mortarmen, along with Corporal Bennett and his Machine Gunners, developed a rigorous training schedule that was overseen by the Platoon Sergeants of Hades First and Second Platoons.

To my knowledge, this was the first integrated weapons section in Afghanistan since the start of the war nine years earlier. By the time my Section Leaders were done training their ANA Soldiers, they would be trained and capable to employ our M240B medium machine gun and 60mm mortar weapon systems effectively in both training and combat.

Our three Mortarmen under the command of Sergeant Smith trained their five Afghan Mortarmen counterparts on the T&R standards of the 60mm mortar. Classes taught by my Marines to the Afghan Soldiers focused primarily on the TTPs of the 60mm mortar gun system, which included sinking the baseplate, mounting the gun, prefire safety checks, large and small deflection elevation changes, direct lay, employment in the offense and defense, firing handheld, nomenclature, and preparing ammunition.

Our seven Machine Gunners, under the command of Corporal Bennett, trained their four Afghan Machine Gunners on various TTPs of the M240B medium machine gun, which included disassembly and reassembly, weapons maintenance, rates of fire, talking guns, employment in the offense and defense, capabilities and limitations, immediate and remedial action, basic gun drills, and how to construct range cards.

In order for the Afghan Soldiers to effectively sustain the weapons knowledge my Marines were teaching, we had to conduct practical weapons employment. The CAC, along with the integrated weapons section, did this through integrated live-fire weapons ranges. With the help of our Commanding Officer and his command team, who were absolutely vital to the successes of the CAC, we were able to conduct training on a live-fire weapons range named Juarez Firing Range, which was located in the desert roughly one kilometer northwest of FOB Geronimo. Juarez Firing Range was a reset training range previous battalions operating out of FOB Geronimo had constructed for sustainment training.

My Platoon Sergeant and I were able to develop courses of fire that would be a good measuring tool to see what type of standard to set for our Afghan partners to judge both their measures of performance and measures of effectiveness. Because time was always a limiting factor on training, our ability to test our Afghan Soldiers on their weapons systems was limited to one day of fire per weapon.

The latter part of the second week was broken down into three live-fire days. On Wednesday, my Marines tested the Afghan National Army Soldiers on the M16-A4 and the M249, on Thursday they tested firing the M240B medium machine gun, and on Saturday they tested the employment of the 60mm mortar gun system.

Developing the overall scheme of maneuver, believe it or not, was actually more difficult than conducting the range. There was a lot of behind-the-scenes actions that had to be conducted, and the biggest trial we faced was getting our battalion to buy off on and believe in the effectiveness of the live-fire confirmation training. Thanks to our Commanding Officer, who conducted the behind-the-scenes deals, we were able to conduct the live-fire weapons ranges.

Developing an overall course of fire and scheme of maneuver was difficult because we did not have enough time to make our Afghans experts, so we had to measure their standard of success on the weapons by making sure they had a general understanding of the weapon system and a general ability to employ that weapon system. They were not going to have the luxury of entire weeks devoted to firing the weapon to gain proficiency; they had a week and a half of classes and three days of live-fire confirmation.

Chapter 49

At 0600 on Wednesday morning, the entire combined action company, consisting of 120 Marines and Afghan Soldiers from Hades First, Second, and Weapons Platoons conducted their twenty-minute tactical column movement to the Juarez Firing Range. Upon arrival at the range, our Marines swept the area for IEDs, and then we posted security to the north, east, south, and west to provide protection during our courses of fire.

Preparations for the range included obtaining paper "zeroing" targets, setting them up, determining the amount Afghan Soldiers per course of fire and relay, and determining where the live-fire lanes would be located. My Marines and Afghans would conduct their course of fire from both the thirty-six-yard and one-hundred-meter firing lines. They would fire three courses of fire from the thirty-six-yard firing line.

The three courses of fire included one course of fire of three rounds with shot adjustments made after the conduct of fire; a second course of fire of three rounds with shot adjustments made after the conduct of fire; and a third course of fire of four rounds with final shot adjustments made—a total of ten rounds fired.

From the one-hundred-meter firing line, as part of the CAC, the Afghan Soldiers conducted their one-hundred-meter confirmation fire. These courses of fire included one course of five rounds from one hundred meters with adjustments made after the course of fire and a second course of fire consisting five rounds from one hundred meters with final adjustments made, for a total of ten rounds fired. Once all firing was completed, each member the CAC would have fired a total of twenty rounds.

With a combined action company of both Marines and Afghan National Army Soldiers, there was sure to be many moving parts during the course of this live fire. The biggest thing that had to be taken into account was making sure my Marines understood every order passed and the Afghan Soldiers listened to the Marines and understood their commands without question. All commands came from the Marines, and the Afghan Soldiers would do what they were told on the firing line. Safety had to be paramount, and the ability for all tasks and commands to make their way down to the lowest Marine on the firing line had to be smooth.

"Gentlemen, everyone bring it in for your safety brief. I am First Lieutenant Bodrog, your Officer in charge (OIC). Next to me is First Lieutenant Miller, your Range Safety Officer (RSO). Overseeing the conduct of the range will be our Platoon Sergeants standing next to us. Both the OIC and RSO will be colocated on the firing line behind the ANA Soldiers conducting the course of fire. Today is our live-fire confirmation portion of training. This practical application will test your skills and knowledge on the employment of the M16-A2 service rifle. Our course of fire will be as follows. We will fire three courses of fire from the prone position. The courses of fire will consist of two relays of three rounds and one relay of four rounds from a distance of thirty-six yards. You will then conduct two relays of five rounds from the one-hundred-meter firing line for your confirmation.

"In order to qualify, you must hit the paper target located downrange on the wooden pallets in front of the berm. Your left and right lateral limits will be the targets my Marines place downrange for the ANA Soldiers to your left and your right. At all times your weapons will be pointed downrange. At all times you will obey the commands from my Marines. If you are caught arguing with or disobeying the commands of my Marines, you will be removed from the firing line and fail the qualification portion of your training. If you experience a double feed or stoppage, raise your right foot and my Marines will assist you and perform immediate actions for your rifles. When you are not firing your weapons, you will always face downrange with your weapons on safe and your fingers straight and off the triggers.

"You will have on your person at all times a Kevlar, body armor, protective gloves, eye protection, and ear protection. Are there any questions about the course of fire for today? If there are no questions, stand by for your Range Safety Officer," I said to the Marines and Afghan National Army Soldiers before we kicked off our first ever combined action company live-fire range.

I had no doubt in my mind that the Marines would know exactly what to do at all times, and I put my complete trust and confidence in their actions. They knew safety was the most important aspect of the live-fire event, and they were all serious-faced and focused on what they were about to accomplish.

"Good morning, gentleman. My name is First Lieutenant Miller. I am your Range Safety Officer for the live-fire portion of you training that we are conducting this morning. First, recite the four weapons safety rules," he said to them.

As a group, the ANA Soldiers recited the four weapons safety rules: treat every weapon as if it is loaded; never point a weapon at anything you do not intend to shoot; keep your finger straight and off the trigger until you are ready to fire; and keep your weapon on safe until you intend to fire. Once they were finished, Lieutenant Miller continued his safety brief.

"Gentlemen, the fifth and unofficial safety rule is to know your target and what lies beyond and in between it. PSOs [Personal Safety Officers], ensure you watch for short shooters. Soldiers on the firing line, at all times safety is paramount for the conduct of my live-fire range. Marines, I'm trusting you with maintaining a high state of alert while coaching our Afghan counterparts on the firing line. Marines, if you observe any unsafe action, clear your Afghan's rifle, make it condition four, wait for the course of fire to be over, and remove your counterpart from the line.

"Safety for this range is dependent on each and every one of you knowing your roles and responsibilities as safety personnel. Every

Marine is a Safety Officer on my range. During the course of fire, I will be located behind the firing line with the OIC. If there is an injury on the line, the Corpsman and safety vehicle will be located directly behind me to conduct treatment. In case of an air CASEVAC (Casualty Evacuation), we will either determine a helicopter landing zone or evacuate you to the HLZ located on Forward Operating Base Geronimo for evacuation to Camp Dwyer or Camp Leatherneck.

"A red star cluster fired from a Marine means all Soldiers will cease fire because a training injury has just occurred. Marines, ensure that if a Soldier is within fifteen degrees of another Soldier's muzzle, cease-fire. Marines, at the end of the courses of fire, ensure accountability for all rounds either expended or not expended. Are there any questions about my range?" said Lieutenant Miller, looking confident as the Afghan Soldiers stared at him as if thinking to themselves, *Why do they put so much emphasis on being safe during a live-fire range?*

"Roger. If there are no questions for either the OIC or myself, Marines, ready your ANA Soldiers on the firing line for their first course of fire. My Platoon Sergeant, Staff Sergeant Salazar, will be calling all commands from this point on," said Lieutenant Miller, eager and ready to kick off our first ever integrated live-fire range.

With that, my Marines on the firing line had the Afghan Army Soldiers line up into eight relays of fifteen shooters and prepared them for their courses of fire. With a thumbs-up from my Personnel Safety Officers (PSOs) on the line, signaling that they were good to go, Staff Sergeant Salazar shouted the commands that allowed them to fire.

"PSOs on the line, are we ready? Roger! Soldiers on the firing line, this will be the live-fire confirmation portion of your training. Soldiers on the firing line, you will be firing three courses of fire in order to qualify with the M16-A2 service rifle. The first course of fire will be the firing of three rounds at your paper target in a time limit of one minute. The second course of fire will be firing three rounds at your paper target in a time limit of one minute. Your third and final course of fire will be firing four rounds at your paper targets in a time limit of one minute. ANA on the firing line, with your weapons pointed downrange, condition four, and finger straight and off the trigger, assume a good prone position. Marines on the firing line, let me know when your Soldiers are set," he said to the PSOs, ensuring all safety conditions were met and understood.

"Roger. RSO, I confirm all set. Soldiers on the firing line, at this time sight in on your targets. Marines, ensure the Soldiers are sighted in on their targets. ANA, this is your preparation time. PSOs, thumbs-up when we are set." The PSOs gave Lieutenant Miller's Platoon Sergeant the thumbs-up, and he continued.

"Roger. Soldiers, at this time with your weapons pointed downrange, go condition three. PSOs, ensuring the weapons are downrange, give me a thumbs-up when we are ready to fire." At this time the PSOs gave the thumbs-up again, and Staff Sergeant Salazar continued.

"Shooters on the firing line, go condition one and make ready. PSOs, give me a thumbs-up when ready. Roger. All set! Shooters on the line, at this time you may commence firing. Targets!" He yelled targets, which was the brevity code and command to fire.

I watched my Marine PSOs hovering over their Afghan shooters like hawks, ready to swoop down at any minute and crush their prey if they made a mistake. If the Afghan Soldiers messed up or threatened the safety on the range, I had comfort knowing my Marines and the Marines from First Platoon would be there to mitigate the risk.

As Lieutenant Miller's Platoon Sergeant shouted commands, my Marines up and down the firing lines relayed them to one another. Simultaneously, our linguists on the firing line shouted the English commands in the Afghan Soldiers' native language of Dari.

"Cease-fire, cease-fire! PSOs, ensure the weapons are pointed downrange and that your shooters are condition four. Soldiers on the line, at this time stand! Once all weapons are condition four, make your way downrange to your targets to check your shots and make spot corrections," Staff Sergeant Salazar yelled down the firing line after the first course of rounds was fired.

For the Marines in Hades First and Second Platoons, these commands were routine and muscle memory, but for the Afghan

Soldiers of the CAC, they were not. They looked at my Marines in humility because of their professionalism and ability to follow simple orders, ensuring the flawless conduct of fire and safety of the range.

"Marines, once you see the targets, mark the shots and make any corrections on the rifle needed. Is everyone good to go?"

At this time the PSOs had made corrections and gave him a thumbs-up.

"Shooters, at this time, make your way back uprange to the firing line. Once you reach the firing line, remain facing uprange until told to face downrange," he yelled to them, ensuring safety remained paramount, the PSOs were tracking, and commands were understood.

For the next two courses of fire, Lieutenant Miller's Platoon Sergeant redundantly shouted the same commands until it was muscle memory for our Afghan Soldiers. The only major difference in courses of fire was the last one, where instead of firing three rounds, the Afghan Soldiers fired their last four rounds at the targets. For the next seven relays consisting of all the Afghan Soldiers in the CAC, all commands came from him and were vetted down to the lowest-ranking Marine on the firing line.

Once all firing was conducted at the thirty-six-yard firing line, he then moved the entire company of Soldiers to the one-hundred-meter firing line and conducted their final two courses of live-fire confirmation.

By the end of the course of fire, our results were very surprising, to say the least. Every Afghan Soldier who conducted the live-fire evolution hit the paper targets and qualified on the M16-A2 service rifle. Some of the Afghan Soldiers even had tight shot groupings, which surprised my Marines. A few of the shooters hit all over the place on their paper targets, but every one of them hit paper.

Our evolution was successful, and the standard my Marines and I had set out to achieve was met. This was a huge win because this was the first time our Afghan Soldiers had ever fired our NATO M16-A2 service rifles. Before our NATO weapons were issued to them, they had carried and fired AK-47s. For every one of them to hit paper and qualify on a weapon they had never shot before was monumental and historic. This showed us that at a small level, the Afghan Soldiers could be relied on in a combat situation to generate effective fires on the enemy. This proved to us that they were retaining the information from their periods of instruction and were able to apply it in a real-world scenario.

CHAPTER 50

With the successes my Marines and Afghan National Army Soldiers achieved during the conduct of the integrated live-fire rifle range, we took the next step in our training with respect to weapons training. We were now going to raise the bar again and attempt to test our luck by training them on crew served weapons, which included the M240B medium machine gun and the 60mm mortar system.

Two days later, my Marines of the integrated weapons section conducted their live-fire crew served weapons training at the Juarez Range. The conduct of the integrated live-fire M240B medium machine gun range had few differences compared to the integrated live-fire rifle range. One of the only differences was that we would be firing from the one-hundred-meter firing line with M240Bs only, not the thirty-six-yard and the one-hundred-meter firing lines like with the M16-A2s.

Another small difference was that instead of the 120 shooters we'd had two days prior, we now had nineteen who were part of the CAC's integrated weapons section. Corporal Bennett, my Machine Gun Section Leader, developed a scheme of maneuver for the course of fire that took into account all periods of instruction from the week prior.

From a distance of one hundred meters, we would have both Marines and ANA Soldiers fire two hundred rounds of 7.62mm each. During the live-fire portion, my NCO would both sustain and test the skills of his Afghanistan Soldiers on certain aspects for the M240B medium machine gun. The skills that were to be tested were the ability to perform talking guns, different rates of fire, barrel change drills, and dead gunner drills.

My weapons section Marines had more than a week's worth of "dry runs" and "dry fire" classes with their Afghan Soldiers and were now getting to the point of maximum redundancy. That showed my Platoon Sergeant and I that the weapons section Marines were anxious to see what their Afghan counterparts could do with live rounds. They also wanted the pride of knowing their instruction was paying off and being retained.

In live-fire drills such as talking guns, dead gunner, and barrel changing, there is no room for error. When dealing with a third world-military, safety must be at the forefront at all times. There is a huge potential for short rounds, friendly fire, and rounds exploding in a shooter's face. At first, the entire Marine leadership of the CAC was hesitant to allow my Machine Gunners to do any other type of live-fire confirmation training than just firing the weapon at the target. But honestly, we all wanted the feeling of knowing just how good our integrated weapons section was, albeit as long as it was conducted in a safe manner. In combat there are no do-overs.

Utilizing generally the same concepts and commands as we did two days prior with the integrated live-fire rifle range, we took a step back and let the Machine Gunners do their job on the range. All commands came from Corporal Bennett, and he controlled the firing line with flawless precision, making sure all the Marines understood the course of fire and maintained safety standards with respect toward the Afghan Soldiers firing the M240Bs.

I harp on safety a lot, but it had to be maintained in this situation even more so because we were not dealing with United States Marines. We were dealing with a foreign national Army in which the Soldiers had no concept of safety or even right and wrong by American standards. These are people who do not care if they live or die. These are people who generally do not have the concept or mental capacity to understand the value of life because they think true life is a spiritual one with Allah in heaven. These are people who think, believe, and more so want to die during Ramadan so they can go straight to heaven faster. (Our Soldiers constantly informed us that death on a battlefield is glorious and something for which to strive. However, death on a battlefield during the Muslim religious holidays, such as Ramadan or Eid al-Fitr, will send a Muslim worshipper straight to heaven with Allah and his virgins ten times as fast.)

The conduct of the machine gun range was generally flawless as Corporal Bennett gave commands for the courses of fire to be shot. Thirteen out of the fourteen Afghan Soldiers performed admirably and had retained the knowledge of their education when they conducted their live fire. It was outstanding to see Afghan Soldiers, who two weeks ago had zero knowledge of the capabilities and limitations of the M240B, grasp, understand, and execute drills such as rates of fire, barrel changes, and talking guns as if they had been doing it for years. It was impressive and outstanding that my Marines had brought them to this level.

The only problem we faced was with one Afghan National Army Soldier who kept short shooting. This Afghan Soldier, who my Marines had given the nickname Baby Face because he cried on numerous occasions when yelled at by my Marines, had already been identified as a weak element by my Marines in the CAC. As all Marines know, once someone is identified as weak, it is an inherent responsibility of Marines to exploit it and purge it so it does not cause pestilence within the group.

Baby Face's weakness was constantly exploited to the point where my Marines and Afghan Soldiers were making him cry and hate life on a daily basis. It was *awesome.*

When it came to training, this was the same Afghan Soldier who would not touch a carbon-covered machine gun because he did not want to get his hands and fingers dirty cleaning and conducting general maintenance. Thus, because he did not like getting dirty, his fellow Afghan Soldiers constantly had to clean his weapon, which they did not appreciate one bit.

Baby Face would wear blond wigs on what Marines referred to as "Man-Love Thursdays." This was a day of the week when Afghans were notoriously known for having homosexual relations with one another and little boys. There is a famous Afghan saying: "women are for children; boys are for pleasure." Every Thursday, this Soldier would always paint his nails different colors and refuse to conduct manual labor so he could be clean and nice when he made love to his Afghan Commander. (Yes, he painted his nails and refused to work so that his Afghan Commander could sodomize him.) These actions were not rare and were quite common among the Afghan military.

It was also a quite common standard operating procedure that the new and youngest Afghan Soldiers' rite of passage was rape by the Afghan Commanders and fellow Soldiers in charge as a way to maintain order, status, power, and discipline.

When it came to the live-fire portion of his training out at the Juarez Range, three Machine Gunners swarmed over Baby Face as soon as he got behind the machine gun to fire. Baby Face had a Marine behind him, one to his left, and one to his right like a trifecta of brotherhood. This was done so there would be no room for error.

As soon as Baby Face started to conduct his course of fire, he began to short shoot ten meters in front of himself. After he received his first warning, he again short shot with the M240B medium machine gun. As he shot the machine gun, he literally shook like a scared child and ducked his head between his arms as if he was trying to hide in the sand because of the gun's loud noise. After this second round of short shooting, Corporal Bennett gave him his final warning and told him if he did it again, he would be kicked off the range and removed from the integrated weapons section. Little did this Afghan Soldier know that my Machine Gun Section Leader was serious.

Only a few seconds after my Machine Gun Section Leader issued his warning, the Afghan Soldier short shot again and started laughing hysterically. At this moment, before the Afghan Soldier even realized what he had done, Corporal Bennett ran over to where he lay in the prone position facing downrange behind the weapon.

Corporal Bennett yelled, "Click, click!" at the Afghan Soldier, ordering him to immediately clear the weapon.

With rounds still in the chamber, the Afghan Soldier tried to open the machine gun feed tray. Without hesitation, Corporal Bennett slammed his hand down on the feed tray cover to prevent rounds from exploding in the

Afghan Soldier's face. My Machine Gun Section Leader then cleared the weapon himself, looked at the Afghan Soldier, who was still lying in the prone position, and repeatedly started to yell at him, even kicking his rib cage (which was covered by his bulletproof vest), for his negligent actions.

I don't think anyone on the line blamed him. Even the Afghan Soldiers knew what their aloof Soldier had done was wrong and commended Bennett for saving Baby Face from possible injury or death. After all, if it hadn't been for my Marines on the line and my Machine Gun Section Leader, the Afghan Soldier could have potentially blown his face off. I would rather the Afghan Soldier take some bruises than lose an eye or half his skull.

After my Machine Gun Section Leader was done disciplining and correcting the deficiencies of Baby Face, who was now crying hysterically, the Afghan Soldier picked himself up and took a walk of shame off the firing line. He was instantly fired by myself with the approval of my chain of command and sent back to the Afghan Kandak located on the south side of Geronimo.

Knowing he was no longer part of the integrated weapons section for the combined action company, he threw a little fit in which he yelled and cursed at the Marines as if we were responsible for his negligence and failure to follow simple weapons instructions and procedure. He even raised his unloaded (condition four) rifle at a few of my Marines and made the verbal noise of "*Pow, pow.*" Without hesitation, the Afghan Section Leader ran over to him and continually smacked him in the face until he apologized for his unprofessional conduct toward my men.

All in all, qualification for both the M16-A2 service rifle and M240B were successful minus the incident with the one Afghan Soldier. The ANA, regardless of mental capacity, could definitely grasp the practical application of firing our NATO weapons.

The last round of qualification for the Marines and ANA Soldiers as part of the combined action company was the 60mm mortar day and night fire. The mortar shoot would be the real testament of training because of how much could go wrong with both high-explosive and illumination rounds, especially in the hands of Afghan Soldiers.

CHAPTER 51

Since the inception of the CAPs and CAC, Sergeant Smith and his Mortarmen had been conducting 60mm mortar dry runs with their Afghan Mortarmen. This was essentially a week and a half of nonstop training.

During the second week of training, every attempt my combined action company made to conduct the day mortar live fire was repeatedly canceled and rightly so. It was a hard sell to approve Afghan Soldiers to fire mortars right outside our FOB.

Another reason for cancellation was location. The Juarez Firing Range was directly in the middle of the desert in an area where local nationals constantly walked their herds of camels and sheep. When my battalion did not cancel our range, my Marines had to cancel the mortar fire because of sheep and camels in the 60mm kill zone. Because of our ROEs and strict adherence to them, dropping 60mm high explosives on Afghan animals was not allowed, even though every one of us subconsciously wanted to do it.

It was a shame too because we had tons of United States government and taxpayer money to give away to the locals for incurred damage, and it would allow us to determine if we were getting effective rounds on target.

First Lieutenant Miller and I administered the mortar range. However, the conduct of fire was run by my Mortar Section Leader and his Mortarmen. My Marines provided security for the range and placed wooden pallet targets approximately one to three kilometers away from the 60mm mortar system; these pallets served as targets to hit with the high-explosive rounds.

The courses of fire that were to be conducted involved the Afghan Mortarmen sinking baseplates, plotting the direction and distance of the target, making the gunfire capable, and ultimately dropping high-explosive rounds on top of the target. This was done under the strict supervision of Sergeant Smith's weapons section Marines. He personally made sure to double-check and correct any mistakes the Afghan Soldiers made, ensuring proper rounds on target. Then, once the gun was laid in on the target, the ANA Soldiers would drop the rounds in the tubes.

After almost two weeks of nonstop classes, it was go time. Once the gun was fire capable, the five Afghan Mortarmen on the range were then given ten rounds of 60mm high explosive each. Five rounds were for two single-fire missions, and the other five rounds were going to be utilized for two separate fire-for-effect missions. Once Lieutenant Miller and I gave the range safety brief, we cleared the range hot and allowed both our Marine and Afghan Mortarmen to take control and operate.

Aside from the uneasiness everyone on the firing range felt, especially as we watched our Afghan Soldiers conduct two fire-for-effect missions, the mortar fire was conducted flawlessly. The targets that had been positioned one to two clicks away from the guns were all destroyed by effective mortar fires.

The Afghan Soldiers proved their worth to my Marines by their successful conduct of all three live-fire ranges. Over the last four days of live fire, my Marines continually raised standards and set the example for future integrated or partnered units to follow. What made it even better was that we were conducting after-action reports and documenting all of it so it could be used again. To our knowledge at the time, nowhere else in Afghanistan were Marines and Afghan Soldiers integrated like we were, and nowhere else were combined units conducting the level of training we were executing on a daily basis.

After the Afghan Soldiers were done firing, Lieutenant Miller and I had our men burn all excess mortar increments and police the range for cleanliness. We then called the Juarez Range cold and patrolled back to FOB Geronimo. For the Mortarmen, their day fire portion was over. Training for the rest of the day entailed preparation for an illumination shoot at night.

The night illumination mortar fire was more restrictive than the day fire. Our CO and Company First Sergeant came out to view the night shoot and to make sure everything ran smoothly. Night considerations are much different than day, and because of the low visibility coupled with the inexperience of our foreign partners, there was always potential for something to go wrong.

My Mortarmen plotted all azimuths and set the gun up on the target. All the ANA Soldiers did was drop the rounds in the mortar tubes. It was another check in the box for the Marines in the CAC. It was one more evolution that raised the bar and set the standard for the Marines of Hades Platoon as part of the combined action company. We were still setting the example for all units across Afghanistan to emulate and follow. We were now fully capable of conducting myriad day- and night-related combat missions throughout our AO and adjacent battlespaces.

CHAPTER 52

One of the biggest keys to success for any leader is to have competent men so he can have the ability to delegate authority down to the small unit levels to empower his small unit leaders. Personally, I feel this way of thinking, which is also a purely Marine way to think, has been lost over the years, especially with the advent of technology, bureaucracy, and the ability to centralize command. Leaders must trust their subordinates and resist any and all temptation to micromanage if possible, unless circumstances dictate otherwise.

This way of thinking directly applied to the conduct of the integrated live-fire ranges. There is nothing scarier than a third-world Afghanistan Soldier dropping live mortar rounds down a mortar tube to blow up pieces of Afghanistan. It was only through empowering my Sergeants, Corporals, and junior Marines that this was made possible both in theory and application. A good leader gives his Marines the plan, allows them to come up with a way to execute it, supervises them, and—when he has to—corrects them. A good leader, through strict supervision, fosters mental growth and allows his subordinates to think through scenarios and problem solve, which enables them and their men to grow.

In this case, the results the CAC produced on the live-fire ranges resulted directly from the way my Platoon Sergeant and I decentralized our responsibility down to the lowest level. It was as simple as telling our Squad Leaders that we were going to shoot a live-fire range and making them responsible for coming up with a training plan and scheme of maneuver. All we did was oversee and supervise while they conducted the actual training. We made spot corrections when it was absolutely necessary. The *S* in BAMCIS, which denotes supervision, must be enforced and applied. BAMCIS is a military acronym for begin planning, arrange reconnaissance, make reconnaissance, complete the plan, issue the order, and supervise.

This photo was taken on 27 July 2010 at FOB Geronimo. The Marines of Hades Second Platoon get their first "eyes on" their ANA Soldier counterparts, who they will train, mentor, and lead for the rest of deployment.

Already on training day one, mediocrity and lack of discipline plague the Afghan ranks. Unreliable Soldiers were an ongoing problem for the Marines of Hades Second Platoon, especially during training. The Afghan Soldiers had the ability to quit anytime they wanted to.

Sergeant Brown (left) and Sergeant Guthrie (right) are conducting snapping-in drills, utilizing the help of our linguist. Snapping in is a process of rifle familiarization that occurs before a rifle range.

This photo was taken on the Juarez Firing Range. The ANA are receiving a safety brief before they execute their live-fire M16-A2 rifle range. To the left of the linguist is Lieutenant Miller (Hades 1) and to the right is Lieutenant Bodrog (Hades 2).

This photo was taken on Juarez Firing Range. Here, the ANA have been broken down into relays of fifteen shooters per course of fire. Organization, planning, and discipline were traits the Marines in the combined action company constantly tried to ingrain into the Afghan Soldiers.

The CAC is conducting their integrated live-fire rifle range to qualify the ANA on our NATO M16-A2 service rifle and M249 SAW. The result from this day was that every ANA Soldier qualified with the M16-A2 and M249 SAW.

Marines and Afghan Soldiers mark shots on their paper Battle Sight Zero (BZO) targets used for the live-fire qualification.

This picture was taken inside the dining facility at FOB Geronimo. Marines utilized the dining facility to conduct classroom periods of instruction for the ANA. Classes taught included but were not limited to doctrine, history, rifle disassembly and maintenance, tactics, patrolling, offense, defense, etc.

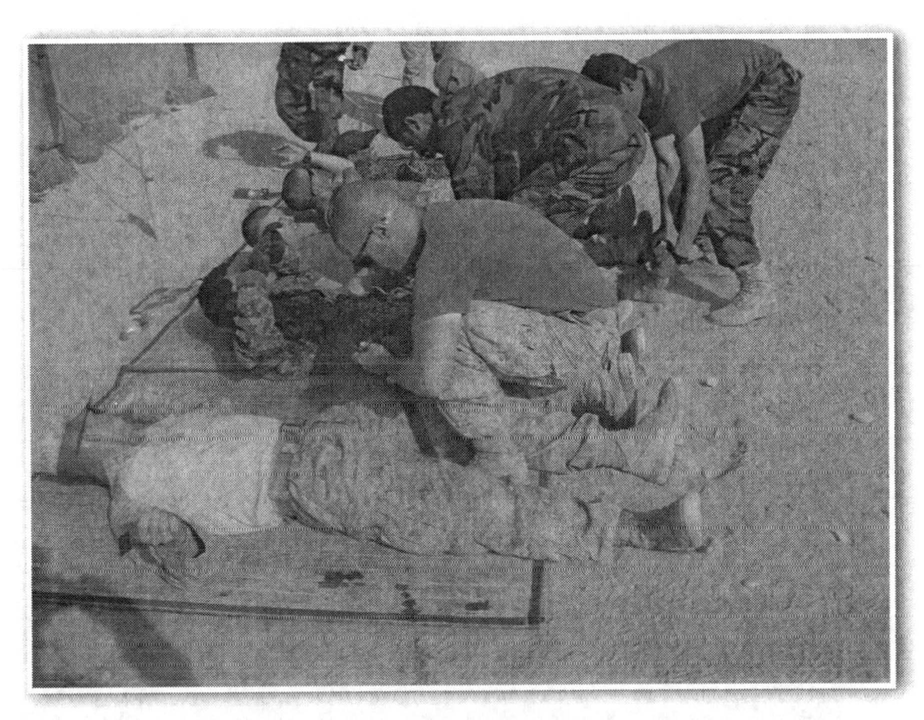

This photo was taken in the LSA for the CAC aboard FOB Geronimo. Here we see the Marines and their ANA counterparts conducting classes on first aid and combat lifesaving. Marines depicted (from front to rear) are Lance Corporal Taylor, Lance Corporal Blomstran, Lance Corporal Gerrity, and Sergeant Brown.

In this picture, my Marines are instructing the ANA on the conduct of room clearing tactics, military operations in urban terrain (MOUT), and the proper way to clear a compound.

In this photo, my Marines are teaching the ANA how to look for IEDs in doorways and how to conduct proper room clearing. Patience was always a virtue when instructing these Soldiers.

In this photo (from left to right), Lance Corporal Curtis, Corporal Bennett, and Lance Corporal Truehaft are working with the ANA on how to achieve proper combat marksmanship.

Private First Class Sisca supervises the disassembly and assembly of the M16-A4 service rifle by the Afghan Soldiers. Every day the Marines of the combined action company drilled the Afghan National Army Soldiers on disassembly and assembly of the M16-A4, M249 SAW, and M240B medium machine gun until they became proficient.

Corporal Bennett and Lance Corporal Curtis work with the Afghan National Army Soldiers on how to achieve proper combat marksmanship by getting in a good fighting stance to conduct combat glides.

Lance Corporal Blomstran works with his Afghan battle buddy on patrolling TTPs. Marines would patrol around FOB Geronimo for hours until their Afghan counterparts mimicked and understood their every move.

Private First Class Sisca instructs the ANA Soldiers in MOUT techniques as per Marine Corps doctrine. The Afghan Soldier with his arms around him is Rahulla. Rahulla was a former mujahedeen warrior.

Lance Corporals Choi and Ortiz physically demonstrate room-clearing techniques with the ANA.

This photo was taken in August 2010 at the dining facility on Geronimo. The Soldier to the left is the Afghan Platoon Commander, and to the right is the Afghan Platoon Sergeant for Hades 2. Staff Sergeant Lebron (right) and Lieutenant Bodrog (left) sit next to their Afghan counterparts, discussing the plan of the day. Sergeant Brown (middle) is supervising the conduct of both the Marines and Afghan Soldiers at a distance, making sure they stay engaged for classes and are not sleeping.

This photo was taken in September 2010 in the LSA for the combined action company. First Lieutenant Freedman (left) is discussing future operations of the CAC with Captain Armas (center) and First Lieutenant Bodrog (right).

In this photo, an Afghan Soldier—part of our integrated weapons section—practices dropping a mortar round into the 60mm mortar tube to ensure correct technique.

Lance Corporal Eicher prepares a 60mm high-explosive (HE) mortar before firing on Juarez Range. The course of fire for each Afghan was one to three rounds in adjust and then a fire for effect of two to three 60mm HE mortars.

Sergeant Smith drops a mortar round in the tube to register the mortar system. Leading by example, Sergeant Smith demonstrates the correct way to register his gun, sink his baseplate, and drop a round in the mortar tube in order to prepare the Afghan Mortarmen for their live-fire confirmation.

ANA Soldier Mohammad Din (a.k.a. Curious George) fires a 60mm HE mortar. Sergeant Smith supervises the Afghan Mortarmen to ensure safety and proper mission conduct.

Lance Corporal Eicher and Afghan Soldier Mohammed Din (a.k.a. Curious George) swab and clean the mortar tube after conducting successful firing aboard Juarez Range.

This photo was taken during Operation Mako, Trek Nawa, Afghanistan.
The ANA explains to the local nationals that both the Marines and Afghan Army will be utilizing the compound as a temporary patrol base.

This image shows the Marines of Hades First Platoon as part of the battalion's CAC.

This photo depicts the Marines and Afghan National Army Soldiers of Hades Second Platoon as part of the battalion's CAP and CAC.

This photo depicts the Marines of Hades Second Platoon proper with their leadership. It was taken at FOB Geronimo on 30 August 2010.

Front row (left to right): Sergeant Olds, Corporal Morris, Lance Corporal Vancamp, Private First Class Sisca, Lance Corporal James, Lance Corporal Hall, and our linguist.

Second row (left to right): Sergeant Brown, Corporal Berry, Lance Corporal Brown, Lance Corporal Castro, Corporal Truehaft, Lance Corporal Gerrity, Lance Corporal Blomstran, and Doc Williams.

Third row (left to right): First Lieutenant Bodrog, Staff Sergeant Lebron, Sergeant Guthrie, Corporal Mount, Lance Corporal Lamoreaux, Lance Corporal Rivera, Lance Corporal Choi, Lance Corporal Ortiz, Lance Corporal Taylor, Lance Corporal White, Doc Greenough, First Sergeant Olea, and Captain Armas.

This photo depicts Hades Second Platoon leadership. From left to right are Sergeant Olds, Sergeant Brown, Sergeant Guthrie, First Lieutenant Bodrog, Staff Sergeant Lebron, Corporal Mount, Corporal Berry, and Doc Greenough.

This photo depicts the CAC's integrated weapons section.

Top row (left to right): Corporal Bennett, Lance Corporal Lowe, Lance Corporal Oliver, Lance Corporal Curtis, Lance Corporal Lowe, Lance Corporal Jenks, Private First Class Johnson, Lance Corporal Oberman, Lance Corporal Eicher, and Sergeant Smith.

Bottom row: ANA Soldiers.

This picture depicts the Marine and Afghan leadership of the combined action company. Shown in this photo is the guidon for the combined action company.

Front row (left to right): Staff Sergeant Salazar (Hades 1, Platoon Sergeant); First Lieutenant Freedman (Executive Officer for Lima/ Hades CAC); and Staff Sergeant Lebron (Hades 2, Platoon Sergeant).

Back row (from left to right): Gul Agha (ANA Platoon Commander for Hades 2); First Lieutenant Bodrog (Hades 2, Platoon Commander); Sergeant Sayeed Agha (Hades 1, Platoon Sergeant); Captain Armas (Commanding Officer); First Sergeant Olea (Company First Sergeant); First Sergeant Entazaar (Hades 1, Platoon Commander); First Lieutenant Miller (Hades 1, Platoon Commander); and Sergeant Tay Gee Dee (Hades 2, Platoon Sergeant).

PART V

Missions of the Combined Action Company

Be polite, be professional, but have a plan to kill everyone you meet.
—General James Mattis (USMC)

Greater love hath no man than this, that a
man lay down his life for his friends.
—John 15:13

When the tiger kills, the jackal will profit.
—Afghan Proverb

CHAPTER 53

With the live-fire confirmations successfully conducted, the Marines of the CAC, and more specifically my Marines and Afghan Soldiers of Hades Second Platoon, were now ready to start conducting integrated combat operations across Task Force Third Battalion, Third Marines AO. In particular, we were ready to go into the battlespaces of India, Kilo, Lima, and Weapons Companies and conduct combat operations in support of their missions or schemes of maneuver.

No sooner had we finished live-fire confirmation than we received our first mission the following day, Sunday, 6 August 2010. Our first mission was a clearing operation north of Geronimo in an area known as the Koshrabad region. Our mission was to depart the FOB via a dismounted security patrol and utilize our ANA Soldiers to systematically search and clear every compound, mosque, cornfield, and haystack north of FOB Geronimo to find weapons caches and IEDs the Taliban were possibly hiding.

My CAP departed friendly lines at 0700 on Sunday morning and conducted the four-and-a-half-kilometer movement northeast, clearing everything in our path. It took hours to clear every piece of terrain, and it was very time-consuming. In the process, however, my CAP conducted numerous amounts of interaction with the local populace to win their trust and confidence. To our disbelief, they had not seen Marines or Afghan Soldiers in quite some time from what we were told, and they were glad we were providing security for the area in support of our COIN mission.

Many locals greeted my platoon with chai tea, watermelon, or other types of food to show their appreciation for our efforts. Sometimes patrolling and working hard in weather that tops 130 degrees Fahrenheit is seen and admired by the local nationals. Some go out of their way to give Marines and Soldiers thanks in the form of food and drink.

The clearing operation north took roughly ten hours. At around 1700, my platoon arrived at PB Sheklay Khor, a patrol base located roughly five kilometers north of Geronimo. As we walked into friendly lines, I remember congratulating all my Marines with my Platoon Sergeant on our first CAP patrol and clearing operation. It was a good feeling and an amazing feat, one that deserved a little reward from their leadership. We settled down at the PB to regroup and refit because later that night my platoon would set the bar even higher and conduct a combined night patrol during which my Afghan Soldiers would colead.

I can honestly say, and my Marines would agree, that patrolling at night with the ANA Soldiers was one of the most difficult tasks a unit could achieve. However, if a unit could build the ANA Soldiers' confidence and give them the tools they needed to be successful, that combined unit would be unstoppable and become limitless.

The main logic any unit had to remember was that many of the Afghan people and Soldiers had very bad eyesight, especially at night. The Afghan Soldiers themselves were ridiculously frightened to patrol at night because they lacked proper night-vision assets and were afraid of what they could not see. It was lack of comfort and the uncertainty of what lay in the night that truly bothered them. That said, a mother bird pushes her baby out of the nest to teach it to fly; the correlation was the same with my Marines and our Afghan counterparts.

A combined unit had to give the Afghan Soldiers no alternative and force them to become comfortable in an uncomfortable environment. That was why my platoon was so successful. We literally gave the Afghan Soldiers no choice in the matter and had their leadership back us up on all occasions when we could. There could be no bargaining with them in instances such as this. A Marine unit must remember that as long as there are Afghan Soldiers present on a patrol, the ROEs can almost literally be thrown out the window. I will use the term *puppet* very loosely, but if a Marine unit can get their Soldiers to unquestioningly follow them, the Taliban and the enemy in Afghanistan will be put in a dilemma on the battlefield and have nowhere to run or hide. The Afghan Soldiers have different ROE limitations, and with them in the lead, they can help and support the local population in ways Marines cannot.

Marines are very limited to what they can and cannot do because of the ROEs in Afghanistan, but the Afghan Soldiers are not. If a unit is smart, they can use these rules to their advantage. All they have to do is train their counterparts in a way that is beneficial to the mission and the law. For instance, Marines are not allowed to go into or search compounds; the Afghans can. Marines cannot conduct night raids without certain levels of approval, but the Afghan Soldiers are not limited by any means when it comes to night raids. Marines are not allowed to search females; the Afghan Soldiers can. In essence, by the time my CAP got really good at conducting combat operations, my Marines essentially provided the lead security while the Afghan Soldiers did the work and heavy lifting.

Later on that night, my combined squad-sized patrols cleared south of PB Sheklay Khor, marking our first night clearing operation. Overall, the operation was very successful and had only a few minor hiccups. The hiccups, of course, were that some of the Afghan Soldiers complained about visibility and were afraid of becoming lost. It was a mundane concern but not a legitimate mission-critical one. My Marines went everywhere with their Afghan Soldier counterparts during patrol, and accountability was a lesson constantly learned and enforced.

As my squads came back inside friendly lines from their night patrols, a truly remarkable thing started to happen. My Marines complimented the actions of their Afghan Soldiers and then started debriefing both Marines and Afghan Soldiers on the patrol with the help of our linguists. From their after-action points, it became apparent that the Afghans were learning what we were teaching them.

Afghan Fire Team Leaders, when sitting in LP/OP positions, were checking their men to make sure they were not falling asleep. Afghan Squad Leaders were following the orders of my Squad Leaders without complaint. Individual Afghan Soldiers followed the orders of their Afghan Fire Team Leaders and Marine counterparts without question. By no means was our night patrol perfect, but as a CAP we were definitely coming together as a single entity. The lessons from our training were starting to take root and grow.

After a rigorous schedule of night patrolling, I rested my Marines and ANA all morning as a small reward. By 1600, my platoon was rested, refitted, and ready for the four-and-a-half-kilometer movement back to our FOB. Some of my Squad Leaders wanted to test their Marines and Afghan Soldiers on the way back and did everything they could to make the patrol arduous. The Marines did well, but I could tell some of the Afghan Soldiers were getting angry and just wanted to get back.

My Squad Leaders, knowing the Afghans hated to get wet, decided to have some fun. They patrolled back through thick-mudded farm fields. They purposely went through canals and streams to soak their Marines and Afghan Soldiers. My Squad Leaders also started to make geometric patterns in their routes back, making circles in their patrol routes and double-backing just to extend the length of the patrol and confuse the enemy, who was most certainly watching.

With good intent and a little comedy, they pushed the Afghans out of their comfort zones and made their patrols back miserable. It was all in good fun and essential to making the unit stronger. The Soldiers soon learned that this was done in order to be a "hard target." The chances of getting blown up by an IED were greatly reduced by patrolling through farm fields and canals. It was also a direct order from me. My Marines were never to follow straight lines, roads, or trails because of the IED threat. Thus, they were ordered to conduct hard patrolling.

No one got hurt, and everyone made it back to Geronimo.

CHAPTER 54

No sooner did we return to friendly lines at FOB Geronimo than we were tasked with our next follow-on mission. Reports from the battalion's combat operations center regarding exact details were very sketchy, but we were told by our Company Commander that the Taliban had assassinated a family in Kilo Company's AO. What made this an even more critical mission was the fact that the assassinated family had a friendly personal and working relationship with our Battalion Commander. He was now taking this personally.

Our Battalion Commander immediately ordered my CAP to conduct a deliberate clearing mission to capture or kill the enemy. Truck Platoon would be our escort to COB Jaker, Kilo Company's main base. From there we would be briefed on our fragmentary order and conduct our mission.

With all of our combat gear and very little water and chow, my CAP arrived at COB Jaker at 2300 that night. It was about a forty-minute drive from FOB Geronimo to COB Jaker, and the biggest fears at night were two things: missing a turn and falling off the uneven dirt roads into a canal or getting blown up by IEDs. Thank God neither of the two ended up happening on our mobile convoy movement; however, these thoughts always infected the very cores of the minds of me and my Marines.

When we arrived at Jaker, my Platoon Sergeant and I met up with the very confident but obviously distraught Kilo Company Commander. Kilo's CO let us know that his Marines were currently at the compound where the parents and their four children had been brutally murdered and that they were aware my integrated platoon was going to be conducting a relief-in-place and clearing mission in the general vicinity to capture or kill the Taliban who had murdered the family.

In my own opinion, this was a job for the Afghan Uniformed Police or Afghan National Army in Kilo's AO, not my men. At this point in our deployment, we were supposed to start transferring power and authority over to them to facilitate their responsibility for taking over the security and protection of Afghanistan. *We are Marines, and we fight battles. We are not policemen trying to solve a murder mystery*, I thought. It didn't matter though. Our Battalion Commander saw something we did not, and he had requested my CAP by name to carry out his orders. Regardless of our opinions, it was an honor to be his right-hand punch.

As soon as Kilo's CO completed issuing our FRAGO, Truck Platoon transported my platoon and I a click and a half south to six separate lines of departure. From these lines of departure, my Marines and Afghan Soldiers of the combined action platoon were tasked with conducting a deliberate clear, from east to west, to capture or kill the alleged Taliban who had murdered our Battalion Commander's Afghan friends.

My CAP inserted into six different departure points from which we started our clearing operation. I split each of my squads into alpha and bravo elements at these positions and placed one senior leader with each squad to facilitate command and control.

As soon as all my Marines were staged in their positions, I gave the order to begin the clear. My Marines had maps of the local area and knew what compounds they would be clearing during the conduct of this mission. They were mainly utilized to push the Afghan Soldiers and drive them during the course of the clearing mission. My Marines were responsible for maintaining the inner and outer cordon security positions for their ANA Soldiers, who were responsible for leading the clear of all compounds in the surrounding area.

This way of clearing was the standard operating procedure for the CAC. As I have addressed previously, the ROEs were very limiting and restrictive toward Marine operations, almost to the point where our hands were tied and we could not do anything except blindly walk through villages and enemy terrain as poster boys of a social agenda, just waiting to get shot at.

To get around this, Lieutenant Miller and I, along with the leadership of the CAC, developed a unique concept of conducting cordon, knocking, and searching. Marines would direct the ANA Soldiers to the compound that needed to be searched. Once we arrived at the objective, my Marines would set up security around the compound to provide the inner and outer cordon. From there, the ANA would conduct either a hard or soft knock on the door of the compound and commence searching with the approval of the local national who owned the compound.

This worked very well for us. The Marines liked it because the Afghan Soldiers dealt with the greedy requests of the local nationals, who always had something to whine and complain about. The Afghan Soldiers liked it because Marines were giving them security and safety while legally respecting the cultural aspect of not invading the local nationals' privacy. This empowered the ANA with a sense of purpose and responsibility.

This was the standard operating procedure my Marines used throughout the rest of the deployment with our Afghan counterparts because it worked. During the course of this clearing mission, my Marines and my Afghan Soldiers cleared more than two kilometers of enemy terrain, more than three hundred mud compounds, and more than two hundred local nationals in the darkness of night. It may not seem like a large feat, but when you consider my Marines were leading a foreign national Army that did not speak English, lacked night-vision assets, and had very limited combat experience and field time, you can begin to appreciate how big of an accomplishment it really was.

The entire clearing operation lasted roughly five hours from start to finish, and my reinforced platoon reached our western limit of advance, a main supply route named Route Keystone, at around 0500.

My Second Squad had it the worst during the entire mission, having to provide security for the compound where the family had been slain while simultaneously conducting the clear. It was a grisly and brutal scene seeing a family that had been unrecognizably hacked to death, some with their heads cut off. For my junior Marines and especially the younger ANA, the sight and smells definitely rattled their bones. Cleaning up blood and body parts amid the screams of those in the compound who were still alive was not something they had expected to do on this night.

The alleged Taliban who murdered the family were nowhere to be found and escaped our grasp that night. They were on the run, however, because they knew from the strong clearing presence my CAP conducted that they were now being hunted by both Marines and ANA.

The clearing mission was successful, with our biggest friction points being the lack of comfort that our ANA had operating at night coupled with the communication barriers. We did not find the Taliban responsible; however, our clearing efforts ensured they were not still in the area. For the most part, my Marines used close proximity hand and arm signals to convey intent, but some barriers still remained between our two units. This was mostly solved with my Marines patiently reinforcing all commands to the ANA, who would mistakenly search a compound twice without realizing it or get lazy and sit down to rest or sleep between clearing terrain or compounds.

Once consolidation occurred at our limit of advance, my platoon loaded up our trucks, which had been providing blocking positions to the north and south on the main road in the area, and we headed back to Geronimo for a debrief.

My Marines, while on board our mounted vehicles, conducted accountability checks for their personnel and gear to make sure nothing was lost or left behind from the clearing operation. Then they conducted the mounted security patrol back to FOB Geronimo.

During our debrief, our CO explained the full story of what had happened the previous night. My men and I soon learned that the family that was murdered in Kilo Company's AO had not been murdered by the Taliban. Directly from our intelligence sources we learned that the Afghan father of the family that was brutally murdered had reneged on a dowry between himself and a thirty-two-year-old Pakistani man for marriage to his thirteen-year-old daughter.

Apparently, from what our intelligence sources were reporting, the Pakistani man did not have enough money to buy the girl from the father and became enraged because the father had promised the man his daughter. In a rage, the Pakistani man had left the compound only to return that same night with some buddies of his to abduct the Afghan man's daughter.

The Pakistani man had then come back to the compound after he abducted the daughter and shot and killed her father and her brothers and stabbed and hacked her mother and sisters to death, leaving only one of her brothers alive to tell the story. He had done this because he felt his honor was challenged, and he needed to restore it.

Ultimately, this became an epic Afghan love story with a tragic ending, so it seemed—one that was not at all that uncommon in this part of the world.

CHAPTER 55

By the time the debrief was over and the truth was revealed, my Marines and the Afghan National Army Soldiers were mentally and physically exhausted. Our Company Commander decided to give us a few days off to rest and refit, and he let First Lieutenant Miller's CAP take over sustained combat operations while my Marines and Afghans regained their strength.

My CAP decided to take the morning and afternoon off for rest and refit, but they had a great idea for the night to improve camaraderie. My Marines decided to have a video period of instruction that night with their Afghan counterparts to bring everyone closer together as a fighting unit. The movie they were going to watch in the chow hall of FOB Geronimo was *Rambo, Part Three*, which depicts Sylvester Stallone as Rambo, who comes to the aid of mujahedeen fighters during the Soviet-Afghan War.

It was amazing to watch both my Marines and the Afghan Soldiers rooting for Stallone as he laid waste to the Russian military. They even found it comical that he played *Buzkashi*, a polo-like game played in Afghanistan that utilizes the headless carcass of a goat instead of a ball and could be played for days. It definitely hit home for our Afghan Soldiers, who despised the Russians. It was comical to see them cheering for an American too.

Many thought Rambo battling the Soviets was a real event that had taken place, and the ANA became even more enthralled of my Marines and our American forces for helping them defeat the Russians during the Soviet-Afghan War. For what little knowledge the Afghan Soldiers did have, many never forgot their own history and who helped them along the way, even if Hollywood did help in the propaganda war.

It was a great spectacle to sit in the background of the FOB chow hall and watch the expressions of the Marines and Afghans. My Marines identified with Sylvester Stallone and the winner mentality of the United States. The Afghans identified with the people, culture, and atmospherics of the movie, especially the mujahedeen. Many even thanked my Marines at the end of the movie for what the United States had done for Afghanistan during the Soviet-Afghan War.

It was both an epiphany and cathartic at the same time, and I personally think it renewed some type of loyalty the Afghans harbored toward my Marines. Even if the movie was fiction, the Afghans had found some sort of solace that the United States had beaten the heck out of the Russians in the movie.

Over the course of the next week, missions were generally focused on local security patrols and refocused on fine-tuning our TTPs with our Afghan Soldiers by building upon and sustaining our critical combat skills and continuing actions.

From this point on, all the local security patrols my Marines conducted were fully integrated and combined squad-sized patrols. The patrolling areas my CAP focused on while back at FOB Geronimo were mostly rural tribal villages three to five kilometers to the north, east, and west of the FOB called Sharakala, Khosrabad, and Socksees.

Sharakala was a small town of opium farmers and wheat growers directly three kilometers northwest of Geronimo. Its village was a large tribal region that stretched nearly three kilometers directly northeast from Geronimo to PB Sheklay Khor. It was generally a passive region in which the local nationals kept to themselves. Most people in this tribal area were farmers and animal growers who were very friendly to Marine patrols.

Khosrabad was a village in the "green zone" directly east of FOB Geronimo. This area characteristically had a high population of farmers and merchants. It was a very fertile area filled with crops such as watermelon, corn, and okra. Although it was very highly populated, many of the locals kept to themselves and tended to their farms, not wanting to be bothered by the Taliban or Marines.

To the immediate west of Geronimo was a town known as Socksees. It was a very small local village, roughly a kilometer in size, of opium farmers. The people there were a very shady group. Their faces looked like a mix of cold and death. Although they were not hostile, the villagers openly supported the Taliban and were not secretive at all about growing poppy to fund the insurgency.

What made these areas of vital strategic importance was that they bordered the Nawa and Marjeh Districts, which afforded the Taliban safe havens and the ability to control and influence decisions and thought processes of the locals. This meant my Marines and Soldiers had a responsibility and opportunity to earn the trust and confidence of these locals and destroy the bonds they had with the Taliban in order to bring them to our side.

The conduct of my integrated patrolling efforts usually lasted from four to six hours per patrol to each of these three areas. The patrols were Marine led, but the face of the patrol belonged to the ANA Soldiers. Marines were the security of the patrol, but my Afghan Soldiers were the visage of interaction and the tools for clearing the compounds.

The locals in the Nawa District didn't necessarily mind the Marines, but they despised the Afghan Uniformed Police and loved the Afghan National Army Soldiers. This was because Marines were a very rugged and fearsome entity, and the people were intimidated by us. After all, with our high-tech gear, body armor, and sheer stature, we must have looked like spacemen to these people.

The Afghan Uniformed Police Officers were local Pashtus, and many treated the population badly because they were inherently corrupt. After all, most village elders had appointed many of these men (some of whom were former Taliban fighters) to the police force from their own villages, thus creating their own personal Army. The Afghan Police would rape, rob, cheat, steal from, and kill local nationals, most of the time on direct orders from their village elders. This had the tendency to make them illegitimate in the locals' eyes.

The local nationals loved the Afghan National Army because of the very simple fact that the Soldiers were outsiders and were not from the Helmand Province. They were foreigners, and for that reason, they were interesting and mysterious to the Afghans. The ANA treated the locals with respect and dignity, never too tough or too easy on them, unlike the Afghan Police. For the most part, the Afghan Soldiers were firm, fair, and generally concerned about the needs of the people.

The Afghan Soldiers considered the locals of the Helmand Province inferior country folk of a lesser race; therefore, they treated them like children. For this reason alone, the locals loved and protected the Afghan Soldiers because the Soldiers pitied them and took care of them.

During the course of dismounted patrols, my ANA Soldiers asked the locals questions on a number of topics. They asked them about their jobs, their families, or just how their days were going in an effort to spark an interest in them. We also tried to gather intelligence, writing down the locals' names and the grid locations of their compounds. My Afghan Soldiers extracted as much information out of the locals as possible to facilitate our intelligence gathering. To the locals, someone asking how their day was or what they did for a living was encouraging, and it instilled trust.

When my Marines and Afghan Soldiers were not patrolling, we conducted training. For the most part, training ran as usual. From 0600 through 0730, physical training was conducted. Classes started from 0900 through 1200 after the morning chow break. From 1200 through 1400, my integrated platoon then took another chow break, and classes resumed at 1400 and culminated at 1700.

With our ANA gaining more field experience, classes were now geared toward sustaining the knowledge they had learned. Since the majority of our missions involved clearing buildings, we taught the Afghan Soldiers a lot about compound searches. My Marines continued to instruct them on how to use compact mine detectors to find IEDs, taught tactical site exploitation when searching a compound, trained them in ways to tactically question and read body language of locals, and gave them daily medical classes in case of a combat casualty.

My Marines even let the Afghan Squad Leaders teach more classes because of their gains in sustaining knowledge and increased proficiency. The Afghans explained to the Marines their country's history and the role of America in Afghanistan. They tried to enhance my Marines' understanding of their military customs and courtesies and provided them with stories of what it was like growing up in war-torn Afghanistan. It was interesting to see the maturity and interest of both sides during these classes and the level of commitment and shared honor being fostered inside the CAC.

CHAPTER 56

Most religions are open to interpretation; some are fanatical and die-hard, some are unrestrictive and loose, and some are right in the middle. The biggest detriment to the training and conduct of daily operations was the Afghans' religion and their holy month of Ramadan. Their version of the Islamic religion during Ramadan forbade them from participating in the conduct of military training from sunup to sundown down every day. The Muslim holy month of Ramadan severely crippled the fighting capacity and operational effectiveness of the CAC. What made this month even worse for my Marines was the fact that we were all mandated by most of our higher leadership to be overly sensitive toward Muslims and the Afghan Soldiers during this month so as not to offend them. Ramadan was an excuse for terrorists to commit horrible acts of cowardice and atrocities against coalition forces not only in Afghanistan but throughout the world. We had to be on guard against these threats at all times. It was not like Christmas or Chanukah or other nonviolent holidays; Ramadan was serious, and we were infidels to these people. Our ANA knew this and took advantage of it every chance they could. They used Ramadan against my Marines as a way of getting out of almost all daily training evolutions, patrols, and operations.

As soon as Ramadan came on 11 August 2010, it was like a light switch turned on, and the mental and physical capacity of our Afghan Soldiers went from competitive training to combative confrontational training. The leadership of the CAC had to revamp all the training schedules to meet the demands of Ramadan and how they were interpreted by our Soldiers.

During Ramadan, our Afghan Soldiers prayed five times a day, did not smoke or dip tobacco, and fasted from sunup to sundown. It took a toll on their bodies to make this kind of commitment. Since their bodies lacked good nutrition anyway, the Afghan Soldiers resorted to being lazy and therefore slept all day and did little to no work, all at the expense of my Marines.

My Marines and I had to eliminate physical training in the morning and could only conduct classes from 0600 to 0900 every day because of their religious constraints. Every time my Marines tried to incorporate fitness or classes that exceeded our 0900 timeframe, the Afghan Soldiers and even their platoon leadership became defensive and complained that we were intruding on their religious customs. They would then quit and walk back to their tents to go to sleep, acting like they didn't know us or hadn't seen us before.

Most of the complaining was just a spectacle. It was a widely known fact, especially to my Marines, that the majority of Afghan people we encountered were generally lazy and just wanted to be left alone, especially during their religious holidays. The beauty of this was that my Marines and I were not Muslim, and we were forced to go out of our way to appease our Afghan Soldiers so we did not offend them or turn them into Taliban.

We were informed by our higher-ups and desk warriors that we could not drink, eat, dip, or smoke in front of them. This was a lie my men tested and proved not to be true. Our "pious" Afghan Soldiers did not care one bit, especially because we were Christian and not subject to their religious customs. They even told us that since we were not Muslims, we did not have to make special considerations. Some of these Afghan Soldiers even continued to smoke, dip tobacco, and consume energy drinks with my Marines during Ramadan.

This kind of passive and lazy attitude by the Afghan Soldiers toward my Marines only lasted for a few days until my CO and the leadership of the CAC met with the Afghan Kandak leadership. The Afghan leadership was appalled by the behavior of their men with respect to training and the lack of integrated operations.

Their Afghan Colonel, Colonel Gul Mohammad, and their Executive Officer, Major Abdul Latif, informed us that Ramadan, especially the fasting, could be negated if it was detrimental to the human body, particularly during times of warfare. For us that meant the Afghan Soldiers could train because it was their job to do so, and the Muslim religion allowed them to eat and drink during Ramadan because their mission trumped their fasting because it was part of a greater good. I thanked God my CO had done all he could to bring the CAC back from the dark pit it was lying in by working tirelessly with the leadership of the Afghan Army to restore it to its original form.

In fact, the ANA Colonel and Major were so angry that our Afghan Soldiers were using their religion against my Marines as an excuse to get out of training that they took the CAC's ANA Soldiers on a twelve-hour nonstop patrolling operation without Marines during which they forced them all to eat and drink.

After that day, training got better, and our own Afghan Soldiers knew their social game was over because their leadership had squashed it. My Marines still respected their culture, obeyed the law of the land, and allowed them to fast during the day, but they now had a deeper respect for the leadership in the Afghan ranks and knew where the line was drawn.

This was something my Marines could have never done and would never have done, and they were glad the Afghan leadership had come through for the survival of the CAC. When it came time to conduct missions, the Afghans were now expected to maintain a physical and nutritional standard so they could successfully conduct business.

CHAPTER 57

During the month of Ramadan, my CAP conducted our next integrated operation, known as Operation Big Wave, on 18 August 2010. Since this was going to be a multiple-day sustained operation, our Afghan Soldiers were not able to participate because of their duties to Ramadan.

The purpose of Operation Big Wave was to deny the Taliban freedom of movement along our main supply routes in the Nawa District. The CAP from Hades First Platoon was blocking from north to south along key routes in the vicinity of PB Meinert for this operation in an effort to push the Taliban west toward the Helmand River.

PB Meinert was a small base in the northernmost part of India Company's AO, located directly north of COB Spin Ghar. As with all positions in India Company, the men at Meinert constantly received enemy fire, and IEDs were continuously found around its position. The Taliban were known to operate in this area; however, up to this point in the war, they had not been able to penetrate because of the spectacular resolve of the Marines of India Company.

Once the CAP of Hades First Platoon was established in their blocking positions in the vicinity of PB Meinert, my platoon was then to conduct a helicopter insert to the east side of the Helmand River and establish our blocking positions on main supply north-to-south routes to deny the Taliban freedom of movement east to west across the Helmand into Nawa through areas such as COB Spin Ghar and PB Meinert.

The operation lasted for four days, during which time my platoon established two defensive positions. We gained and held the high ground overlooking main roads that ran through our operational box, set up four M240Bs that pointed down possible enemy avenues of approach, and dug in for the sustained combat operation.

The days were very long and hot, averaging 130 degrees Fahrenheit or hotter during the day. The nights, however, were very cold, averaging low thirties. For lack of a better description, it was pure desert conditions. It didn't matter though, because the scenery was outstanding, and the mission was noble. Sitting on top of the cliffs above the Helmand River, overlooking the terrain thousands of feet below, was a breathtaking sight neither my Marines nor I will ever forget.

Over the course of the next four days, traffic was generally very slow or very fast paced, averaging either only few vehicles or tractors per hour or many per hour. However, direct from our intelligence reports, the traffic we were witnessing was said to be very unusual for the region. This usually meant that the traffic we experienced was from Taliban.

The Taliban were definitely denied freedom of movement from north to south in the Nawa District during this operation, and the proof of it was in the patterns of traffic we experienced on the east side of the Helmand River.

My Marines searched a total of 133 vehicles and more than three hundred local nationals during this operation. My Third Squad ended up recovering a small weapons cache of four AK-47s with full magazine clips. It was not a very rewarding find by any means, but we achieved mission accomplishment by denying the enemy freedom of movement on the main supply routes running north to south on the eastern side of the Helmand River. They now had to find a different way to cross the river to kill our men. Intel reports heavily suggested that the Taliban were unable to cross into the Nawa District from Quetta, Pakistan, and therefore tried their luck south through Garmsir or north through Lashkar Gah.

On the morning of 22 August 2010, from our HLZ, known as HLZ Rebel Yell, my Marines and I consolidated our forces on a precipice overlooking the Helmand River and extracted via two CH-53 helicopters back to FOB Geronimo. That was the last time my platoon conducted an operation on the east side of the Helmand River.

CHAPTER 58

When my Marines and I returned to FOB Geronimo, Staff Sergeant Lebron and I ensured they all took a well-deserved rest for the rest of the day. We had faced above 130-degree temperatures for the last four days, and our bodies were pretty bruised and beaten from climbing up and down the jagged cliffs along the Helmand River.

The mission had been a success, as my Marines and I would find out over the course of the next few days. Success was measured on the basis that because of the actions of both Hades First Platoon and Hades Second Platoon, there had been zero significant events such as IED or small arms attacks in both India and Kilo Companies' AOs for a total of one week after our departure from the east side of the Helmand River. Our efforts denied the Taliban the ability to control routes in and out of our AO that they would have used to deliver and transport materials to kill our forces.

The next morning, 23 August 2010, the CAC undertook the task of creating an integrated and organic mobile maneuver element. Now our CAC and our CAPs had capability of self-lifting our combined unit and could go anywhere in the AO in support of other platoons and companies without relying on Truck Platoon, Motor Transport, or other battalion assets to escort us around the battlespace, which freed up more men for the fight.

Our mobile element consisted of two MRAPS, two MATVS, two seven-ton armadillos, and four Afghan Ford Ranger combat vehicles. What made this mobile element very effective was the fact that both Marines and ANA were fully integrated in all the military vehicles. We were able to keep unit integrity, and integrated vehicles gave us that much more of a tactical advantage against the enemy and our restrictive ROEs.

As all Marines know, MRAPS, MATVs, and seven-tons are by nature very heavily armored and very slow. They are not the best vehicles for quick maneuvers and usually drive from point A to point B very slowly and methodically. This is a good thing when traveling in an area where there is a potential for IEDs or indirect fire that could kill a platoon full of Marines. However, in an environment in which one is taking small arms fire or the enemy is on motorcycles, these vehicles cannot maneuver fast enough to react and neutralize the situation. That was the beauty of our new mobile element.

Like a little armada, our integrated mobile element had the ability to be both defensive and offensive, with the slow Marine vehicles being used for shielding enemy fires and taking the brunt of an IED blast while the smaller, quicker Afghan vehicles could be used to maneuver and chase down the possible enemy. The CAC now had the ability of being both defensive and offensive.

Sergeant Smith and his combined weapons section undertook the task and responsibility for the maintenance, preparation, and command of the vehicles in the mobile element. Every day they found time to train with their Marines and ANA on employment of the vehicles.

Training initially included tactically driving around the internal perimeter of FOB Geronimo, testing both maneuverability and ability to conduct immediate actions drills such as recovery of a downed vehicle or what to do in an IED attack. My Marines and Afghan Soldiers rehearsed these drills day in and day out over the course of the week until the actions became muscle memory.

Training also included the sustainment of the TTPs my Marines and ANA conducted on Geronimo through the actual application of driving on Afghan roads known to be laced with IEDs. My mobile element routinely conducted daily route familiarization, insertion, and extraction of our combined forces in and out of numerous objectives. This ensured that my drivers knew the routes in the AO and that we kept true to our COIN roots by constantly interacting with the population. The endstate of all this ensured the quick and speedy reaction time of the CAC in the event that we were activated and needed to support a sister platoon or company anywhere in the AO quick, fast, and in a hurry.

Throughout the week, we devoted time to training for upcoming operations. Dismounted and mounted patrolling missions were mainly squad patrols, with the occasional overnight combat operation directly west of Geronimo in the Sharakala and Socksees villages. Much training still needed to be accomplished to better our Afghan partners, and the clock was against us. Ramadan and Eid al-Fitr would end in September, and at this point the Afghan Soldiers were still only working about six hours a day.

CHAPTER 59

Training up until August 31 was usually conducted in the morning hours from 0600 through 0900–1000. My CAP conducted myriad sustainment trainings ranging from the integrated live-fire ranges with our M4s, M16s, M240Bs, M249s, and 60mm mortars on the Juarez Firing Range. We conducted numerous battalion combat missions and utilized our mobile element to transport us throughout the AO.

My Marines and I tried to cram in as much information as possible with respect to the learning capabilities of our counterparts so they would not lose the standard they achieved during the month of Ramadan.

My Marines and I were only in Afghanistan for seven months; the Afghan Army was there for good. We had to train them to the best of our abilities and make them the most professional Soldiers possible before we left in December. They needed to be ready to fight the enemy and conduct COIN without our help.

Our next big mission came on the night of 31 August 2010. My Marines and I were in our hooches when at about 2130 we heard the loud sounds of gunfire and explosions approximately three kilometers directly west of the FOB.

The situation we were briefed by our CO was that Afghan Uniformed Police Officers had been conducting a mounted patrol through the fields to our west when they had gotten stuck in the muddy and wet ground. While they were stuck, they came under fire from at least six enemy forces from the Sharakala village, which was known to support the Taliban. They were in trouble and were requesting help from our battalion to defeat the enemy.

Less than twenty minutes after the firefight started and my platoon was briefed on the mission by Hades 6, we stormed out of the gates of Geronimo to reinforce the Afghan Uniformed Police Officers who were under fire. In less than twenty minutes, the entire CAC, minus our weapons section, conducted a dismounted patrol and literally ran three kilometers in zero illumination and wearing all our protective equipment to the village of Sharakala.

When my integrated platoon reached the town, we regrouped in preparation to have our ANA clear the entire town and capture or kill the enemy shooting at the Afghan Uniformed Police Officers. Both artillery from an area south of us known as Fiddler's Green and our own integrated 60s mortar section (firing at maximum effective range) provided continuous illumination and fire support for our clearing operation.

The illumination support was outstanding and very accurate. In fact, the illumination rounds were so accurate that my Marines and ANA were literally dodging artillery illumination canister shells falling to the earth as they cleared the village. It was amazing and very accurate! The artillery shells were more of a threat to me and my Marines and Afghans than the potential enemy within the village.

It was funny to even think about the accuracy of the rounds. One of the spent illumination canisters in particular that fell from the sky was so dead-on accurate that it hit and killed a local villager's goat no less than twenty meters away from my Squad Leader calling in the grid to fire. Of all the things one can remember from a deployment, I still remember the loud shrill of "*baaa*" before the goat was struck and killed by an illumination canister that fell to the ground from overhead. (The next day, the owner of the goat brought the canister to Geronimo and asked for battle damage payment. He even asked my CO if he could keep the canister and use it as container to hold water.)

My integrated platoon and the Marines and Afghan Soldiers of Hades First Platoon cleared the entire town in roughly three hours. From the time the firefight commenced to the time it took both units within the CAC to reach the village of Sharakala, an hour had already gone by, and the enemy had more than enough time to flee. Our Afghan Soldiers cleared the compounds and locals within the entire town, only finding personal shotguns and ammunition used for home security. At around roughly 0300 that morning, empty-handed, the CAC returned to friendly lines at FOB Geronimo.

The next morning, through hearsay and rumors my Marines were able to extract from our Afghan Soldiers, we soon discovered the truth of what had happened the previous night. From what we were informed, the Afghan Uniformed Police Officers were stranded three kilometers west of Geronimo and their vehicles were stuck in the mud. They were without cell phones or lines of communication and thus started firing their weapons to get the attention of the personnel at Geronimo because they were scared and alone. Knowing Marines would run to the sound of gunfire and support them, they made up a story that the Taliban was firing at them, reported it to our COC, and requested help. This was all done in an effort to hide the fact that they were irresponsible, unprofessional, and reckless. This could have gotten my men killed.

Thus, because of this lie, not an uncommon virtue in the Afghan military service, the men of the CAC had been sent out to investigate and clear Sharakala. These kinds of stories were not uncommon. The kicker was that Marine units had to treat the Afghan military as a legitimate partner against the Taliban even though most of the time their results violated integrity, rule of law, and every ethical and moral standard to which Marines hold themselves. My Marines always did their best to stay true to the mission and the legal ramifications surrounding every mission, even if our third-world military partners did not.

CHAPTER 60

The next operation my men took part in was known as Operation Western Resolve. It was a combat operation in which the CAC expanded the western border of our AO in an effort to support adjacent units and their battlespaces. First Reconnaissance Battalion was currently operating in the area, which was essentially the middle ground between Marjeh and Nawa, and they were culminating their operations and consolidating their forces north to COB Reilly.

COB Reilly was located north of Geronimo in an area called The Five Points, and it too was located between Marjeh and the Trek Nawa-Nawa areas. First Reconnaissance Battalion had engaged in numerous kinetic instances with the Taliban (reportedly killing more than one hundred enemy fighters) in the Trek Nawa-Marjeh area to our west, and because they were about to consolidate at Reilly to prepare to move to the Sangin Valley, we were tasked to take back the area they would be leaving.

It was a seventeen-day operation that lasted until 20 September 2010. The CAPs from Hades First and Second Platoons were to rotate patrolling schedules in and out of this area during the operation.

All it meant for the men of the CAC was that combat security patrols would be longer, the chances of kinetic activity increased, and key terrain we had been previously denied going to, such as key villages and main supply routes where IEDs were known to be, was now ours to patrol.

For more than three weeks, the CAC conducted mobile inserts and extracts throughout our western border. We conducted reconnaissance patrolling to determine accessible vehicle routes, and we conducted dismounted security patrols to gather intelligence to update our situational awareness for the area. My platoon ended up discovering makeshift terrain models built by the enemy that detailed the layout of FOB Geronimo. We subsequently documented them and destroyed them.

The ANA conducted the COIN aspect of the fight during this time. Local nationals who had not seen Marines or even a military presence in months talked our ears off about the role of opium and the Taliban in the Sharakala and Socksees villages and gave us vital intelligence on them.

Operations during Western Resolve were nonstop and ranged from squad patrols to overnight platoon operations. By the end of the first week, my CAP was tasked with another search and recovery mission, this time for an Afghan woman. From what our reports stated, the Taliban had assassinated a very outspoken woman from the surrounding area who was diligently fighting for education reform and human rights for Afghan women and children.

After repeated death threats and assassination attempts, the Taliban eventually kidnapped and killed her and then dumped her body parts all over the Marjeh and Nawa borders, which was now our area. The Marines and ANA of the CAC searched the area for days, finding only bloody clothing. We did not recover her body. Keeping the population intimidated, fearful, and uneducated was the Taliban's goal so they could maintain control. Murder and intimidation campaigns were effective methods of enforcement.

Our overnight combined platoon and company operations usually entailed establishing temporary PBs and running about four squad-sized patrols out of the PBs to various areas of interest. My Marines never used the same PB twice and always remembered to pick PBs that were located on terrain that offered tactical advantage and could be both easily defended and abandoned quickly.

CHAPTER 61

The end of Ramadan came on 13 September 2010, and it could not have come sooner for me or my Marines. We were at the climax of frustration with our counterparts and their inherent ability to be nothing but lazy and confrontational for the last month. Luckily the Afghan Soldiers we placed in leadership positions both spoke English and kept order; otherwise, Ramadan could have been far worse. My Marines and I marked the end of Ramadan with a platoon clearing operation created by our CO.

The clearing operation took place in the vicinity of PB Sheklay Khor. Directly five hundred meters south of the PB was a small village in which, according to credible intelligence my Marines and I received, a Taliban Commander resided. The mission of my CAC was to conduct cordon and knock on every compound in the village to locate and detain the Taliban Commander and his accomplices.

My integrated platoon departed north from Geronimo at 0300 that morning and made the four-kilometer night movement to a staging point east of the village. It was a long and arduous movement through canals and muddy terrain, undoubtedly characteristic of all of my patrols and the terrain in the many parts of the Nawa District.

By the time my platoon was in place at our attack position, it was around 0530.

At this time my Commanding Officer gave me the approval, and my Platoon Sergeant and I commanded our CAP to conduct the systematic clearing of the village.

The mission did not last long, and its execution was peppered with irony. No sooner did my platoon make the four-kilometer movement in the pitch-black of the night, reach the village, and begin the clearing operation than my Commanding Officer received a call over his radio from the battalion COC informing him we had to abandon the mission and return to base because the air condition (AIRCON) had turned red.

Red air was a disaster for Marine units on the ground because it meant troops in contact or in need of air support were virtually out of luck unless they had a motivated or crazy pilot supporting them. Our ROEs and the air quality prevented air support during condition red. AIRCON red was when the ceiling of the sky is literally right over your head, the sand in the air makes it almost impossible to see, and the density of the air clogs all mechanical and tactical gear or equipment, making even the simplest military operations a disaster.

Personally, I feel like AIRCON red gives the enemy the advantage over Marines because the enemy knows that when the air is red, Marines are not out patrolling. It seriously limits our ROEs, and any thinking enemy can take advantage of these shortfalls in our tactical surfaces and gaps. As Marines we pride ourselves on training like we fight. It is ridiculous that because of a negative air condition all operations stop, especially in a war zone. Regardless of my own personal bias and the bias of every Marine that day, we immediately followed our orders and returned to base, making the four-kilometer movement back to Geronimo.

My Marines rested for the remainder of the day. I especially didn't like messing with their heads, so rest was a condition that was ultimately granted, especially because we would be right out the door again shortly.

The next day my integrated platoon conducted Operation Surge. This was an operation in Lima Company's AO designed to reinforce their patrols around COB Toor Gar. Lima Company was very short on manpower and were lacking in their ability to patrol their battlespace effectively. Therefore, at the request of my former Commanding Officer, Captain Shields, my new Commanding Officer gladly went out of his way to support a sister company, his colleague, and the Marines in Lima's AO.

From 14 September 2010 through 15 September 2010, my integrated platoon conducted ten patrols throughout the battlespace of Lima Company while Hades First Platoon finished up Operation Western Resolve back at Geronimo.

During these patrols, which usually lasted roughly five hours each, my Marines visited the bazaars, Afghan Police Stations, and even an Afghan wedding after being invited by the Afghan groom. My Marines and Afghans provided security, cleared compounds, and tended to the needs of the local nationals if they encountered medical problems. It was not the sexiest of missions; however, working for our old company gave us a good feeling, which was mutual for the Marines of Lima Company, who severely needed a good day's rest from their nonstop hard work throughout the deployment. As a Commander, I was elated to see my Marines who had been selected to stay at Toor Gar early on in the deployment and hear stories of how much good work they were conducting.

During one of our last patrols for Lima Company, my First Squad took enemy contact via a squad-sized Taliban force three kilometers north of COB Toor Gar. The enemy engaged my integrated squad from a little over five hundred meters away but did not get any effective rounds on my Marines. My Marines immediately returned fire on the enemy, apparently wounding or killing one of them in the process, and tried to close with and destroy them before they egressed.

By the time Sergeant Olds and his integrated squad arrived at the area from where they had been fired at, the only thing left was a blood trail and tire tracks from a motorcycle, which was driving east in the direction of the Helmand River. Whoever had fired at my Marines was long gone and now headed toward Pakistan.

My platoon returned to Geronimo on the afternoon of 15 September 2010, after a job well done in Lima Company's AO. We had another successful mission under our belts and one that had enabled my Platoon Sergeant and me to return to FOB Geronimo with all our Marines intact. For anyone in a leadership position, the biggest burden of a leader is ensuring the safety and safe return of his or her men. For a Marine, especially a Platoon Commander, there is no greater love one can have than love for his Marines.

CHAPTER 62

My integrated platoon had an inherent ability to be a victim of our own successes, and we felt this time and again from the missions that came down on us. When we returned to Geronimo, apparently our reputation and accomplishments had spread so far that we were tasked to assume the role of the regimental helicopter quick reaction force during the course of the Afghan general political election period lasting from 17 September 2010 through 20 September 2010.

To sum it all up, my CAPs task was to support any platoon, company, or battalion inside the Regimental Combat Team Seven (RCT-7) AO, known as AO Guadalcanal, if they came under attack during the course of the elections. As a student of history, I was humbled to be a main effort for an operation named after a famous WWII battle in which my grandfather was involved. I hoped it was a sign from God that he was watching over my platoon. Hades First Platoon would be the battalion's mobile maneuver element and provide QRF support if any unit in the battalion's AO came under attack during the course of the election period.

Over the next four days, my men were put on a continuous sixty-minute strip alert. This meant my CAP had to be ready to load a helicopter with all chow, weapons, military gear, and ammunition within one hour.

During the course of the elections, our battalion intelligence section received numerous credible intelligence reports and warnings that local Taliban leader Mullah Abash, who was located in Kilo Company's AO at this time, was planning a major attack to disrupt and sabotage the local elections.

These reports came to fruition when Mullah Abash and three of his accomplices conducted an assassination attempt in which they shot and killed my fellow Platoon Commander and friend from Kilo Company First Lieutenant Scott Flemming on 17 September 2010. To honor his memory, I will not go into details of the event. However, I will say that to my knowledge, during the course of writing this memoir, Mullah Abash has still never been killed or captured. Every day I pray for the capture or killing of this terrorist scumbag so Lieutenant Fleming and his family will have justice.

CHAPTER 63

No other operation during our time as the CAC solidified our hours of training and operational capabilities more than the conduct of supporting Operation Mako. Operation Mako was an India Company combat operation designed to deliberately clear a portion of their battlespace from east to west into an area known as Trek Nawa, clear out weapons caches, and uproot enemy forces.

Trek Nawa was a lawless area and a haven for the Taliban. It was located eight kilometers northwest of FOB Geronimo and directly east of Marjeh. It was the gray area between both Nawa and Marjeh in which the enemy had free reign to plan and conduct operations against Marines because the local nationals gave them support and shelter out of fear for their lives. Strategic value was never determined for the Trek Nawa region; therefore, Marine presence was limited because of the lack of tactical importance. With limited Marine presence, it had become a hotbed and breeding ground for Taliban and insurgent violence and activity, especially after the culmination of Operation Moshtarak back in June.

The area of Trek Nawa was a dichotomy of both arid ground and wetlands. The southern portion of the region was very desertlike with few compounds and even fewer local nationals. As one moved farther north into Trek Nawa, the area was characteristically very muddy and wet with ten-foot-deep canals spread out literally every twenty meters. The people of this area were very insidious and evilly stared at Marine units with cold gazes and eyes filled with fiery hatred and death. The local Afghans here had been brainwashed by the Taliban and knew no better than to obey their every command, even though Marines and coalition forces did their best to help them and win their trust and confidence in the COIN aspect of the war.

The people of this region were characteristically the same people military units and even civilians read about in topics dealing with firefights. They went out of their way to throw women and children in the middle of a firefight to be sacrificed to turn the population against our units. They are the same people who will run at you with an AK-47 in one hand and a baby in the other because they know we cannot shoot babies. This was the reality and the enemy we were fighting. No amount of training could prepare anyone to deal with this reality. No matter how fast a Commander's "OODA Loop" can strategically process real-time events, images of women and children being sacrificed in the name of Islam will leave a stain in one's memory bank. (OODA is an acronym developed by USAF Colonel Boyd; it stands for observe, orient, decide, and act.)

These were the choices and dilemmas my young eighteen- and nineteen-year-olds had to face when dealing with an uncivilized and irrational enemy. These are the stories the civilian population does not know about, especially when they prejudge decisions or scenarios our young Marines face in combat based off television reports or news articles.

I mean, what would you do if you saw a baby or child placed on an IED for the sole purpose of blowing you up when you try to save him or her? This was the reality and the truth about the enemy we faced, and this is what units in this area faced on a daily basis. Life had no value to our enemy, and he would go to extremes to beat us because he had no limits, but we did.

The staging area for my CAP was located at COB Reilly in Second Battalion, Sixth Marines' (2/6) AO. Prior to arriving at our staging area, my CAP received our operations order at PB Poole, a PB named after a Marine who gave his life during combat operations in the Nawa District. This was India Company's most western PB and was located on the Nawa/Trek Nawa border along Route Olympus. Route Olympus was the most feared route in the entire battalion AO because of the constant IED and enemy threat units faced.

India Company's Commanding Officer gave a very confident and thorough operations order to both my Marines, the Marines of India Company, and our Afghan Soldiers on the morning of 21 September 2010. My integrated platoon was tasked as a supporting effort for the mission and ordered to provide northern blocking positions for India Company as they cleared an area inside Trek Nawa from east to west. This blocking position would prevent Taliban from escaping north during India Company's clearing mission. My orders were to kill or capture all enemy fleeing north during India's clear.

Directly following the operations order, my combined platoon was to conduct a mounted security patrol northwest to stage at COB Reilly, also known as The Five Points. From there, our mission was to coordinate with the Marines located at the COB, develop a plan to patrol south in their AO, and then set up multiple squad blocking positions to the north of India Company to deny the enemy egress to the north.

My Marines were staged out of COB Reilly because part of the operational box that was going to be utilized for India Company's operations was in 2/6s AO. For this particular mission, 2/6 gave permission for us to use their battlespace to defeat the enemy and reinforce their Marines.

The India Company operations order culminated at 1100 on the morning of 21 September 2010. Once it was finished, my men conducted backbriefs and did rehearsals of concepts with the Marines of India Company out of PB Poole. This was done to ensure everyone was tracking on the plan and their tasking statements.

At 1500 on the same day, my CAP departed friendly lines at PB Poole for COB Reilly. We arrived at COB Reilly at approximately 1530, a half hour later. We staged our daypacks, linked up with the command at the COB, and gave our intentions report to the Company Commander of 2/6. Our plan was to conduct a movement to contact from Reilly three kilometers south to set up a PB and then set up blocking positions from north to south in support of India Company's main effort mission.

What helped us the most was listening to and gaining guidance from both 2/6 and First Reconnaissance Battalion, who were currently colocated with the grunts at Reilly. First Reconnaissance Battalion had been operating in the area to reinforce 2/6 for the past month. At the time my platoon arrived, Recon was consolidating and preparing to move to Sangin, Afghanistan, for the remainder of their deployment.

From what my Platoon Sergeant and I learned, Recon had apparently killed roughly one hundred enemies in the Trek Nawa area over the last month and a half. Under their guidance, which I took to heart, the first thing we were instructed to do was to get out of open terrain and establish a PB. After discussion about the best time to conduct operations, I heeded their warnings and traded the safety of darkness for the speed we could achieve during daylight hours in setting up our PB. Nothing else mattered in their experienced minds than setting up a base of operations first because they knew the enemy in the area. Hell, they had killed most of them.

They explained to Staff Sergeant Lebron and me that establishing a PB with good cover, concealment, and overwatch was key to being successful in the kinetic area of Trek Nawa where we were about to go. They informed us that the enemy in the area used trigger lines and murder holes to set up ambushes against Marine units and were very well prepared. The last bit of advice they gave us was that once our PB was established, we should stand by for contact with the enemy.

CHAPTER 64

At 0430 the next morning, my Marines and the Afghan Soldiers of Hades Second Platoon broke into alpha and bravo elements and then departed friendly lines at COB Reilly to establish our PB three kilometers to the south and support India Company's main effort mission.

Our alpha element had both First and Third Squads, myself included. The alpha element was the forward element, and it had one specific job: to establish the PB at all costs. The rear element, or the bravo element, was the inner maneuver element. It consisted of my Platoon Sergeant and Second Squad. Should the alpha element take contact, the rear would maneuver on the enemy while the lead element double-timed to the PB.

My bravo element was positioned roughly five hundred meters to the northeast behind my alpha element. They were the diversion and the outer maneuver element. As the alpha element pushed south, the bravo element conducted patrols around the alpha element, allowing zero enemy infiltration that would prevent the accomplishment of the mission to establish a PB. We attempted to conduct a hybrid of satellite patrolling to confuse the enemy, who were watching our every move and studying my patrolling techniques.

The movement south was quick, and my Marines and Afghan Soldiers were on their toes as they felt cold chills running up and down their spines and across the backs of their necks. We felt like strangers in a foreign land—outsiders, unwelcomed by all. The eeriness of the Trek Nawa region gave off a strange, grim vibration, and we felt like death surrounded us. As we patrolled farther and farther south, the locals would dart in and out of compounds and make sneering noises at us. They hid behind mud compound walls and then popped out again, whispering of our movements and actions to enemy cohorts who stood behind the walls of the compounds. Village elders and military-aged men would mean mug my Marines and hold babies in their hands while they took the index fingers of their opposite hands and ran them across their throats as a signal to say we were going to die. My Marines and I laughed, standing firm and ready to arrange a meeting between them and their Allah in heaven with their promised virgins.

My Afghan Soldiers and linguists, on the other hand, were scared beyond belief and clung to their Marine counterparts as they hurriedly tried to push us faster and faster to establish our PB.

The alpha element patrolled roughly three kilometers south of COB Reilly and established a temporary PB between two main roads in the area at approximately 0700 that morning. I immediately had our interpreter command our ANA to remove the local nationals who lived in the compound so my CAP could establish a safe haven for my Marines. (This was a tactic both First Recon and 2/6 had been using in the AO.) The sense of an approaching fight flowed through the air, and every one of us could smell the danger of something about to happen.

Once the local nationals fled the compound, my Marines and Afghan Soldiers immediately scanned the inner perimeter for primary IEDs and secondary and tertiary directional firing charges. We then secured the area and established overwatch positions, placing our designated marksman and medium machine guns on the rooftops to cover a 360-degree perimeter.

With the bravo element still providing my alpha element security outside the PB, I sent out a reinforced fire team of six Marines and six ANA Soldiers from our newly established position to conduct linkup and escort my bravo element into the compound. Once this was done, the reinforced fire team conducted local security patrols in our immediate vicinity to scan the immediate area and adjacent compounds, making sure no one was sneaking up on us or planning to attack us.

Once my bravo element was inside friendly lines at the PB, I had Sergeant Brown, who was in charge of that element, rest and refit his men for thirty minutes. I then sent his element back outside friendly lines to conduct local security patrols in the immediate vicinity and relieve the fire team currently out there. At all times my CAP strived to have one element outside the wire of the PB and two back for a QRF and to provide security.

Once everything was in order and operations out of the PB were continuous, the morning went by very slowly and quietly for us. My alpha element went out on a dismounted security patrol for a few hours and discovered a few pictures of local nationals carrying AK-47s, but nothing out of the ordinary. Sergeant Olds and his element came back inside the wire at around 1200 with nothing unusual to report. Sergeant Brown left a few of his Marines and ANA at the PB for security and then took his squad out next to conduct local security patrols. He came back inside the wire at roughly 1330 that afternoon, again with nothing to report other than that everything seemed unusually quiet for an area known for its inherent kinetic activity.

At 1400, Sergeant Olds patrolled his squad of six Marines and six ANA out of the PB to set up blocking positions on our southern tactical limit of advance in support of India Company's main effort mission. Roughly twenty minutes after his squad departed friendly lines, the sounds and impacts of India Company's clearing mission could be felt and heard by all of us still inside the PB once their Company Commander declared his troops were in contact.

Marine Cobras patrolled the skies above us. We watched their pilots fire rockets and ammunition at enemy targets below. Light antitank weapons (LAWs) were blowing up and destroying the walls of enemy compounds, 60mm mortar rounds started rocking the earth as they exploded on the ground, and 40mm high-explosive grenade rounds from their M203 grenade launchers were blowing up all enemies who remained in their path. The explosions lasted for more than an hour, and the look on every Marine's and Afghan's face was priceless as they all sat at our temporary PB with smiles of appreciation for India Company closing with and destroying the enemy directly to our south.

Our silent screams of elation were short-lived. Twenty minutes into the fighting, Staff Sergeant Lebron and I started to get a bad feeling. We looked at each other from inside the PB, both instinctively knowing something was about to happen to Sergeant Olds and his integrated squad directly south of our position. The enemy would soon be fleeing north and run right into our Marines on the border. They were alone and unafraid with the enemy egressing right toward them.

Feeling an uneasiness and inability to relax, I remember saying to my Platoon Sergeant with an urgent excitement, "Staff Sergeant, usually I would never go with you in the same patrol, and we both always make sure we are separated in the event something happens to one of us but—"

Before I could even finish my sentence, he replied, "I feel you, sir. Usually you and I will be in separate elements, but I have a feeling something bad is about to happen, and you and I both need to be there for it." The feeling we had was almost mutually precognitive, as if we had an inherent sixth sense telling us something did not feel right and our men were in danger.

We grabbed a majority of Third Squad and their ANA, minus few Marines and Sergeant Guthrie, our Third Squad Leader. We left our Third Squad Leader behind with Sergeant Brown to guard the PB in our absence and conduct local security patrols to make sure the enemy did not infiltrate our position. If the worst were to happen, Sergeant Brown would assume the role of Platoon Commander while Sergeant Guthrie assumed the role of Platoon Sergeant.

My Platoon Sergeant grabbed Corporal Mount and his fire team of Marines and Afghan Soldiers, and we all departed the PB in a blaze of fury. We double-timed our movement south, hurriedly heading in the direction of First Squad.

We were no more than five minutes out the door of our temporary PB when we receive an urgent call from Sergeant Olds that his combined squad was caught in an ambush and was taking effective enemy fire.

As his squad had patrolled our southern limit of advance, a few young local national boys had started yelling, throwing rocks, and pointing at him and his men. This caught the squad's attention and methodically sucked my Marines and Afghan Soldiers into an ambush position and kill zone. Once Sergeant Olds and his squad were committed and sucked in by the young Afghan decoys, they hit an enemy trigger line, and the Taliban opened up fire on them and the two Afghan boys from up to three separate flanking positions.

It was a beautiful ambush position by the enemy on my Marines. They had done their homework, and we had to give them credit. It was an L-shaped ambush initiated from compounds and mud-walled buildings from the west and then reinforced from separate compounds from both the southwest and south.

By the time Staff Sergeant Lebron and I received the call, our squad was pinned down and engaging the enemy three hundred meters to their south and west. A five- to seven-man Taliban fire team had my squad engaged with effective fires from PKM machine guns and AK-47s. Sergeant Olds and his squad responded by rocking away with their rifles, semiautomatic weapons (SAWs), and M203 grenade launchers, targeting, blowing up, and destroying the compounds in which the enemy was located.

With all the noise and destruction my Marines were causing to kill the Taliban, it became difficult to find the exact location of my squad. I radioed back to my PB to request immediate air support to kill the enemy engaging my squad.

I then radioed Sergeant Olds to fire a white star cluster in the air to signal his exact position so we could locate him. In all the chaos and thunder from the grenades exploding and machine gun fire, plotting a grid or tracking their position with a GPS would take too long. Besides, the enemy already knew where they were and had a tactical advantage at this point.

Less than two minutes after I gave the command to fire the white star cluster, we honed in on their position and ran full speed to their location. A feeling of uncertainty laced with excitement filled our bodies as adrenaline pumped our heavy muscles into action and led us in the direction to reinforce our Marines who were pinned down. As we ran toward Sergeant Olds and his squad, only one thought flowed through our minds: to help our Marines by killing the bastards who wanted to kill us.

There was no doubt in my mind that the enemy thought he had us licked and did not expect what happened next. Within about ten minutes of Sergeant Olds's radio transmission and contact report, we arrived on scene to reinforce First Squad, who were pinned down in a trench.

The situation on the ground reminded me exactly of Range 410 out at Enhanced Mojave Viper in Twentynine Palms, California. My Marines were caught in an L-shaped ambush and were getting engaged from three hundred meters to the south and three hundred meters to the west by AK-47s and PKM machine guns.

I ran up on my pinned-down squad and placed myself behind the wall of a compound directly north of their position to observe the battlefield and conduct command and control. I gave the order for Staff Sergeant Lebron to take the majority of the squad he was with and maneuver from north to south on the enemy located west of First Squad's position to outflank and suppress them. I then dove into the trench with my Radio Operator, Lance Corporal Ortiz, and linked up with my Squad Leader, Sergeant Olds.

I immediately ordered my Marines and Afghan Soldiers to stay engaged with the enemy to the south and west while my Platoon Sergeant maneuvered on the enemy. As if the gates of Hades opened up, my Marines started to pick up their rates of fire, sending hundreds of rounds downrange at the enemy compounds. They then opened up with a barrage of 40mm grenades from their grenade launchers and rocked even more compounds with their LAW rockets.

After a few minutes of engagement, I received a call from my Platoon Sergeant to shift fires south, as he was now engaged with the enemy to our west. As my Marines and I shifted fires south, we heard the gunshots and fire coming from our west and knew at this point that our Marines and ANA had gained advantage over the enemy, taken the ground, and had them on the run.

Within about five minutes, air came on station, and Staff Sergeant Lebron and my Marines were able to force the enemy to egress southwest, successfully cutting off their fires. Once Marine Cobras started flying overhead and firing on the compounds we were being ambushed from, all enemy fire and activity ceased. This was not uncommon because the enemy feared helicopters and their destructive capabilities. Helicopters stayed on station another twenty minutes and then departed to reinforce India Company and their troops, who were still in contact.

It was almost as if a light switch went off. The precise moment the Cobras departed, my Marines and I taking cover in the trench line were engaged again, this time from five hundred meters to our southwest and two hundred meters to our south. I then received a call over the radio from my Platoon Sergeant. He identified an enemy shot spotter behind a compound to our south. He relayed to me the position of the spotter, and my Marines and I began to sight in.

The spotter, who ran in and out of the compound directly to our south, was in all black, talking on a cell phone, and pointing at my Marines and me. After almost twenty seconds of constant watch, we noticed that every time we raised our rifles to sight in, the spotter disappeared behind a wall before we could squeeze a round off. Then when the spotter emerged, gunfire would begin again. The spotter was walking the rounds of their shooters onto our position.

At this moment, my Marines positioned themselves to the south and waited like predators stalking their prey for this alleged spotter to surface again. Within seconds, and as plain as day, the spotter emerged from behind the shadows of the compound wall. My Platoon Sergeant called it right down to the smallest detail. An enemy spotter emerged, talking on a cellular phone, dressed in all black, and literally pointing at us while walking the enemy shooters and their rounds onto our position.

That was all the evidence my Marines and I needed to destroy the enemy. I remember I had three Marines and two Afghan Soldiers pointing their weapons in the direction of the spotter during this moment of realization. No sooner was the spotter identified than I heard Sergeant Olds's voice over my radio: "Sir, I confirm the enemy spotter two hundred meters to the south, all black on a cell phone, pointing. I am engaging."

Without hesitation, and acting under the premise of special trust and confidence in my Squad Leader, I replied, "Take him out!" Sergeant Olds had one of his Marines squeeze the trigger of his M4 service rifle, sending a single 5.56mm round over a distance of two hundred meters in the direction of the enemy. Seconds after the round left the chamber of his Marine weapon, piercing the air as it traveled, the round exploded through the front and back of the enemy shot spotter's head, parting his cranium like Moses parted the Red Sea. With that single shot, all fire suddenly ceased, and everything went dead quiet. My Marines and I waited in the trench for a few minutes. Then we started to maneuver on the position of the enemy spotter.

During this time, Staff Sergeant Lebron and his squad kept firing on the enemy to the west while pushing from north to south, effectively guarding our western flank. They ended up clearing the compounds to our western flank using their Afghan Soldiers and found only blood trails and spent rifle round casings. We assumed we killed a few enemies to our west; however, the Taliban were good about sanitizing their areas of combat prior to Marine units coming on scene, which had most likely occurred in this case.

About fifteen minutes went by before my Marines and I reached the destroyed spotter for the conduct of a battle damage assessment, but the results were obvious. The spotter had been destroyed by a head shot. The spotter had also been stripped from head to toe and policed by the enemy in the adjacent compound. They left behind only a few unspent rifle rounds in the compound rooms from which they shot at us.

I remember the joy and elation I felt as the spotter lay there, facedown in a pool of his blood. I was grateful that my Marines were still alive and that the enemy was dead. My Marines and I consolidated at the site where the spotter had been destroyed. Then we pushed south to clear a village the remaining enemy from the building had fled to.

After twenty minutes of clearing the area with our Afghan Soldiers, we found no more enemies and subsequently received no more fire. That fact alone solidified my confidence that the dead enemy had been a shot spotter. My Marines had been engaged by a fire team reinforced of five to seven enemy forces from two or three separate positions only thirty minutes ago, and now we were receiving zero contact.

During this time, India Company, who was to our south, was wrapping up their operation and egressing back to PB Poole. I made the decision at the same time to consolidate back at our temporary PB, regroup, and then get back as soon as possible to COB Reilly before any more uncertainty was thrown our way. The mission was officially over, and I was responsible for bringing my men back safely once again.

On our way back, my platoon encountered zero resistance from any enemy. It was crazy. Just eight hundred meters south of our PB, we had been caught in an ambush and were engaged with the enemy for more than twenty minutes. Then, after one round was fired through the cranium of an enemy spotter, all enemy activity had ceased. It was amazing; however, we were all subconsciously still on edge, thinking all hell might break loose again.

Once my Marines and I returned to the temporary PB, we broke down our defensive and support-by-fire positions and prepared to egress north in echelons back to COB Reilly. Even though our Afghans had trouble with this formation during training at Geronimo, there was no getting around utilizing it at this point, and they learned to use it really quickly.

Again, I broke my platoon into alpha and bravo elements for the dismounted security patrol north. The bravo element was on our eastern flank, providing security to the east, while the alpha element provided security to the west. The primary mission was to get to back to the safety of COB Reilly. The secondary mission for both elements was to directly support each other to set the conditions for the main mission of returning to the COB.

I will never forget the uneasiness my Marines and ANA Soldiers felt as we patrolled out of Trek Nawa, heading north for The Five Points and

COB Reilly. I had never seen or witnessed my ANA Soldiers acting as afraid as they were during that time. They literally thought they were going to die. It was as if my CAP was departing the gates of hell itself as all its demons tried to pull us back in.

Little children pointed their fingers like guns at the heads of my Marines as we passed compounds. Fathers and village elders stood by us with babies in their hands, pointing their fingers at us in the shapes of pistols. Military-aged males stared at us and whispered words to men waiting behind compound walls regarding whereabouts of our patrol, its size, and our current activity. Little children stood on rooftops, acting as surveillance with cell phones in one hand and pointing at my Marines and Afghan Soldiers with the other as we made our way back north to COB Reilly.

Fearing the enemy may try to get a tactical advantage on my platoon, I made the decision to rapidly change our egress route back to COB Reilly. By pulling an audible on our patrol route out, we were able to confuse the enemy to the point of disorientation so he was unable to locate or engage my Marines and Soldiers.

My platoon returned to Reilly that night at around 1730. Upon arrival, Staff Sergeant Lebron and I immediately conducted a formal debrief with the leadership of 2/6.

We wanted nothing more than to get our Marines safely back to FOB Geronimo and out of this AO. Call it luck or a close call, but the enemy had almost caught us with our pants down. At roughly 1840, after our debriefs were conducted, my platoon and I thanked the command at COB Reilly for their hospitality and support in allowing us to utilize their AO for the mission. My CAP loaded up our mobile vehicles, and we made the one-and-a-half-hour journey southeast back to Geronimo.

Without a doubt, if we had not listened to the stellar wisdom of the Marines located at Reilly prior to the conduct of operation, the outcome would have been far worse. As a leader, anytime you or your Marines are in unfamiliar territory, it is always best to swallow your pride, ego, or reputation and show humility to the units operating in the area. They know both the enemy and terrain better than you do, and for the safety of your men, you would do right to shut up, listen, and take notes.

The operation in Trek Nawa solidified the existence and confirmed the value of our CAP and the CAC. Our existence and the proof that the combined action platoon and company worked was cemented by our victory, with help from the blood of the dead enemy spotter who was now fertilizing the desert ground.

During the engagement, the few Afghan Soldiers who had not cowered in the trenches had returned fire along with my Marines in an effort to suppress the enemy. When Staff Sergeant Lebron and I had run toward my First Squad to reinforce them, the Afghan Soldiers who were with us, and even the Afghan Platoon Commander, ran toward the sound of gunfire. They were ready, and I was now confident that when we left Afghanistan to redeploy back home, our ANA had the confidence and training to take the fight to the enemy without our help.

I remember during the ride back to the FOB, Staff Sergeant Lebron informed me that he even had to tackle the Afghan Platoon Commander during the assault because he was running full speed at the enemy without even firing at one point. As he explained it, he told me the Afghan Platoon Commander looked as if he was doing a kamikaze run toward the enemy shooters, running ahead of his Soldiers, who he left far behind him. In an act to save the life of the Afghan Platoon Commander, my Platoon Sergeant had done what he did best: protect the lives of the men.

We were lucky that day. The firefight had all the ingredients to make a potential disaster for both my squad and platoon. The quick thinking and sound judgment of my Marines paid off that day. As I look back on the event now, I think the enemy must have thought he had the upper hand until he saw my squad outflanking him from the north to cut off his fires to the west. He also did not take into account that we would eliminate his shot spotter and neutralize his ability for command and control of fires.

When we returned to Geronimo, my Platoon Sergeant and I decided to let our Marines and Afghan Soldiers rest for the remainder of the night. The next morning, we conducted a formal debrief with our CO and our Marines. The premise of the debrief was to go over the time line of events that occurred the day prior. Our ROEs were so restrictive that sometimes Marines were investigated or charged when they killed an enemy, and we wanted to inform them that what they had done was right.

We also wanted to reassure the Marines that their command was behind them 100 percent. COIN is a very difficult type of warfare, and the worst feeling Marines can have occurs when their leadership and brethren abandon them at critical moments. Not that this was the case, but my Platoon Sergeant and I felt we needed to commend our Marines for killing the enemy, protecting one another, and defeating the Taliban threat. They deserved a pat on the back. The last reason we had for conducting the debrief was to check the mental status of my Marines and Corpsmen to ensure there were no issues that would prevent them from doing their job for the rest of the deployment.

CHAPTER 65

Our next combat operation occurred on 24 September 2010. The operation was to support a platoon in India Company at PB Skullet. PB Skullet was another PB in India Company's AO located in an area that constantly faced the enemy threats of IEDs or firefights.

The night prior to our receipt of the operation, the Marines and Sailors at the PB were attacked by a fire team of Taliban fighters. Utilizing machine guns and RPG complex fire attacks, the enemy and the Marines at Skullet stayed engaged throughout the night. After a night of fighting and almost completely out of ammunition, the Marines were victorious, taking zero casualties and defeating the enemy with both air support from Cobra helicopters and their own superior firepower.

Upon arriving at Skullet, my platoon was to conduct a BDA and reinforce the men there by helping them patrol their battlespace until they recovered from the firefight, received a much-needed resupply of ammunition, and were able to reassume control of their patrolling areas.

After my platoon arrived, we immediately conducted the BDA and resumed the hunt for the Taliban responsible for the attack. As we patrolled the area around Skullet, we soon noticed that the ground and shrubbery were literally still smoking and on fire from the amount of ammunition shot by both the Marines at the PB and the Cobras that had provided support during the engagement the night before.

My platoon assessed the damages, only finding pieces of clothing, sandals, and blood trails; however, there was nothing significant to report. We concluded that the extreme amount of firepower and ammunition dumped on the enemy from the Marines at Skullet and the Cobra helicopters, and the subsequent fire caused by the ammunition burning the terrain, had destroyed virtually all evidence. It was unrecognizable.

Throughout the day, my platoon patrolled the immediate battlespace for the Marines at Skullet to help them recover from the previous enemy attack. That night, the Marines at India's PB were resupplied and refitted and reassumed control of their battlespace.

The next day, my platoon received our next mission from our CO via radio transmission from Geronimo. We patrolled seven kilometers south to an area in Kilo Company's battlespace known as Checkpoint Wrightsman. Checkpoint Wrightsman was a military checkpoint on a main supply route. It was built in honor of our fallen Marine Corporal Wrightsman. The area around the checkpoint saw significant roadside bombs and IEDs, did not have a strong Marine presence, and was only reinforced by the unreliable and mostly corrupt drug-addicted Afghan Uniformed Police Officers.

When my platoon arrived, lo and behold, we found that the Afghan Police had abandoned the checkpoint for fear of getting shot at or blown up. My Marines and ANA were on our own to defend it.

No matter. As Marines we work well with less, and in our case it was one less unit to get in the way of our military business. For two straight days, my CAP secured Checkpoint Wrightsman, stopping and searching more than seven hundred vehicles and personnel driving north to south along the main supply route. For my Marines and me, securing an area named after the fallen brother we had recovered from the bowels of the Helmand River was a rewarding honor for the memory of his legacy.

CHAPTER 66

On the afternoon of 26 September 2010, my Marines and I conducted a battle handover of Checkpoint Wrightsman back to Kilo Company's Marines and their Afghan Uniformed Police Officers. Our mobile element extracted us back to Geronimo, where we conducted rest and refit. Over the course of the next week, training resumed with our ANA Soldiers. At this point in our training, the Afghans were confident and committed to the lessons we were teaching.

Corporal Berry, my Second Squad First Fire Team Leader had trained our foreign counterparts so methodically in the realm of tactical site exploitation that they could best any junior Marine in the CAC and battalion in terms of employment and application. Throughout the last two months, Sergeant Brown had brought our partners up to a standard of conceptualizing a basic understanding of English, coupled with a respect for American history and Marine culture. Having them understand our culture and assimilate them into it was key to bringing us together as a fighting unit.

Sergeant Olds and his squad had turned his gaggle of mediocre Afghans into physical studs and hardened trained warriors. Sergeant Guthrie and his squad had made their Afghan Soldiers into tactical gurus, making them professionals in their abilities to conduct searches of houses, room clearing, and employment of our compact mine detectors to locate possible IEDs.

Since the end of Ramadan and Eid al-Fitr, our schedule had gone back to normal, and the hours my CAP was not training were spent conducting both mounted and dismounted security patrols from Geronimo. Teaching and instructing the Afghans became a marathon, and we were now sprinting to the finish line. Training a third-world military that has only been around for a few years and then shaping and forming them into a capable and effective fighting force to defend their country was honestly not thought possible and given very little credit and recognition. My Marines truly surpassed an unthinkable feat in this respect.

Training at this point in the deployment became routine for the men of the CAC. No questions were asked, and orders were obeyed. Staff Sergeant Lebron and I had legitimized the Afghan Platoon Sergeant and Platoon Commander, as had Lieutenant Miller and his Platoon Sergeant. Even though our CO and the leadership of the CAC controlled all operations and training, we still brought our counterparts to the table, knowing full well that their opinions did not matter but giving them the credit they deserved.

The value that this gave our counterparts in front of their men was priceless because the men started to see their leaders as legitimate and competent. Eventually, all credit for the conduct of operations went to the Afghan leadership when they were in front of their Soldiers even though in the background my Marines controlled the strings. Most of all, I believe the Afghan Soldiers saw their leaders partnering with us and fighting alongside us, whether it was in nightly meetings or on the battlefield, and they believed in the cause and mission more than anything.

Every morning from 0600 through 0730, physical training was conducted, followed by chow, which lasted until 0900. Six hours a day were then devoted to classroom instruction and training six days a week, with Friday being their only day off because it was their holy day.

By the first week of October 2010, our Afghan Soldiers were technically and tactically proficient in many aspects of the Marine Corps doctrine. There were now Afghan Fire Team Leaders leading squad patrols who utilized and grasped the concepts of hand and arm signals and patrolling formations.

These same Fire Team Leaders conducted immediate action drills for scenarios involving enemy contact, IED attacks, sniper fire, and indirect fire. During class instruction, our Afghan Soldiers were more attentive, started to fall asleep less and less out of respect for my Marine instructors, and genuinely wanted to work with my Marines on everything they did.

My Marines and Afghan Soldiers were by no means equal, and they never would be, but they were being competitively groomed and brought together through the hardships and burdens they were bearing together, both in the classroom environment and during combat operations. The sense and feeling that Marines in our present-day could form, train, and lead a foreign third-world military just like our brothers of the past during the Vietnam War was now reality.

Instead of having CAPs, we now had a fully functioning combined action company. It was concept born through a simple idea discussed by Marine Bing West in his book *The Village* that was expanded upon by my battalion and CO and made reality in the hearts and minds of my Marines. It was a reality that was earned into existence through the hard work and sacrifice of a few motivated Marines and sustained through training and practical application that surpassed expectations and was cemented in blood.

CHAPTER 67

After a week and a half of nonstop patrols and classroom instruction conducted from Geronimo, the Marines and Afghan Soldiers of Hades Second Platoon were tasked with the next operation, known as Battalion Operation Sledgehammer. The mission tasked my Marines and Afghan warriors to be the main effort for the battalion during the conduct of this operation.

The overall intent behind this mission was that my platoon would be the battalion main effort and lead the deliberate clearing from west to east of every compound in a four-kilometer operational box. The OP box was carved out of Kilo Company's AO, and we were to confirm or deny the validity of our intelligence reports, which had concluded that there were Taliban Commanders—along with weapons caches and munitions—in the vicinity of our operational box. My CAP was to capture or kill these enemy fighters if we encountered them.

For this mission, my platoon had a special guest directly attached to us. That guest was a female reporter from the *Washington Times* named Sara Carter, and she was going to embed with my integrated platoon over the course of the next few days.

The mobile element of my CAC escorted my CAP to the staging area on the morning of 6 October 2010. The staging area for this operation was going to be PB Skullet, located roughly six kilometers from our objective areas. This was where we would initiate the operation. PB Skullet soon became known as a comedic "black hole" for the Marines of Hades Second Platoon for the simple fact that once we arrived, we always seemed to get sucked right back into the gravitational field of the PB, and no matter how hard we fought, we could not escape it.

After arriving at PB Skullet and meeting with the leadership there, I conducted my operations order to my platoon. My scheme of maneuver broke my platoon down into three different squads to maximize our efficiency and efficacy in clearing four kilometer-sized grid squares consisting of more than one thousand local national compounds. For the rest of the day, my Marines and Afghan Soldiers rehearsed the proper procedures and concepts for room clearing, tactical questioning, mine detection, and tactical callouts of local nationals from their compounds.

Over and over again, my Squad Leaders and I rehearsed the routes to our objective areas, the compounds each combined squad was responsible for clearing, and all actions and inactions that could come about from the conduct of this operation. In a nutshell, rehearsals of concepts (ROC drills or walks) were our moneymaker, and every Marine and Afghan had to know his job from the highest to lowest level, especially in the absence of leadership.

At 0400 on 7 October 2010, Operation Sledgehammer kicked off, and my platoon departed friendly lines at PB Skullet and made the six-kilometer movement to our objective areas. We spread apart by time, with each squad departing ten minutes behind the other, and arrived at our three separate objectives by 0530 that morning. At 0600, I gave the order to my Marine and ANA Squad Leaders listening over the radios, and Operation Sledgehammer was underway. No sooner had the operation commenced than one of our Afghan Soldiers had a negligent discharge. No one was hurt in the process; however, the ability of surprise was lost.

Second Squad, led by Sergeant Brown, was located to the north of the three objectives and had our CO and our embedded *Washington Times* reporter attached. I was located with Sergeant Guthrie in the center with Third Squad, and to the south was Staff Sergeant Lebron with Sergeant Olds and First Squad.

Coordination, command, and control of friendly fires were essential because our units were right on top of one another. We had to ensure that all fires were directed to the east toward the Helmand River to prevent friendly fire incidents. The hardest part of the operation was battle tracking and making sure each of my integrated squads was maintaining integrity and staying on line during the systematic clear. In this manner, each squad was both able to mutually support one another and have fire deconfliction because they knew where each other was located.

For close to twelve daylight hours, my Marines and Afghan Soldiers conducted the nonstop deliberate clearing of every compound in the proximity of our four grid squares. It was a long and arduous task, frequented by many tactical pauses for our Afghan Soldiers, whose job was to search every compound and local national along the movement from west to east toward the river. Met with this friction, my CAP had to endure the unforgiving Afghan terrain of endless canals and cornfields filled with thick mud and deep water. These canals were notoriously known for shattering the ankles of Marines on patrol.

With all of that and the constant presumption that there was an enemy in our midst and IEDs under our feet, coupled with 120-degree heat, sleep deprivation, and lack of chow and water, the clearing of more than four kilometers was a very intense mission. It is in these most miserable times that one truly measures himself and his platoon and truly knows their value. I will not lie; a twelve-hour clearing operation under these extreme conditions was miserable, but it was our job all the same. It was both honoring and humbling to stand beside my men during the conduct of this operation, and all of our operations for that matter.

Throughout the clearing operations there were many high-value individuals and compounds my Marines and ANA had to locate and conduct raids on. Many of the individuals we were looking for were high-level Taliban Commanders, and the compounds we were to search were their alleged homes and safe havens.

One enemy Commander we were still looking for in particular was Mullah Abash, who was still at large. To our dismay, during the course of the entire clearing operation all we were able to recover were some rifle shells and a possible IED power source. It was as if our intelligence had gotten it wrong, the Afghans tipped the enemy off, or all of the Taliban had fled either south to Quetta or east to Pakistan for the winter. There was nothing to be found and no one to be had. Our four-kilometer twelve-hour clearing operation yielded my CAP zero intelligence finds as we reached our limit of advance west of the Helmand River.

Empty-handed and staring at the mountains and cliffs above the river to the east, my CAP consolidated on the banks of the Helmand and then patrolled two kilometers west. We then arrived at a compound known to belong to Mullah Abash. At this point, my CO and platoon leadership were pissed, and we wanted nothing more than to try to disturb a "hornet nest." In saying that, I had my integrated platoon take over Mullah Abash's alleged compound and dwell in the Taliban Commander's house as a way of getting payback for the man responsible for killing First Lieutenant Flemming.

In my mind, now that we were in Abash's compound, he was either going to get pissed off and try to attack us or get scared and run away. Hoping to strike gold, all my platoon found was potluck. We ran PB operations out of Abash's compound for the remainder of the day and into the night. However, if there were any enemy in the area, they were long gone by now. With supplies running low and the promise of finding anything of intelligence value diminishing by the hour, my CAP broke down the temporary PB at the known Taliban Commander's compound at 0500 the next morning and made the six-kilometer movement back to PB Skullet.

In my mind, the operation was a successful failure. My CAP had successfully cleared every compound in the operational box; however, we had failed to find the intelligence we had been assured was there. The positive benefit of the mission was the impact it had on our embedded reporter. She had nothing but compliments, and she expressed disbelief toward the combined operations and actions that my Marines, partnered with the Afghan Soldiers, had been able to accomplish. She was amazed at how far the CAC had come and could not believe my Marines had brought the ANA Soldiers to a standard that could be concluded as proficient and effective. It was nice to hear these kind words and opinions expressed by her, though my mind was clouded with anger at not finding anything during the operation.

Our patrol back to PB Skullet was met with even more friction when my Platoon Radio Operator, Lance Corporal Ortiz, received a transmission from our Battalion Operations Officer that our orders were to stop our return to base, recock, and refit in order to reclear the entire operations box again. At this point, even my CO was irritated, not only because our Operations Officer told this to my Lance Corporal but because our own battalion was convinced that there was some type of intelligence in the area we had cleared, and they were not going to be satisfied until they found it.

To this day, other than the information I was given, I will never know what our highers thought we overlooked or missed when they ordered us to reclear the entire four-kilometer operations box.

Ill-equipped with supplies to continue our mission, my platoon ended up returning to PB Skullet that morning on 8 October 2010 for a twenty-four-hour rest and refit. A lot of confusion as to what was going on and what we were supposed to find plagued our minds as the men who sat behind the desks made the decisions. Someone making that decision was internally bent on the notion that during the clear my platoon had to have missed numerous weapons caches and Taliban.

Frustrated and always looking out for the best interests of the men under his command, my CO left my CAP at PB Skullet to go to the battalion COC and request a change of mission and orders from his superiors. Disobeying a direct order would have gotten him and all of us fired. He returned to PB Skullet later that day and informed us the orders would remain the same. Obeying the orders of my higher, my platoon rested and recocked for the follow-on mission of Operation Sledgehammer II on the morning of 9 October 2010. Just the same as the conduct of Operation Sledgehammer, my CAP broke down into three squads and recleared the entire four-kilometer operations box. Beaten, bruised, and battered, my worn-out Marines and Afghan

Army Soldiers held up in a compound that night, again finding zero intelligence throughout the AO.

Having patrolled more than fifty-five kilometers in the last three days, through muddy terrain, deep canals, and quagmires of cornfields and under the embrace of the unforgiving heat of the Afghan sun, the men in my CAP were getting mentally and physically exhausted. There was simply no intelligence to be had, and our intelligence was not right on this particular mission. Out of all the hundreds of local nationals we encountered, tactically questioned and exploited, not one gave any hints or particular details of Taliban whereabouts or locations.

There is no doubt in my mind that at one point there had been weapons caches and Taliban Commanders in the area. However, through all the weeks of planning for the mission, it is my own personal opinion that our intentions were leaked through the "loose lips" of our Afghan counterparts who were aligned with the Taliban. This was done to reveal our intent and warn them to flee before we arrived.

On 10 October 2010, my Marines and I left the security and safety of the temporary PB we had established during the conduct of Operation Sledgehammer II and once again patrolled six kilometers back to the confines of PB Skullet. Tired and worn out, my Marines and I consolidated again at PB Skullet, linked up with our integrated mobile element, and made the one-hour mounted journey southwest to FOB Geronimo.

CHAPTER 68

The same day we returned, my Marines and I were informed that our ANA Soldiers were going to be officially detached from our platoon and sent north to the India Company AO to reinforce positions there. From what we were informed, the First Tolai of Afghan Army Soldiers, which is their First Platoon, was overdue to be relieved in India's AO, and the Third and Fourth Tolai, who both Hades 1 and 2 were training, were scheduled to relieve them.

This word came very suddenly and took every one of my Marines by surprise. It goes without saying that things can change in an instant in the Corps. Our combined action platoon and combined action company had served as both the main and supporting efforts for two battalion operations, ten company operations, and numerous platoon operations over the course of the last four months. Now our days of training our Afghan Soldiers were coming to an end quick, fast, and in a hurry. As shocking as this news was, all of my Marines within the CAC were more than confident that any unit that received our ANA would benefit greatly.

Anything worth doing is worth giving 110 percent so it is done right. As was the case almost weekly, my CO culminated a training week with an integrated company formation and gave out awards for both Marines and ANA who had earned them through hard work and effort. The awards were either letters of appreciation, verbal recognitions, or Benchmade knives. These were given to commemorate both Marines and Afghan Soldiers for a job well done. Our last day as a combined action company and combined action platoon was no different.

With the battalion's Combat Cameraman present to take pictures, our Commanding Officer and his First Sergeant, like the true professionals they always strived to be, conducted the final formation of the CAC. All of the Marines and Afghan Soldiers of the combined action company stood in formation in the rear of our LSA for the last time as a combined unit as the names of award recipients were read off.

As the awards process culminated and the formation ended, it was cathartic and rewarding. At the same time, it felt like our Sisyphean task was over. It was cathartic because my Marines and I had accomplished a feat few believed was possible and even fewer thought would work. It was rewarding because my Marines and I had succeeded in created a fully integrated combined action platoon and combined action company, and now they were off on their next mission for the overall good and future of Afghanistan.

If anything was certain, it was this: Future military units, in an effort to enhance the transition of lead security to their Afghan partners, could now use the training techniques and lessons learned from our missions to enhance their own proficiency and combat capabilities against the enemy. These lessons and TTPs would particularly enable transition of lead security from Marine units to their Afghan counterparts.

The Marines of the CAC had created a cornerstone and a foundation that could be used as a premise or building block for the future transfer of authority and lead security responsibility to the government of Afghanistan by United States and NATO forces.

Our ability to be an unstoppable fully integrated maneuver element throughout the battalion's AO was now officially over with the departure of our ANA Soldiers. With the support of the ANA, our platoon had been able to go to places that Marine-pure platoons could not venture because of our ROEs. The ROEs that limited our capabilities in this fight did not limit our Afghans, who had become the spearhead of the CAC.

As with all of my platoon formations, Staff Sergeant Lebron and I made it very professional and ceremonial for our men. He and I walked up to each individual Afghan Soldier, thanked him, and congratulated him for efforts in service to my platoon and company and his country. Concordantly, the Afghan Platoon Commander and Platoon Sergeant, after viewing the actions of Staff Sergeant Lebron and myself, went up to all of my Marines, shook their hands, and gave them thanks for their service in enhancing the future of their country.

After the formation, my Marines shook the hands of their Afghan counterparts, thanking them for a job well done and an experience they would not forget for as long as they lived. From Private First Class up to the rank of First Lieutenant, every one of my Marines had taught and learned a great deal from these third-world Soldiers, and each Soldier was now a better warrior through learning from my Marines and Sailors.

My Platoon Sergeant and I, wanting nothing in return from our Afghan counterparts, gave each of them our own personal KA-BAR field knives as a gesture and parting gift for a job well done. Excited and grateful for everything our Marines had taught them, they offered us chai tea for one final sitting before we disbanded.

At the conclusion of our tea, we each shook each other's hands like men for the last time and parted ways. As the Afghan Soldiers left our LSA one by one, my Marines and I knew we had set them up for success and that the country of Afghanistan and its inhabitants would be a little bit safer from the Taliban.

EPILOGUE

The future of the combined action company was the topic of discussion over the next few days with our Commanding Officer and the higher echelons of power within our battalion at Geronimo. After much debate, plans were in the works for the training and integration of another Afghan unit, the First Afghan Tolai. The First Tolai would come from India Company to Geronimo over the course of the next month and slowly start moving into the LSA.

My Marines and I had done our best preparing our ANA Soldiers for sustained combat operations. Our battalion was eager to bring the First Tolai to the same level of preparedness and professionalism our former partners were now at. With the deployment coming to an end and Second Battalion, Third Marines, getting closer to relieving us in the middle of November, the decision was made.

After much debate, it was decided that training would resume for the Marines of Hades First and Second Platoons. Our company would train the unit of ANA Soldiers from the First Tolai by the middle of November. Having written down all our training TTPs and having saved all class material, we were confident that training would begin much better than before.

While the planning for this was going on, our next mission manifested itself on 12 October 2010. Our orders were to return to PB Skullet, where the conduct of our operations would be based. The mission was to conduct security patrolling operations in the vicinity of PB Skullet and an Afghan Uniformed Police station located three kilometers to the northeast. My Marines were tasked to conduct twenty-four-hour security patrol operations for a downed Combat Logistics Battalion vehicle near the Afghan Police Station until it was repaired and able to self-life back to Camp Dwyer.

Simultaneously, while this mission came down to us, we received news that a gas tanker full of fuel located a few kilometers northwest of Skullet had been reportedly blown up by Taliban forces.

On a constant alert and with their gear staged and ready, Hades First Platoon departed the gates of Geronimo first to lead the way and reinforce the Marines at PB Skullet in securing the area around the gas tanker. While Hades First Platoon went to secure the area, my platoon followed them out of the gates second to guard the downed CLB vehicle and their Marines.

For two days, my Marines and I secured the downed vehicle with simple rotation plans while First Platoon dealt with the gas tanker and tried to hunt down the enemy responsible for its destruction. I broke my platoon up into three squads and put each squad on twelve-hour rotations from PB Skullet to the Afghan Police Station and back.

Hades First Platoon was on autopilot, needing very little guidance at this point. Lieutenant Miller and his Platoon Sergeant were aggressively in control of the situation and waited like predators for the Taliban to return.

Over the course of the two days, my Marines guarded the downed CLB vehicle and its Marines and Sailors. Zero incidences occurred, and our Combat Logistics brethren were no doubt relieved that they had grunts to protect them. When their wrecker vehicle was fixed, the Marines and Sailors even thanked us before their departure. The phrase, "No better friend, no worse enemy," made famous by the legendary Marines Corps General James Mattis remains true for all Marines in or out of the Corps. This type of camaraderie is unique and primarily found in the Marine Corps. It is ingrained in all Marines to always come to the aid of one another no matter how great the cost or risk.

As is the case with anyone who is a victim of his or her own successes, rest time for my platoon was short-lived, and our next follow-on mission was handed down to us when we returned to PB Skullet later that morning. Always lacking enough Marines to patrol the enormous battalion AO, Kilo Company requested battalion support in opening a new patrol base north of their district center. As a battalion entity, Hades Second Platoon was sent to the task.

Direct from the mouth of my Commanding Officer, my platoon was to immediately consolidate and then patrol southeast to Checkpoint Wrightsman, located in Kilo Company's AO. Once there, we were to reinforce the Afghan Uniformed Police (if they were sober and present) and then proceed to establishing and constructing a PB in the vicinity of the checkpoint. In honor of our fallen Marine, the patrol base was going to be named after him once it was established and fortified.

My platoon returned to Checkpoint Wrightsman within the hour. At the time of our return, CP Wrightsman was being torn down and was no more than two main supply routes separated by a canal, with large mud fields opposite the routes. It was very humbling that my platoon had the honor of securing the checkpoint during its construction by our combat engineers.

Once all HESCO walls were in place, our defensive positions were set up, and our communication assets were in place, I radioed to Kilo Company's COC the following words: "Kilo Main, Kilo Main, this is Hades 2, PB Wrightsman, radio check, over."

Acknowledging receipt of transmission, the Marine on the other end of the radio replied, "PB Wrightsman, PB Wrightsman, this is Kilo Main. Lima Charlie, Oorah, and *Semper Fi,* Marines!"

My platoon conducted dismounted combat operations in support of Kilo Company until 20 November 2010. The order was then given to hand the PB over to Kilo Company and the Afghan Uniformed Police.

By the end of November, our deployment was coming to an end. Second Battalion, Third Marines, slowly started to filter into Geronimo, eager to take the helm and run the show. At the same time, Afghan Soldiers from the First Tolai began to move into our LSA. Immediately, the Marines and Corpsman from both Hades First and Second Platoons began training them. With little time to waste, our Marines did their best to train the new Afghan Soldiers in an effort to set our relieving unit up for success during their future combat operations in the Helmand.

A few days after training commenced, and while the process of relief in place and transfer of authority (RIP/TOA) was going on between our two battalions, I received terrible news that two more of my friends from my Infantry Officer Course had been killed, this time in Sangin, Afghanistan. My squadmate and friend from The Basic School and Infantry Officer Course (IOC 4-09) First Lieutenant Robert Kelly had been killed. Three days later, I received more terrible news that my other friend and classmate from IOC First Lieutenant William Donnelly IV had also been killed by Taliban. By the end of the deployment, three of the finest Lieutenants I had the pleasure and opportunity of serving with were gone, and many more of my classmates had been wounded.

By 7 December 2010 (Pearl Harbor Day), my platoon loaded up on helicopters and flew out of Geronimo, homebound for Hawaii. With the final pieces of transition going on, most of the battalion was en route back to the United States and civilization. Knowing that most of us would return to Afghanistan within a year for a second deployment, we focused on our families and friends waiting for us all back at home.

About the Author

Mark A. Bodrog was born in Roebling, New Jersey, in 1984. After receiving a bachelor's degree in criminal justice from Rutgers the State University, he joined the Marine Corps to become an Infantry Officer. He served two combat deployments to Afghanistan as both a Platoon Commander and Executive Officer.

CPSIA information can be obtained at www.ICGtesting.com
Printed in the USA
LVOW05s1321181213

365910LV00013B/175/P